Timesaving Tips for Organizing Piles of Papers

- ✔ When you pick up a piece of paper, ask yourself, "What is it? Why do I have it? What am I going to do with it?" If you don't have a good answer, throw it away or recycle it.

- ✔ If you find within your piles some task that needs to be done, write it on your Master List.

- ✔ If you need to keep a document, put it in a file folder.

- ✔ If you don't need a document any longer, throw it away!!! (Or recycle it.)

Timesaving Tips for Setting Up Your Filing System

- ✔ Use new file folders.

- ✔ Write file labels by hand.

- ✔ Use expandable file pockets to hold your file folders. Avoid hanging files.

Timesaving Tips for Using Your Master List

- ✔ Use a letter- or legal-sized piece of paper.

- ✔ Write on every line.

- ✔ Don't worry about priorities.

- ✔ Review the list throughout the day and ask yourself, "What's the most important thing I must do now?"

- ✔ Look at your list before you go home at night and ask yourself, "What's the most important thing I must do tomorrow?"

- ✔ When you've completed 50 percent of the items on page one of your list, transfer the unfinished items to page two, consolidating your list, and then throw the old list away (or put it in a file labeled "Old Lists").

Timesaving Telephone Tips

- ✔ Make a list of the items that you want to discuss with the person you're calling.

- ✔ Arrange the sequence of the items so that the most important items will be discussed first.

- ✔ Have at your fingertips the files or other papers to which you'll need to refer.

Time Management For Dummies, 2nd Edition

Cheat Sheet

Timesaving Voice Mail Tips

✔ When you listen to your messages, speed them up so that you can get through them quickly. (This feature may not be available on all voice mail systems or home answering machines.)

✔ If you've got long-winded callers, limit the length of time that a person can leave a message to 60, 90, or 120 seconds at most. (When you record your message, tell callers that they have only 60 seconds to leave their messages.)

✔ I know this may sound like it's defeating the purpose of the voice mail system, but if you're getting too many calls, try limiting the number of calls that your voice mail box can hold. When your box is full, the caller will be told something like: "This voice mail box is full." Now the caller will have to call someone else, call back later, or send a letter or e-mail message.

Timesaving E-Mail Tips

✔ Try to keep your e-mail message on one screen. If a message takes more than one screen, you should shorten it.

✔ If you're including a list of items, use a bulleted or numbered list. It's easier to read (like this list).

✔ If you must send a long message, attach the file as an enclosure. Write a brief description of the message in the subject line. The e-mail message itself should be a more detailed description of the enclosed file.

✔ When you attach a document to an e-mail message, write a brief but thorough description about the document you're sending. Don't forget to include the purpose of the document, detailed instructions regarding what the recipient is supposed to do with the document, and the date you need a response.

...For Dummies®: Bestselling Book Series for Beginners

Praise for Jeffrey Mayer

"The most tangible and immediate result of Mayer's work is a clean, organized desk where once there was a cluttered nightmare."

—Richard Roeper, *Chicago Sun-Times*

"Some people even give a session with the dean of the desk cleaners as a birthday gift for the CEOs in their lives."

—*People*

"Jeffrey Mayer is 'Mr. Neat the Clutterbuster.' He makes molehills out of messy mountains of paper."

—Jim Freschi, *USA Today*

"Jeffrey Mayer tells clients how to efficiently manage their time and their paperwork."

—Kevin McCormally, *Kiplinger's Personal Finance Magazine*

"Jeffrey Mayer is the messy manager's solution to piles of files."

— Annetta Miller, *Newsweek*

"Jeffrey Mayer describes his approach as a crash course in how to get organized."

— Thomas J. Brazaitis, *The Plain Dealer*

"Jeffrey Mayer helps business and professional people create order out of disorder."

— William Gruber, *Chicago Tribune*

"*If You Haven't Got the Time to Do It Right, When Will You Find the Time to Do It Over?* is filled with timesaving tips that Jeffrey Mayer has picked up from an obsession with doing things quickly."

— Alexa Bell, *Investor's Business Daily*

"Jeffrey Mayer can clean your desk and get you organized in just two hours."

— Ronald E. Yates, *Chicago Tribune*

"Jeffrey Mayer, author of *Winning the Fight Between You and Your Desk* receives about $1,000 for helping offices combat clutter."

— Lucinda Harper, *The Wall Street Journal*

"Jeffrey Mayer's *Winning the Fight Between You and Your Desk,* is a guide to the joys of personal computing."

— Mark Mehler, *Investor's Business Daily*

"Jeffrey Mayer's *Winning the Fight Between You and Your Desk* tells you how to get organized at work with your computer. I need this one, even if you don't."

— Larry Shannon, *The New York Times*

"Jeffrey Mayer's organizing strategy relies heavily on the use of two pieces of common office equipment — a wastebasket and a computer."

— Robert A. Devaney, *Washington Times*

"As companies move toward the paperless office, Jeffrey Mayer has begun encouraging executives to supplement clean desks with efficient computer usage."

—Mukul Pandya, *The New York Times*

"Jeffrey Mayer's *Winning the Fight Between You and Your Desk* is concise, focused, well-organized, and easy to read — just as it should be from someone who is paid $1,000 to clean up an executive's desk."

—Scott Pendleton, *Christian Science Monitor*

"When I consulted with Jeffrey Mayer several years ago to improve the management of my time, I told him that the real test of his work would be measured by recidivism. In other words, how much would my behavior have changed a year or two later? Jeff's contribution passed with flying colors! His deceptively simple ideas and techniques have persisted and brought about a permanent improvement in how I handle paper flow, meetings, telephone calls, etc. I would recommend him to anyone as a time management consultant."

—David Shute, Senior Vice President, General Counsel, and
Secretary; Sears, Roebuck and Co., Chicago, Illinois

"Jeffrey Mayer's *If You Haven't Got the Time to Do It Right, When Will You Find the Time to Do It Over?* is a must read. I've long been a proponent of a 'clean desk' and have kept one myself for more than 25 years. I'm a firm believer in the time management techniques that he espouses in his books, tapes, and seminars. He's got a lot of important things to say. His books should be required reading for anyone who wants to save time, be more productive, and make more money."

—Norman R. Bobins, President and Chief Executive Officer,
LaSalle National Bank, Chicago, Illinois

"My professional relationship with Jeffrey Mayer dates back more than twenty years. I have found Jeffrey to be intelligent, articulate, detailed, and competent in all our dealings. He is an accomplished and successful author of many business books and does practice what he preaches."

— Howard S. Goss, President, Transco Inc., Chicago, Illinois

"Five years, ago, Jeffrey Mayer introduced me to a whole new way of staying organized and focused on both my personal and professional priorities. I'm still using the tips, techniques, and strategies he gave me. They really do work! Jeff is a wizard at helping people stay organized!"

—Richard W. Pehlke, Vice President and Treasurer, Ameritech,
Chicago, Illinois

"Jeffrey Mayer is a talented writer who deals with complex business subjects in a very succinct, meaningful, and practical way. I highly recommend his books."

—Ronald J. Patten, Ph.D., C.P.A., Dean of the College of Commerce,
DePaul University, Chicago, Illinois

"We liked Jeffrey Mayer's *If You Haven't Got the Time to Do It Right, When Will You Find the Time to Do It Over?* so much that we referenced it in our book."

— Paul & Sarah Edwards, Authors, *Working From Home*

"Jeffrey Mayer got me organized. His organizational tips and techniques have helped me to save time. His helpful hints for using ACT! for Windows have made me a much more proficient user. His knowledge and experience has provided me with many valuable tools for improving the management of my time."

—Robert J. Winter, Jr., President, Stein & Company, Chicago, Illinois

"If your time is money, then you've got to read Jeffrey Mayer's *If You Haven't Got the Time to Do It Right, When Will You Find the Time to Do It Over?*. His ideas will save you at least an hour of time a day. He really knows his stuff!

—Arthur S. Nicholas, President, The Antech Group, Chicago, Illinois

"It was my habit for too many years to create piles of 'I Gottas' and 'I'm Gonnas.' Jeffrey Mayer came into my life and I had a huge pile of throwaways: papers, magazines, and books. And he left me with a clean desk, clean closet, clean book case, and a process to assure that the 'I Gottas' and 'I'm Gonnas' were controlled in the future."

—Ben T. Nelson, Retired Executive Vice President,
Harris Trust and Savings Bank, Chicago, Illinois

"Since working with Jeffrey Mayer I have totally revamped my personal workspace in line with his suggestions . . . out with the file folders, and away with the stacks of untended documents! Jeffrey's 'clean desk' approach to getting organized has convinced me that a fresh perspective can bring about positive changes. I leave my office each day with a feeling of accomplishment, and, more importantly, I arrive the next morning in a position of control. His system is simple, effective, and easy to keep moving.

—Bill Jacobs, Chairman of the Board, Office Concepts, Inc.,
Chicago, Illinois

"Jeffrey Mayer reminded me that it's important to manage the paper flow and not let the paper flow manage me. His timesaving tips are invaluable. My colleagues can't believe that my office has stayed organized."

—Gregory A. Browne, ARM; Manager, Insurance Claims,
GATX Corporation, Chicago, Illinois

"Just when all seemed hopeless and I was about to drown in a sea of paper and computer files, Jeffrey Mayer came along and saved me. What he offers can make the difference between success and failure in any field."

—Michael Harrison, Editor and Publisher, *Talkers Magazine*,
Longmeadow, Massachusetts

"Jeffrey Mayer's approach is very straightforward. It employes common sense, purposefulness, and a range of techniques that can be of great value to anyone and everyone. Jeffrey Mayer has identified the secret of success: Use your time to your advantage."

—James Paglia, President, Tassani & Paglia, Chicago, Illinois

"I'm really grateful to Jeffrey Mayer for the time he spent going over my organizational needs and prompting me to organize myself appropriately. I found it most beneficial to have someone take a fresh look at my old habits to help me streamline my follow-up systems, making me more productive and efficient. As a consultant, time is money, and I feel the time spent with Jeffrey Mayer has enabled me to work at a higher level.

—Gerri Hilt, Executive Recruiter, Chicago, Illinois

"Both my husband and I have known Jeffrey Mayer for nine years and are stagestruck with his abilities. He truly delivers what he promises with an incomparable wit. Indecision is an unknown to Jeff. He gets it done. His time management techniques have streamlined our business and personal affairs."

—Ellie Thompson CTC, President, Brookshire Travel Services Inc., Chicago, Illinois

"Jeffrey Mayer's ideas for time management should be a basic primer for everyone entering the business world. His genius is in clearly describing a set of simple tools that provide immediate timesaving benefits no matter how organized or disorganized one may be. If you're sick and tired of stacks of paper, lost memos, missed deadlines, and a general state of administrative chaos, or if you're on the other extreme of time management and are looking for a way to wring out the last 2 percent of efficiency, you will find that Jeffrey Mayer's tools will help you accomplish your objectives."

—J.E. Treadway, Vice President Human Resources, Metromail (An R.R. Donnelley & Sons Company), Lombard, Illinois

"Jeffrey Mayer does the impossible. He makes time management fun. Everyone knows in his or her heart of hearts that he or she is wasting time, and Jeff offers solid suggestions on how to get 65 minutes out of every hour.

—George M. Taber, Editor and Publisher, *New Jersey Business Newspapers,* New Brunswick, New Jersey

"Jeffrey Mayer helped me to clean off my desk. The time he spent with me has helped me become much more efficient and productive. I've recommended his services to a number of my friends and associates."

—Ronald N. Primack, Attorney, Lansing, Illinois

Praise for Jeffrey Mayer's Books

"Jeffrey Mayer's book *If You Haven't Got the Time to Do It Right, When Will You Find the Time to Do It Over?* has been invaluable to me. It has helped me accomplish more work in less time. Jeffrey Mayer's system and time management principles save me five to seven hours per week."

> —Jeffrey W. Durkee, Resident Vice President, Merrill Lynch, Century City, California

"Being able to keep my desk organized and uncluttered all the time is an intriguing prospect. I appreciate your perceptive note and look forward to reading your book, *If You Haven't Got the Time to Do It Right, When Will You Find the Time to Do It Over?*. I take some comfort in knowing that many others have been confronted with this problem — and have solved it."

> —Bill Bradley, United States Senator, Washington, D.C.

"I found Jeffrey Mayer's *If You Haven't Got the Time to Do It Right, When Will You Find the Time to Do It Over?* to be thoroughly enjoyable. It had numerous ideas and suggestions which could be readily absorbed into my short- and long-term activities. Furthermore, his book is now part of my team's reading list."

> —Chris Hutchinson, Product Development Manager, Fisher & Paykel Healthcare, Auckland, New Zealand

"When I discovered Jeffrey Mayer's book *If You Haven't Got the Time to Do It Right, When Will You Find the Time to Do It Over?* almost five years ago, my business life changed — dramatically — for the better. Since then I've used his system exclusively and find that time I was wasting shifting paper from one pile to another has been put to substantially more profitable use. I credit Jeffrey Mayer and his book with helping me and my company grow and prosper. I recommend it without reservation."

> —Chaz Cone, Chief Executive Officer, OPMS Software Manufacturing Group, Inc., Atlanta, Georgia

"Jeffrey Mayer's time management system is practical and more efficient than any other I have ever used. His easy-to-follow methods will help anyone become more organized and help them to better utilize their time. His book, *If You Haven't Got the Time to Do It Right, When Will You Find the Time to Do It Over?*, is a book that I keep available for ready reference. Quite simply, Jeffrey Mayer's methods help me get things done!"

> —Mark Lawley, Photographer, Leeds, Alabama

"Jeffrey Mayer's book *If You Haven't Got the Time to Do It Right, When Will You Find the Time to Do It Over?* has immediate, simple and practical ideas to increase both personal and team productivity. I highly recommend it to anyone who wants to be more organized for maximum results with minimum effort!"

> —Shelly Espinosa, M.S.W., Executive Director, Working Solutions, Thornton, Colorado

"I loved Jeffrey Mayer's book *If You Haven't Got the Time to Do It Right, When Will You Find the Time to Do It Over?.*"

> —M. Bachammar, Stanel Corp., Paris, France

"I thoroughly enjoyed Jeffrey Mayer's *If You Haven't Got the Time to Do It Right, When Will You Find the Time to Do It Over?.*"

> —N.H. Atthreya Ph.D., Director, M M M School of Management,
> Bombay, India

"As a time management expert, I enjoyed Jeffrey Mayer's book *If You Haven't Got the Time to Do It Right, When Will You Find the Time to Do It Over?.*"

> —Sandra Woods, President, Up The Ladder, Toronto, Ontario

"I thoroughly enjoyed reading Jeffrey Mayer's *If You Haven't Got the Time to Do It Right, When Will You Find the Time to Do It Over?.* Many of the principals in his book are common sense, everyday principles that have been systematized for practical application for a clear way of action."

> —Khalid Al-Turki, Al Turki Trading, Contracting,
> Kingdom of Saudi Arabia

"I loved Jeffrey Mayer's book *If You Haven't Got the Time to Do It Right, When Will You Find the Time to Do It Over?.* It's lively, fun to read, and full of good advice."

> —Sarah Hutter, Associate Editor, *Working Mother,*
> New York, New York

"Jeffrey Mayer's concise, user-friendly approach to time management is just what today's managers need. His book *If You Haven't Got the Time to Do It Right, When Will You Find the Time to Do It Over?* is must-reading for any manager."

> —Timothy S. Mescon, Ph.D., Dean of the Michael J. Coles School of
> Business, Kennesaw State College, Marietta, Georgia

"I loved Jeffrey Mayer's *Winning the Fight Between You and Your Desk.* I first read about him in People years ago and was so impressed with his ideas that I kept the article, and I still have it."

> —Dennis Rahilly, Exact Hi-Tech Engineering Communications,
> Cambridge, Massachusetts

"Jeffrey Mayer's *Winning the Fight Between You and Your Desk* is loaded with excellent information and the format made it very easy to breeze through. Thanks for taking the time to write an informative book like this and presenting it in such a useable format."

> —Dr. Scott R. Fladland, Chicago, Illinois

"Thanks for writing *Winning the Fight Between You and Your Desk.*"

> —Samuel R. Phillips, Consulting Engineer, Portola Valley, California

"Jeffrey Mayer has many good ideas in *Winning the Fight Between You and Your Desk.*"

> —Robert B. Mellman, Attorney, Montclair, New Jersey

 ™

References for the Rest of Us!™

TIME MANAGEMENT FOR DUMMIES®

2ND EDITION

by Jeffrey J. Mayer

IDG Books Worldwide, Inc.
An International Data Group Company

Foster City, CA ◆ Chicago, IL ◆ Indianapolis, IN ◆ New York, NY

Time Management For Dummies® 2nd Edition

Published by
IDG Books Worldwide, Inc.
An International Data Group Company
919 E. Hillsdale Blvd.
Suite 400
Foster City, CA 94404
www.idgbooks.com (IDG Books Worldwide Web site)
www.dummies.com (Dummies Press Web site)

Library of Congress Catalog Card No.: 99-62837

ISBN: 0-7645-5145-0

Printed in the United States of America

10 9 8 7 6 5 4 3 2 1

2B/RS/QV/ZZ/IN

Distributed in the United States by IDG Books Worldwide, Inc.

Distributed by CDG Books Canada Inc. for Canada; by Transworld Publishers Limited in the United Kingdom; by IDG Norge Books for Norway; by IDG Sweden Books for Sweden; by IDG Books Australia Publishing Corporation Pty. Ltd. for Australia and New Zealand; by TransQuest Publishers Pte Ltd. for Singapore, Malaysia, Thailand, Indonesia, and Hong Kong; by Gotop Information Inc. for Taiwan; by ICG Muse, Inc. for Japan; by Norma Comunicaciones S.A. for Colombia; by Intersoft for South Africa; by Le Monde en Tique for France; by International Thomson Publishing for Germany, Austria and Switzerland; by Distribuidora Cuspide for Argentina; by Livraria Cultura for Brazil; by Ediciones ZETA S.C.R. Ltda. for Peru; by WS Computer Publishing Corporation, Inc., for the Philippines; by Contemporanea de Ediciones for Venezuela; by Express Computer Distributors for the Caribbean and West Indies; by Micronesia Media Distributor, Inc. for Micronesia; by Grupo Editorial Norma S.A. for Guatemala; by Chips Computadoras S.A. de C.V. for Mexico; by Editorial Norma de Panama S.A. for Panama; by American Bookshops for Finland. Authorized Sales Agent: Anthony Rudkin Associates for the Middle East and North Africa.

For general information on IDG Books Worldwide's books in the U.S., please call our Consumer Customer Service department at 800-762-2974. For reseller information, including discounts and premium sales, please call our Reseller Customer Service department at 800-434-3422.

For information on where to purchase IDG Books Worldwide's books outside the U.S., please contact our International Sales department at 317-596-5530 or fax 317-596-5692.

For consumer information on foreign language translations, please contact our Customer Service department at 1-800-434-3422, fax 317-596-5692, or e-mail rights@idgbooks.com.

For information on licensing foreign or domestic rights, please phone +1-650-655-3109.

For sales inquiries and special prices for bulk quantities, please contact our Sales department at 650-655-3200 or write to the address above.

For information on using IDG Books Worldwide's books in the classroom or for ordering examination copies, please contact our Educational Sales department at 800-434-2086 or fax 317-596-5499.

For press review copies, author interviews, or other publicity information, please contact our Public Relations department at 650-655-3000 or fax 650-655-3299.

For authorization to photocopy items for corporate, personal, or educational use, please contact Copyright Clearance Center, 222 Rosewood Drive, Danvers, MA 01923, or fax 978-750-4470.

About the Author

Jeffrey Mayer is one of the country's foremost authorities on time and business management. For a living, he helps busy people get organized, save time, and become more productive. Jeff's claim to fame is his "clean desk" approach to time management.

He walks into an office that looks like a toxic waste dump — with piles of paper strewn all over the place — and in two hours the desktop looks like the flight deck of an aircraft carrier. So much is thrown away that the wastebasket is filled to the brim, overflowing, and spilling onto the floor. All that remains are a handful of file folders, a pad of paper, a computer, and a telephone. Everything else is neatly filed away.

USA Today dubbed him "Mr. Neat, the Clutterbuster," and *People* called him "The Dean of the Desk Cleaners." *Esquire* stamped him "The Productivity Guru."

Long ago, Jeff realized that if everybody were better organized, they could take more control over their day and would have more time to focus on their most important work. At the end of the work day, they could leave the office, go home, and spend more time with their family and friends.

Jeff's clients realize that time is money, and Jeff's able to help them convert wasted time into time that can be used more efficiently, effectively, and profitably. Jeff's specialty is in teaching people how to improve their follow-up systems. With a good follow-up system, a person's able to spend more time working on the things that are important, instead of the things that keep him or her busy.

Since the founding of his Chicago-based consulting firm, Mayer Enterprises, he has helped tens of thousands of men and women (many are top executives at Fortune 500 Companies) get organized, use their time more effectively, and make more money.

His corporate clients include: American Express Financial Services, Commonwealth Edison, DDB/Needham Advertising, Encyclopaedia, LaSalle National Bank, Merrill Lynch, Navistar, Sears Roebuck & Co., and R.R. Donnelley & Sons Company, just to name a few.

Jeff's been interviewed by almost every major newspaper and magazine in the United States, including *The Wall Street Journal, The New York Times, Newsweek, People, Forbes, Business Week,* and *Fortune.* And he has been interviewed on hundreds of radio and television programs across the United States, including *The Today Show, American Journal, CNN, CNBC,* and *ABC News.*

Jeff also publishes a newsletter — ACT! In ACTion — for Symantec's ACT! Contact management program. If you would like a free sample issue, complete the coupon at the back of this book, or visit his Web site at www.ACTnews.com.

Jeffrey Mayer Would Like to Hear From You

Jeff would like to hear from you. How did you like this book? How did it help you find your life's calling? How can this book be improved? Please share your success stories with Jeff.

Jeff can be reached at:

Mayer Enterprises
50 East Bellevue Place, Suite 305
Chicago, IL 60611
Phone: 312-944-4184
Fax: 312-944-6681
E-mail: jeff@ACTnews.com
Web site: www.ACTnews.com

Jeffrey Mayer Would Love to Speak at Your Next Business Meeting, Conference, or Convention

Jeffrey Mayer would be delighted to speak at your next business meeting, conference, or convention. For date availability, he can be reached at the above address.

Other Books by Jeffrey J. Mayer

If You Haven't Got the Time to Do It Right, When Will You Find the Time to Do It Over?

Find the Job You've Always Wanted in Half the Time with Half the Effort

Winning the Fight Between You and Your Desk

Time Management For Dummies

Time Management For Dummies Briefcase Edition

ACT! For Windows For Dummies

ACT! 3 for Windows For Dummies

ACT! 4 for Windows For Dummies

Success is a Journey

ABOUT IDG BOOKS WORLDWIDE

Welcome to the world of IDG Books Worldwide.

IDG Books Worldwide, Inc., is a subsidiary of International Data Group, the world's largest publisher of computer-related information and the leading global provider of information services on information technology. IDG was founded more than 30 years ago by Patrick J. McGovern and now employs more than 9,000 people worldwide. IDG publishes more than 290 computer publications in over 75 countries. More than 90 million people read one or more IDG publications each month.

Launched in 1990, IDG Books Worldwide is today the #1 publisher of best-selling computer books in the United States. We are proud to have received eight awards from the Computer Press Association in recognition of editorial excellence and three from Computer Currents' First Annual Readers' Choice Awards. Our best-selling ...For Dummies® series has more than 50 million copies in print with translations in 31 languages. IDG Books Worldwide, through a joint venture with IDG's Hi-Tech Beijing, became the first U.S. publisher to publish a computer book in the People's Republic of China. In record time, IDG Books Worldwide has become the first choice for millions of readers around the world who want to learn how to better manage their businesses.

Our mission is simple: Every one of our books is designed to bring extra value and skill-building instructions to the reader. Our books are written by experts who understand and care about our readers. The knowledge base of our editorial staff comes from years of experience in publishing, education, and journalism — experience we use to produce books to carry us into the new millennium. In short, we care about books, so we attract the best people. We devote special attention to details such as audience, interior design, use of icons, and illustrations. And because we use an efficient process of authoring, editing, and desktop publishing our books electronically, we can spend more time ensuring superior content and less time on the technicalities of making books.

You can count on our commitment to deliver high-quality books at competitive prices on topics you want to read about. At IDG Books Worldwide, we continue in the IDG tradition of delivering quality for more than 30 years. You'll find no better book on a subject than one from IDG Books Worldwide.

John Kilcullen
Chairman and CEO
IDG Books Worldwide, Inc.

Steven Berkowitz
President and Publisher
IDG Books Worldwide, Inc.

*Eighth Annual
Computer Press
Awards ≥ 1992*

*Ninth Annual
Computer Press
Awards ≥ 1993*

*Tenth Annual
Computer Press
Awards ≥ 1994*

*Eleventh Annual
Computer Press
Awards ≥ 1995*

IDG is the world's leading IT media, research and exposition company. Founded in 1964, IDG had 1997 revenues of $2.05 billion and has more than 9,000 employees worldwide. IDG offers the widest range of media options that reach IT buyers in 75 countries representing 95% of worldwide IT spending. IDG's diverse product and services portfolio spans six key areas including print publishing, online publishing, expositions and conferences, market research, education and training, and global marketing services. More than 90 million people read one or more of IDG's 290 magazines and newspapers, including IDG's leading global brands — Computerworld, PC World, Network World, Macworld and the Channel World family of publications. IDG Books Worldwide is one of the fastest-growing computer book publishers in the world, with more than 700 titles in 36 languages. The "...For Dummies®" series alone has more than 50 million copies in print. IDG offers online users the largest network of technology-specific Web sites around the world through IDG.net (http://www.idg.net), which comprises more than 225 targeted Web sites in 55 countries worldwide. International Data Corporation (IDC) is the world's largest provider of information technology data, analysis and consulting, with research centers in over 41 countries and more than 400 research analysts worldwide. IDG World Expo is a leading producer of more than 168 globally branded conferences and expositions in 35 countries including E3 (Electronic Entertainment Expo), Macworld Expo, ComNet, Windows World Expo, ICE (Internet Commerce Expo), Agenda, DEMO, and Spotlight. IDG's training subsidiary, ExecuTrain, is the world's largest computer training company, with more than 230 locations worldwide and 785 training courses. IDG Marketing Services helps industry-leading IT companies build international brand recognition by developing global integrated marketing programs via IDG's print, online and exposition products worldwide. Further information about the company can be found at www.idg.com.   1/24/99

Dedication

To my wife Mitzi, and my daughter DeLaine.

I love you both very much.

Acknowledgments

There are many people who have contributed to the successful creation of both the first edition of *Time Management For Dummies* and the revised edition of this book, and I would like to thank and acknowledge them for their help and contributions.

A BIG Thank You goes to my good friend Kathy Welton, who also happens to be the publisher of IDG's business and general reference books. Kathy brought me into the *...For Dummies* family, and it has been a truly rewarding experience for me. I have thoroughly enjoyed working with Kathy and look forward to a long relationship with both her and IDG Books.

Mark Butler has been a great help to me in the creation of this new edition of *Time Management For Dummies*. We worked very closely in laying out the book, and he offered great insights for ways in which we could improve upon the first edition. Thank you, Mark, for all that you've done.

I would also like to thank my Project Editor Mary Goodwin and Tina Sims, my Copy Editor, for their contributions in making this a great book.

I would also like to thank two dear friends who made major contributions to the first edition of *Time Management For Dummies*. Tim Gallan was my editor on *Time Management For Dummies, Time Management For Dummies Briefcase Edition, ACT! For Windows For Dummies, ACT! 3 For Windows For Dummies*, and *ACT! 4 For Windows For Dummies*. Tim has played a huge part in my success as an author.

The other person I would like to acknowledge is my dear friend Stacy Collins, who as Brand Manager, oversaw every aspect of the creation of the first edition of *Time Management For Dummies*.

I would also like to thank Mimi Sells, IDG's Director of Public Relations, and her colleagues in the public relations department, Catherine Schmitz and David Kissinger, for all that they have done for me in marketing and promoting my *Time Management For Dummies* and my other *...For Dummies* books over the past five years.

And I can't forget the Production people who put this book together, so thanks to all of them for making these pages look so good.

Publisher's Acknowledgments

We're proud of this book; please register your comments through our IDG Books Worldwide Online Registration Form located at http://my2cents.dummies.com.

Some of the people who helped bring this book to market include the following:

Acquisitions and Editorial

Project Editor: Mary Goodwin
   (Previous Edition: Tim Gallan)

Senior Acquisitions Editor: Mark Butler

Editorial Coordinator: Maureen F. Kelly

Acquisitions Coordinator: Jonathan Malysiak

Acquisitions Manager: Kevin Thornton

Copy Editor: Tina Sims
   (Previous Edition: Greg Robertson)

Editorial Manager: Kelly Ewing

Editorial Assistant: Paul Kuzmic

Production

Project Coordinator: E. Shawn Aylsworth

Layout and Graphics: Chris Herner, Angela F. Hunckler, Brent Savage, Jacque Schneider, Janet Seib, Michael A. Sullivan, Brian Torwelle

Proofreaders: Rachel Garvey, Marianne Santy, Rebecca Senninger, Janet M. Withers

Indexer: Sherry Massey

Special Help
   Ted Cains, Nicole Haims, Pam Mourouzis, Rowena Rappaport, Billie Williams

---

General and Administrative

IDG Books Worldwide, Inc: John Kilcullen, CEO; Steven Berkowitz, President and Publisher

IDG Books Technology Publishing: Brenda McLaughlin, Senior Vice President and Group Publisher

Dummies Technology Press and Dummies Editorial: Diane Graves Steele, Vice President and Associate Publisher; Mary Bednarek, Director of Acquisitions and Product Development; Kristin A. Cocks, Editorial Director

Dummies Trade Press: Kathleen A. Welton, Vice President and Publisher; Kevin Thornton, Acquisitions Manager

IDG Books Production for Dummies Press: Michael R. Britton, Vice President of Production and Creative Services; Cindy L. Phipps, Manager of Project Coordination, Production Proofreading, and Indexing; Shelley Lea, Supervisor of Graphics and Design; Debbie J. Gates, Production Systems Specialist; Robert Springer, Supervisor of Proofreading; Debbie Stailey, Production Control Manager; Tony Augsburger, Supervisor of Reprints and Bluelines

Dummies Packaging and Book Design: Patty Page, Manager, Promotions Marketing

◆

The publisher would like to give special thanks to Patrick J. McGovern, without whom this book would not have been possible.

◆

Contents at a Glance

Cartoons at a Glance

By Rich Tennant

page 5

page 61

page 309

page 127

page 185

page 343

page 245

Fax: 978-546-7747 • **E-mail:** the5wave@tiac.net

Table of Contents

Part IV: Looking Out for #1.......................... *185*

Chapter 14: Make Winning Presentations 187

Introduction

If you're like most people, you never have enough time to get everything done at the office. You're working harder and you're working longer, but you still don't feel as though you're making any headway. So you come in early; you stay late; you work weekends; and when you finally get home at the end of a long day, you're so worn out that you don't have any time or energy left for yourself, your friends, or your family. The time management techniques that worked so well for you just a few years ago don't work anymore. Because the world around us has changed in so many ways, your techniques have become obsolete.

We used to believe that we could get our work done if we could just "handle a piece of paper only once!" Today we've still got the papers, and we also have e-mail, voice mail, and wireless communications systems. On our desktops are super-fast computers that are all networked together. And we're all communicating with each other via the Internet.

We were once thrilled when we could send a letter via FedEx and get it to someone by 10:30 the next morning. Today, you just fax it from your computer directly to another computer. And if you want to send someone a document, you just attach it to an e-mail message. When you want information, you log on to the Internet and visit your favorite search engine.

Secretaries and administrative assistants used to sit at their desks typing letters, memos, reports, presentations, and other documents on their IBM Selectric electronic typewriters at 60 words per minute. Today, most of the secretaries are gone, and in their place is a blazingly fast PC that we use to write our own letters, memos, reports, and presentations. Then we use our spell checkers and grammar checkers to correct our mistakes, and send our documents off as faxes or e-mail.

To create complex documents, presentations, and reports, we used to have to get together for long, drawn-out meetings in the company's conference room. Today, our computers are all networked together, and the new groupware products enable a group of people — in different cities — to now work together at the same time to create documents, presentations, and reports.

When you need to speak with three or more people at a time, you just call AT&T, MCI, Sprint, or Frontier to set up a conference call. These sophisticated teleconferencing networks now support audio and data transmission. And with videoconferencing, you're able to hold *virtual* meetings over the Internet.

We aren't handling paper any more! We're handling information. And the time frames we have to make decisions continue to shrink.

To succeed in the 21st century, you've got to do more than just get organized. You have to do a better job of staying on top of all your unfinished work, tasks, and projects, and you accomplish this goal by improving your follow-up systems. With an efficient and effective follow-up system, you can convert the time that's wasted during the course of a normal business day into time that can be used more efficiently, effectively, and profitably.

I call this system *addition by subtraction*. By eliminating the wasted time, you'll have more time to spend on your high-priority items, the things that are most important to you. Then you can get your work done, leave the office at a reasonable hour, and spend the rest of the day with your family and friends doing the things that you enjoy.

When you first start trying to tackle your time managment goals, you may feel overwhelmed by the task. That's where *Time Management For Dummies, 2nd Edition,* comes into the picture. I tell you everything you need to know to start getting organized and using your time more efficiently.

So What's Exactly in This Book?

To make it easy to find exactly the information you want, I've organized this book into seven parts. You can start reading at any point in the book that interests you.

Part I: Improve Your Time Management System

I'll show you how to get organized and help you develop an efficient follow-up system.

Part II: Taking Care of Business

I'll talk about how you can plan your days, manage your meetings, maintain control of the flow of a conversation, and help people make better decisions.

Part III: Improve Your Ability to Communicate Information

I'll talk about how you can improve your ability to communicate information by using the telephone, electronic and old-fashioned postal mail, and voice mail.

Part IV: Looking Out for #1

I'll show you how to make presentations to groups of people, how to promote yourself, how to set goals for yourself, and how to go through life as a winner.

Part V: Time Management on the Go

In this part, I tell you about ways to save yourself immeasurable time when setting up your home office, including the importance of creating a good working environment. I also give you tips that can save you time when you're on the road — whether you're traveling to the next town over or to an entirely different country.

Part VI: Technology and Time Management

The technological advances available today can improve your work efficiency to a degree you never before imagined. But you can't get the most out of these tools until you know how to manage your computer's performance and which computer software is best for you. In this part, I tell you what you need to know about optimizing your time in front of the computer. If you can't be confined to a desktop computer, I tell you about some other techie-type gadgets that can shave time off your work day.

Part VII: The Part of Tens

I'll throw in a bunch of top ten lists to inform you, entertain you, and increase the page count of this book to meet my contractual obligation to IDG Books Worldwide.

Icons Used in This Book

 The Tip icon flags a juicy, bite-size bit of information guaranteed to make your life easier.

 The Timesaving Tip icon points out the kind of tip that's going to save you gobs of time and add years to your life.

 I stuck the Remember icon next to stuff you ought not forget lest a terrible curse befall thee.

 The Technical Stuff icon serves two purposes: For people who like fancy-shmancy computer jargon, this icon lets you know where to look. For people who get nervous just seeing a digital clock, this icon lets you know that there's stuff nearby you don't want to read.

 The Anecdote icon lets you know that I'm about to tell some sort of story, usually a story with a point, but not always.

Part I

Improve Your Time Management System

The 5th Wave   By Rich Tennant

In this part . . .

A less inviting title for this part might be "Clean Up That Mess!" Before you're ever going to be more productive, you need to get organized, and that's what this first part is all about. After a brief overview, I help you clean up your office. Then I show you how to create a Master List so that you can get your work in order. After that, I cover how you can make the most of your daily planner. And last but not least, I discuss the benefits of using ACT!, a computer application that will make any person's life more organized.

Chapter 1

The Time Management Mind-Set

*W*ith workloads that have become swollen by the downsizing fervor, we're all working harder than ever. We're coming into our offices earlier each morning. We're staying later in the evening. When was the last time you even took a 30-minute lunch? How many times a week do you skip lunch?

And though we're putting in all these extra hours, we aren't getting to our important projects, let alone the routine correspondence and the other miscellaneous things that have accumulated in piles on our desk, in our in-boxes, on the credenza, and on the floor. These things wait until Saturday, when we hope to have some uninterrupted time so that we can actually get something done.

So what are we doing during our eight-, ten-, or twelve-hour days? I haven't got the slightest idea, and I'll bet that you don't either. That's probably why you're reading this book at this very moment.

On the following pages, you'll learn some wonderful timesaving tips, techniques, ideas, and strategies that will help you get your work done quicker, faster, and better, and give you more time to spend with your family and friends.

Become More Productive, Efficient, and Effective — Not Just Busy

In today's highly competitive business environment, working additional hours doesn't guarantee that your business will be more successful or that your career will prosper. The only way that you can be successful today is to

Time utilization analysis

While I was meeting with the division manager of a large public company, he showed me a copy of a time utilization survey that his firm had recently conducted. The survey showed that the employees were spending the majority of their time on tasks not directly related to serving their clients' needs. The employees were spending most of their time doing routine office work, shuffling papers back and forth, attending meetings, and answering electronic and voice mail messages. The breakdown is as follows:

Time spent doing office work and attending meetings: 25 percent

Time spent responding to electronic and voice mail messages: 15 percent

Time spent on the telephone: 15 percent

Time spent in face-to-face meetings with clients: 20 percent

Time spent in preparation for those meetings: 25 percent

Upon analysis, it became apparent that many of the company's employees were devoting most of their time to activities unrelated to their clients' needs. Management has now set an overall goal of increasing their employees' client meeting/client preparation time to at least 60 percent of each employee's work week, thus reducing the time spent on administrative activities to 40 percent.

become more productive, efficient, and effective, not just busy. When productivity increases, the quality of your work improves, you get things done on time, and best of all, you accomplish more tasks with less effort. The company makes money, and so do you.

You must remember that you're getting paid for your results, not the number of hours you work. We all have encountered coworkers who try to impress us by bragging about how many hours they put in. They wear their 70- or 80-hour work weeks as a badge of honor. They believe that the extra hours show dedication to company and career.

In many instances, though, the overtime is a smoke screen that covers up inefficiencies and poor work habits. If you analyze the quality of these people's work, the volume of work produced, and the timeliness for completing it, you'll quickly discover that people who consistently work overtime really aren't superstars. In fact, they're just barely getting by. They rarely get their work done on time, and the quality of that work is OK at best. Considering the number of hours they actually work, they're getting a very poor return on their investment.

You've Got to Pace Yourself

Many people don't realize that there's a big difference between working hard and working smart — between being busy and being productive. For most of us, a career will span 30 to 40 years. If you think of a career as if it were a marathon, you realize the necessity to pace yourself over the course of the race.

Sure, there are times when you need to pick up the pace, and then you need to slow down again to catch your breath. Your goal should be to use and conserve energy so that you don't burn out or become exhausted long before crossing the finish line.

The people who work 50, 60, or 70 hours per week are pacing themselves through a 100-yard sprint when they're really in a marathon. They're working as hard as they can, for as long as they can, in the hope of crossing the finish line *before* they collapse. They look at the completion of the next project or task as the finish line, and they look no further. As soon as they have another project to work on, they soon find themselves running another race.

Until recently, most employers didn't care how many hours it took for an employee to get a particular job done. Productivity and efficiency weren't that important because the extra costs could always be passed along to the customer.

That approach doesn't work any longer. The competition is just too fierce. As a result, corporate America's been forced to find ways to cut expenses, increase employee productivity, and improve the quality of their products or services. These goals cannot be achieved by asking employees to work longer and harder. Employees need to be taught to work more efficiently and effectively.

For one thing, working longer hours doesn't necessarily make an employee more productive. Every person has a limit, and there's a point of diminishing returns where additional hours of work don't result in a measurable increase in the quality or the quantity of the work produced. In fact, when a person's putting in too many hours, the probability of making a mistake dramatically increases.

History has shown that these kinds of mistakes can be very costly in time and in money both to the company and to the employee. Studies have also shown that working long hours leads to burnout, increased stress and tension on the job, and additional pressures at home. Today, people need to measure and balance the requirements at work with those of their personal and family life.

ANECDOTE

All work and no play *almost* makes Frank a dead man

Early in my career, I knew a man who worked in sales for a major life insurance company. As a new agent, he sold a phenomenal amount of life insurance and was held up as the model agent that everybody else was supposed to emulate.

It shouldn't surprise anyone that the managers in the office were only looking at his end results — the volume of life insurance sold — not the daily activities that produced the sales. When I analyzed his daily activity, I found that he wasn't working a regular 40-hour work week. He was working more than 80 hours.

This was Frank's typical workday: Each morning he got up at 5:00 a.m. and had one or maybe two appointments before he got to the office. Then he worked a full day, and after dinner, he had one or two additional appointments. Many evenings he didn't get home before midnight.

He followed this work schedule Monday through Friday, week in and week out, for years. He even worked on weekends, with several appointments on Saturdays and occasional appointments on Sundays.

Yes, he was achieving fabulous results in comparison to his colleagues. But he wasn't doing it during *normal* business hours. He was working two jobs. His performance wasn't that of a super salesman; he was merely a man who chose to put all of his time, energy, effort, and life into selling. He never had any time for his wife or children, and he couldn't even enjoy the things that his money could purchase.

One day, the results of Frank's work habits finally caught up to him. He was giving a speech to a group of fellow life insurance agents — telling them what a great salesman he had become — and collapsed in front of the audience. He was rushed to the hospital and spent the next week under his doctor's care. The doctor's diagnosis was that he was suffering from exhaustion.

At the time, Frank was still months away from his 35th birthday. He learned the hard lesson that when you burn the candle from both ends, sooner or later the candle may burn out.

Testing Your Time Management Savvy

We're all looking for ways to do our work quicker, faster, and better. Now if you want to learn how to manage your time better, you've got to become aware of how you're spending your time during a typical business day. So before you dive into this book, I would like to ask you some questions:

1. How long does it take you to find important papers — like that report your boss wants in the next 60 seconds — that are buried in piles on the top of your desk? See Chapter 2 to learn how to transform a desk that looks like a toxic waste dump into one that resembles the flight deck of an aircraft carrier.

2. How many times have you been put in Voice Mail Jail? To get out of Voice Mail Jail, read Chapter 11.

3. Do you find yourself playing endless games of telephone tag with your most important clients? To quickly win the game, turn to Chapter 10.

4. Do you spend your day putting out fires while your important tasks just seem to fall through the cracks? See Chapter 6 for help.

5. Would you like to spend less time responding to your e-mail messages and more time doing your important work? If so, see Chapter 13.

6. Do you find that you don't get to your important tasks until the very last minute? Then check out Chapter 3 for tips on getting the most out of your Master List.

7. Would you like to get your appointment book, calendar, Rolodex file, and things-to-do list off your desk and inside your computer? Then read Chapter 5 to learn how you can use ACT! to take control of your day.

8. Would you like to do a better job of promoting your company and yourself? Then see Chapter 15.

9. Do you spend too many hours each week sitting in meetings that don't accomplish much and leave important issues unresolved? Then read Chapter 7 for help.

10. Would you like to have more time for yourself, your family, and your friends? If so, you should sit yourself down and read this book cover to cover. It's packed with so many timesaving tips, techniques, ideas, and strategies that you'll quickly find yourself doing better work and completing it on time, with less pressure and strain. The time that you once wasted during a normal business day will be used much more productively and efficiently. And as a result, you'll be spending less time at work and more time with your family and friends. Now that's being productive!

Chapter 2

Getting and Staying Organized

• •

• •

*O*n the next few pages, I'm going to show you my fun and easy process for getting, and staying, organized. You should be able to organize your desk in about two hours time, so turn off the phone and close the door — if you're lucky enough to have one — so that you won't be interrupted, and don't forget to bring a dumpster. You'll find that at least 60 percent of the papers on your desk can be tossed, and when you start working on the drawers inside your desk, as well as your file drawers, you'll discover that at least 80 percent of those papers can go.

You Can Save Yourself an Hour a Day By Getting Organized

You probably don't realize it, but most people waste almost an hour a day looking for papers that are lost on the top of their desks — 60 percent of which aren't needed anyway. So that's where I think we should start: with the top of the desk.

Let me describe a typical office:

✔ There are piles of paper everywhere — on the desk, the credenza, the chair, and the floor.

✔ Next to the phone there's a pile of pink phone slips.

✔ The lights on the phone itself are blinking so fast that one would think the phone's about to explode because of all of the new voice mail messages.

- ✔ On the wall there are so many sticky notes that they could be mistaken for a swarm of butterflies.

- ✔ Off in a corner there are piles of unread newspapers, magazines, and trade journals.

- ✔ Your computer is constantly announcing the arrival of a new e-mail message.

- ✔ Somewhere in all of this mess are a calendar, an appointment book, and a to-do list.

Sound familiar?

Well, you're going to get rid of all of those piles of paper on the desk. In just a few hours, you can take a desk that looks like a toxic waste dump — with piles of papers everywhere — and transform it into a desk that looks like the flight deck of an aircraft carrier. You'll throw away so much that your waste-basket (or recycling bin) will be filled to the brim, overflowing and spilling onto the floor. All that remains on the desktop will be a telephone and a pad of paper.

Your goal isn't to have a nice, neat, orderly desk. The desk is secondary. Your goal is to get organized so that you can convert time that's wasted during the course of a normal business day into time that can be used more efficiently and effectively.

With a neat, orderly desk, you'll improve your follow-up systems so that you can do a better job of staying on top of all of your unfinished work. And when you can spend your time working on the tasks that are important, instead of the *things* that keep you busy, the quality of your work improves, and you make more money. A clean desk is the place where it all begins. So let's get started.

Separating the Wheat from the Chaff (Or Is It the Pigs from the Cows?)

The first step in getting organized is to separate the wheat from the chaff. So go through all of the papers on your desk, one piece at a time.

- ✔ If a paper is important, put it in a keeper pile for the time being.

- ✔ If a paper belongs to someone else, create a pile of things to give to your colleagues or coworkers.

- ✔ If you don't need a paper any longer, put it in the recycling bin or throw it away!

In the span of 20 to 30 minutes, you should be able to lighten your paper over-load by more than half, and your wastebasket will soon be filled to the brim.

If you're finding it difficult to part with some of your files or other papers at this time, just take them off your desk and put them in one of the drawers in your filing cabinet. This way, you've got the best of both worlds. If you need the materials at some future time, you know where to find them, and if you find that you don't need them, then you can throw them out in six months.

Organize your keeper pile

Now go through your keeper pile one piece of paper at a time.

- ✔ If there's work to do, note it on your *Master List,* which is a things-to-do list that's written on a big piece of paper. (I'll be describing how you can use your Master List to take control of your workload and workday in Chapter 3.)
- ✔ If you no longer need that particular piece of paper, throw it away. If you do need it, put it in a properly labeled file folder and file it away.
- ✔ If a folder doesn't exist, create one. I'll talk about filing in a few moments.

File the important stuff

If you have papers or files you wish to keep but don't really need right now, file them away. There's no reason to leave them on the top of your desk any longer.

Sort through all those other piles of paper in your office

Now that you've gone through everything on your desk, continue the same process by going through the piles that have accumulated on your credenza, floor, and everywhere else. If there's work to do, note it on your Master List. If you need to keep a document, file it away; and if you don't need it any longer, throw it away!

Don't reminisce or interrupt yourself

While you're going through these papers, your objective is to sift, sort, and catalog each and every one of them. Don't allow yourself to get sidetracked from the task at hand. When you come across a note for a phone call that you were supposed to have returned sometime last week, don't drop everything to make that call. Just note it on your Master List and keep going.

Or, when you find a memo that outlined a project you were supposed to be working on for the past few days but haven't yet begun, don't start now. And when you discover a copy of a letter that you recently sent to a client, customer, or prospect — that's been sitting on your desk for a month — just note on your Master List that you've got to make a phone call, and keep sifting and sorting.

These documents are the items of business that you're looking for. You're going through your piles, one piece of paper at a time, so that you can create a list of everything that you need to do!

While You're at It, Remove the Sticky Notes from the Wall

Many of us use sticky notes in much the same way as we use our piles. They allow us to see what it is that we've got to do. When we need to remind ourselves that we've got something to do — like write a letter, work on a proposal, or return a telephone call — we jot down a brief note on this small piece of paper and stick it on the wall, computer, telephone, or anything else on which it may adhere. Isn't that the *real* reason we got computers?

The problem with this system is that many of us fail to notice, or do anything about, the notes that we've written. The next few paragraphs outline a better way to take down notes.

Write everything down — on big pieces of paper

The habit of jotting down a thought on a piece of paper is a very efficient way of remembering that you've got something to do. Putting things down on paper frees you from having to try to remember what those things are. Now you can use your wonderful brain power for something that is considerably more important.

But when you write notes to yourself on small pieces of paper and then stick them on the wall, you begin to create problems. After you post more than a few of them, you tend to stop paying attention to any of them, and none of them appears to be of much importance. As a result, you ignore the note and forget the task. Even though you see these notes throughout the day, day after day, simply seeing the note doesn't provide you with the necessary motivation to do the task. So the notes remain attached to the wall, the work remains undone, and everything begins to back up.

When there's work to do, such as making a phone call, writing a letter, or following up on something, note it on your Master List instead of a sticky note. A single piece of letter-sized paper, with about 25 lines, can hold the information of 25 sticky notes.

Don't forget to file your notes

The practice of taking detailed notes — especially of your telephone conversations and meetings — is a very good one. But when you don't place your notes inside a file folder along with all the other material on a specific subject or topic, there's the possibility that when you've got to make a business decision, you may not remember that you have this information.

So when you take notes, place the paper in the appropriate file so that you can find it when you need it, and if there's work to do, note it on your Master List.

 Always date your papers. Every time you write something on a piece of paper, you should always put a date on it. This way you can see where things fell chronologically. Records of phone conversations and meetings become useless when you can't remember when they took place.

Dealing with Piles of Newspapers, Magazines, and Trade Journals

Every day, we get stacks of newspapers, magazines, and trade journals, many of which we never even look at, let alone read. Many of us have piled up so much reading material that we wouldn't get through it all if we spent an entire workday just reading.

So what do we do with all of this material? We stick it in a "reading" pile that's never looked at again. Isn't it ironic that we end up feeling guilty because we didn't get around to reading these things, even though our world didn't come to an end simply because we never read that stack of magazines?

We just find it hard to admit that the majority of the information that crosses our desk isn't necessary, and somehow, we get along very well without the information we didn't know we were missing.

So the most important thing you can do when these reading materials cross your desk is to decide what you want to do with them. If you've got newspapers that are more than a few days old, throw them away (or recycle them). If your magazines are more than a week or two old (if a magazine's a monthly, two months old), get rid of them, too. Chances are that the information's already out of date, and for most of us, we have many ways of obtaining important information even if we missed it the first time around.

When you need information on a specific subject, search the Internet. Internet searching techniques are discussed in Chapter 15.

Instead of allowing yourself to feel guilty because you didn't get your reading done, you should focus all of your energies on getting your important work done, done well, and completed on time. You should never lose sleep because you didn't have time to read the latest newspaper or magazine.

Set Up a Reading File

As an alternative to having stacks of newspapers, magazines, and trade journals lying around, why don't you set up a reading file for yourself? When you receive a magazine, quickly skim the table of contents and, if you see an article that you think may be of interest, rip the pages out of the magazine and throw the rest of it away. Then just put the article in a reading file that you can take with you on your next business trip, or read during the commute home.

If you don't want to rip up the magazine, then circle the page number of the article you wish to read in the table of contents or put a sticky note on the page where the article starts; otherwise, you'll never remember why in the world you saved the magazine in the first place. Dealing with reading material in this way will save you a lot of time because you won't have to thumb through an entire magazine to find that article that you wanted to read when you had a bit more time.

Do the same thing with your newspapers. Scan the paper quickly and, when you find an article that's of interest, rip out the page, put the article in a reading file, and throw the rest of the paper away. Furthermore, whenever you're reading anything — a letter, report, memo, newspaper, or magazine, always have a pen nearby so that you can circle or highlight any words, sentences, or phrases that you find of interest.

You may also find it very helpful to write any thoughts, comments, or questions you may have in the margins or on a sticky note. This way, you won't have to reread the material when you pick it up a week, a month, or a year later. With the important information highlighted, you'll know in an instant what caught your eye at the very moment you read the material.

Clean Out Your Desk Drawers

After you've cleaned off the top of your desk, you may want to tackle the drawers inside your desk. This task would include both the drawer that's designed to store your files, the smaller drawers, and the lap drawer.

You'll find that at least 80 percent of the papers in your file drawer can be tossed. That's because your working papers and to-do items have been sitting in piles on the top of your desk. In some of the offices that I've helped get organized, I've found that the file drawers were actually empty. And in others, the drawers contained files that belonged to the previous occupant of the office.

Since most of the papers in these drawers haven't been looked at in quite a while, it should be easy for you to go through them and toss the papers and files you no longer need. If you want to keep some papers and the file's beat up, make a new folder.

Use Expandable File Pockets Instead of Hanging Files

If you find that the files inside your file drawer aren't easy to work with, one of the reasons may be because you're using hanging files to keep your manila folders from falling over. The hanging files themselves can often take up 30 percent of the space of a file drawer — when it's empty.

So as an alternative to using hanging files, you can use expandable file pockets instead. You put your file folders inside the file pockets and then place them inside the file drawer. The file pockets come in various widths, from 1½ inches to 5 inches. In most cases, you'll find the pockets that expand to 3½ inches to be the most convenient to use.

What Does Your Briefcase Look Like?

And finally, once you've organized your office, why not organize your briefcase? Over the years, I've met many people who have a briefcase that they keep filled with work, reading materials, and other things that they never look at. Each night they lug this briefcase home so that they can do some work after dinner. And each morning they bring it back to the office, without ever having opened it.

So take a few minutes and go through all of the stuff that's in your briefcase. If there's work to do, note it on your Master List and plan to do it during regular business hours. If you need to keep something, file it away. The rest should be pitched.

Hard Drive Housecleaning, Anyone?

I know that I started this chapter with a discussion on how to get organized and clean off all the stuff that's accumulated on the top of your desk, but you can't forget about cleaning up the stuff that's inside your computer.

You see, your computer's hard drive is nothing more than an electronic filing cabinet. And no matter how large a hard drive you've got, you've got to do some housecleaning. If you continue to add more and more files and software programs, without deleting the ones you no longer need or use, the drive, like the file drawers in your office, will eventually become stuffed beyond capacity. Until you actually start getting rid of your old computer files and unused programs, you won't realize how much space is being wasted.

In Chapter 24, I show you how to clean up your hard drive, and I give you some tips so that you can get more out of your computer.

It's Easy to Stay Organized

Once you get organized, it's easy to stay organized, but it's going to take some work on your part. There's no avoiding the fact that every day you're going to continue to receive several inches of mail, a bunch of e-mail messages, a lot of voice mail messages, and a handful of faxes.

However, you don't have to allow yourself to lose control of your daily work plan. All you've got to do is continue to add new items of business to your Master List (discussed in detail in Chapter 3).

I'm sure you've often been told that "You should only handle a piece of paper once." In theory, this advice sounds great, but in reality, it doesn't work! You may in fact have to handle a piece of paper many times. But your goal should be to complete your important work, not to try to get rid of those papers as soon as they cross your desk.

So when something comes into your office, don't drop everything so that you can deal with it at that very moment. Instead, just add it to your Master List and plan to get to it at some time in the near future.

Just remember these three steps:

1. If there's work to do, you add it to your Master List.

2. If you need to keep the piece of paper, you file it.

3. If you don't need the piece of paper any longer, you throw it away, pass it on, or recycle it.

Clean Up Before You Go Home at the End of the Day

Before you go home at the end of the day, always spend a few minutes getting organized. Go through your stack of mail, listen to your voice mail messages, and scan your e-mail to see what items of business need to be added to your Master List. Papers that you need to keep should be filed in the appropriate folder or thrown away.

Then spend a few minutes reviewing your Master List and select the specific work, tasks, or projects that you feel are the most important. When you arrive at the office tomorrow morning, sit down and go to work.

Get into the habit of going through all of the things that have accumulated on your desk during the day, and you'll find that it's relatively easy to stay organized. If, after a few busy or hectic days, you find things have backed up and stacked up on you, then just stop cold. Take a half hour to get yourself cleaned up and organized again.

Now it's going to take you a bit of time to get organized. It's not going to happen overnight, but if you do a little bit at a time and stick with it, you'll see amazing results. You'll find that you're able to do a better job of staying on top of your important work, tasks, and projects. You'll feel that you've got much more control over your work and your day. And when you leave the office at the end of the day, you'll pat yourself on the back and congratulate yourself for a job well done.

Your goal is to complete as much *important* work as possible during normal business hours. When you go home at the end of the day, you've earned the right to relax and spend some quiet time with your family, your friends, and yourself.

Chapter 3

The World's Most Effective Follow-Up System: The Master List

● ●

In This Chapter

▶ Creating your follow-up system: The Master List

▶ Using a Master List

▶ Recognizing the limitations of your Master List

● ●

*W*hat does the top of your desk look like? Do you have piles of *stuff* everywhere? Well, if you're trying to stay on top of all of your unfinished work, tasks, projects, and telephone calls and you're doing it by leaving everything out on the top of your desk, then you're flirting with disaster. It's just impossible to keep on top of everything, or anything, when your office looks as if a tornado has gone through it.

Important things get lost, misplaced, or are soon forgotten, and at the very least, it takes a lot of time — wasted time — to find that letter, memo, file, or report when you need it. And why did you begin to look for it in the first place? Because your boss just asked for it, and he or she is standing at your doorway; or someone just called and is waiting patiently, or impatiently, on hold while you frantically search through the stacks of papers on your desk.

You may not be aware of this fact, but most people waste at least an hour a day looking for papers that are lost on the top of their desk. By getting organized, you can convert the time that's usually wasted during the course of a normal business day into time that can be used more productively and efficiently.

With piles of papers everywhere, it does become very difficult, if not impossible, to stay on top of the important things in your life.

In Chapter 2, I described how to get organized and get rid of the piles of papers on your desk top. So if your desk is a mess, go back and read Chapter 2 for the help you'll need to get your office organized. Then come back to this chapter to develop a better follow-up system.

The first few pages of this chapter are meant to convince you that using piles of papers is an inefficient follow-up system. After I get you to agree that you need to change your evil ways, I'll show you how a Master List is a better follow-up system.

Oh Where Did I Put My Calendar?

I know that you've never given this much thought, but many of the things that remain on the top of the desk are left out as reminders of things to do. We think that by seeing a piece of unfinished business, it will remind us to write that letter or make that call, and we'll do it.

In theory, this may sound great; in practice, it just doesn't work! Yes, you do get things done, and you often, but not always, meet your deadlines. You are, however, paying a price: It takes a lot more effort and exertion to get the work done. This occurs because you start working on a project when there's no lead time left. So your stress level is higher than it should be, and I would venture to say that the quality of your work isn't *always* at the highest level that you're capable of producing.

One of the main causes of efficiency problems is the piles themselves. The piles of papers are there to remind you of the tasks you're supposed to do, but you never get to these tasks until the last minute because the papers were lost, buried, and forgotten within the piles.

I'll get to it later

Do you ever go through your in-box and look at the pile of letters, memos, and reports that have accumulated and just put them aside in an "I'll get to it later" pile? Well, you're not alone because almost everybody else is doing it too.

But when you put things aside in this manner, you create problems for yourself. Once you get into the habit of leaving piles of paper everywhere, too many things end up in the "I'll get to it later" pile. But later never comes.

Over the years, I've had many people say to me, "I put things aside, and if I don't get a follow-up call or additional correspondence, I'll eventually throw it away."

Though this system may be an easy way to get through the day, is it the best way to take control of the things that are going on in your business life, and is it an efficient way to manage all of the papers that come across your desk?

When you just put things aside, you're putting yourself in the position of waiting for things to happen, and then you're forced to react to them. You're no longer making your own decisions, and you've lost control of your daily business affairs.

And you don't begin working on the task or project until someone calls to ask, "Where is it?" Now you've got to drop everything to do something that's been sitting around for a month.

But I Know Where Everything Is

Now I know you're going to tell me that you know where everything is, and I'm sure that you do, but the question isn't: "Do you know where everything is?" The real question is: "Do you know what work, tasks, and projects you have to do, and when you have to do them?"

- ✔ Who do you have to call?

- ✔ From whom are you awaiting a telephone call?

- ✔ Who are you supposed to be sending a letter, memo, presentation, proposal, or other piece of information to?

- ✔ Who is supposed to be sending you a letter, memo, presentation, proposal, or other piece of information?

The answer to these questions has nothing to do with whether or not you know that a particular piece of paper is sitting 3 inches from the top of one pile, or 2 inches from the bottom of another.

Just because you *think* you know where something is has nothing to do with your ability to get your work done, get it done on time, or even get it done well. Many times the work will remain undone until someone asks for it, and it's at this time that you must drop everything so you can complete a task that should have been done days ago. Now you have another fire to put out; your whole day is going up in smoke; and you don't even realize that you're guilty of arson.

So instead of leaving things out in piles, you'll find that you can be much more efficient and productive when you keep a list of all of your tasks, projects, and other items of business on what I call a Master List, which is a things-to-do list that's written on a large piece of paper. By writing everything down on your Master List, you give yourself the ability to maintain complete and total control over everything that's going on in both your business and your personal life.

An Efficient Follow-Up System Is the Key to Being Successful in the Business of Life

I know that you work hard, that you put in a lot of hours on the job, and that you're dedicated to your company. But hard work and dedication can only take you so far, and after a while, there just aren't any more hours left in the work day or the work week.

So if you want to become more efficient and effective; improve your ability to stay on top of all of the unfinished work, tasks, projects, and correspondence; and be able to do your work faster and better, then all you've got to do is improve your follow-up system.

Here are some of the things that an efficient follow-up system will do for you:

- ✔ It will help you get your work done well and done on time.
- ✔ It will help you improve the quality of your work.
- ✔ It will give you the opportunity to start your important projects while you've got plenty of lead time.
- ✔ It will help you remember who you're supposed to call and when you're supposed to call.
- ✔ It will give you complete control of your business affairs.
- ✔ You will be able to stay on top of the work you've delegated to others.
- ✔ It will allow you to compress the amount of time it takes to make decisions.
- ✔ You won't have to spend so much time putting out fires, because fewer fires will start.
- ✔ It will give you the ability to juggle lots of balls at once — without dropping any of them — thus avoiding the time-consuming and costly process of dealing with emergencies that could easily have been avoided.
- ✔ You will have complete control over your schedule, your day, and your life.
- ✔ You will have less stress and tension.
- ✔ At the end of the day, you will be able to say to yourself, "I really got a lot done today."

- ✓ You will be able to get a good night's sleep.
- ✓ You will get to stay home on the weekends.
- ✓ You will have more time to spend with your friends and family, doing the things that you enjoy.

With an effective follow-up system, things just don't slip through the cracks. You're able to stay on top of your most important work, tasks, and projects. You get your work done on time, you do it well, and you make it home for dinner.

Now that you're aware of the importance of having a good and thorough follow-up system, sit back and relax as you read the next few pages because I'm going to explain how easy it is to set up an efficient follow-up system.

I start by showing you how to make a Master List of all your things to do. In Chapter 4, I explain how to get the most out of your daily planner. And in Chapter 5, you'll learn how easy it is to put your daily planner inside your computer with the ACT! contact management program.

ANECDOTE

My own follow-up system

As an author, I represent myself as my own literary agent, and in selling my books, follow-up is of prime importance. After I send a proposal, I make it a point to find out if it has been received. (I usually call within two days if I used FedEx or a within a week if I used Priority Mail.)

After I'm told that my proposal was received, I ask the editor how long it will be before the publisher and acquisitions people expect to get around to looking at my proposal. And after they've had a chance to look at it, how long will it take them to decide whether or not they want to make me an offer to publish my book.

By making these phone calls, I learn a lot about the people with whom I'm dealing. Some answer their own phone. Others have their calls screened by an assistant or secretary. And a small handful actually return my calls.

Once I have the opportunity to speak with them, I can get a pretty good idea of their interest just by the tone of their voice as they talk to me. Some are friendly and cordial and are happy to hear from me; others are short and curt and speak to me as if I were a nuisance to them.

Based on these conversations, it is easy for me to identify both the people I should continue following up with and the people who have already decided to turn me down. Most important, by calling, I know who's interested and who isn't. And with this information, I can continue to move forward. (I was once told that "If you're not being rejected, you're not trying hard enough.")

I've learned that if I contact enough people, sooner or later I will find someone who not only likes my books but wants to buy them. That's how I've sold nine books, including the book you are holding in your hands.

What Is a Master List?

The basic concept behind using a Master List is that by writing everything down in an orderly, meticulous way, you can do a better job of staying on top of all of your unfinished work, tasks, projects, and correspondence. When you put things down on paper, you don't have to remember that much. You do, of course, have to remember where you put the piece of paper.

Now I know that you've been writing things down for years, but you just haven't been doing it methodically.

- ✔ You've been writing names, addresses, and phone numbers on sticky notes and sticking them onto the wall.
- ✔ You've been keeping to-do lists on the backs of envelopes.
- ✔ You've been scribbling notes to yourself on any piece of paper that you can get your hands on.

So yes, you've been in the habit of writing things down, but the manner in which you've been doing it isn't a very efficient or effective way of staying on top of all of your unfinished work.

By using a Master List to keep an itemized inventory of your unfinished work, you have an organized, systematic, and compact format for maintaining control of your workload and your workday.

Shouldn't I only handle a piece of paper once?

How many times have you heard the old adage: "You should only handle a piece of paper once"? But that advice just doesn't work in the high-pressure business world of the 21st century. And besides, you're dealing not only with paper but also with voice mail, e-mail, many different kinds of computer files, and all the wonderful things that are available over the Internet.

So you shouldn't be concerned if you handle a piece of paper once, twice, or a dozen times. The number of times you handle a piece of paper isn't important; what is important is that you make a decision about what you're going to do with that piece of paper.

When something crosses your desk, make a decision — *now* — instead of waiting to see what happens next.

- ✔ If there's work to do, note it on your Master List.
- ✔ If you need to keep it, file it away.
- ✔ If you don't need it any longer, pass it on to someone else, put it in the recycling bin, or throw it away.

You don't need to keep unneeded or unnecessary papers in a pile on the top of your desk for the next six months.

Getting the Most out of Your Master List

Over the next few pages, I'm going to show you how to set up and use a Master List. Much of the information might sound like common sense — because that's what it is — but you'd be surprised by how many people don't practice these simple techniques.

Use a big piece of paper

It's my suggestion that you keep your Master List on a big piece of paper. That way, you've got 25 lines on a page with which to list your projects, tasks, and the other items of business that you must do or follow up on. And because you're using a big piece of paper instead of a sticky note or the back of an envelope, you've got enough space to include not only such information as names and phone numbers, but you can also include things like the purpose of a phone call and any other pertinent information. If necessary, you can even write this additional information on a second or a third line.

Don't skip lines. When you're adding items of business to your Master List, make it a point to use every line so that you can get 25 items listed on a page rather than 12.

Write everything down

The key to making your Master List work for you is to make sure that you write everything down. The more tasks, projects, calls, and other to-do items that you put down on paper, the greater your ability to control the events that are taking place during the workday.

Add additional pages to your Master List

When you've used up all of the lines on the first page, don't be afraid to start a second one. It's common for most people to have a Master List that's one or two pages in length.

Cross off completed tasks

When you've completed a task, project, or other item of business, give yourself the pleasure of crossing it off your list. Don't just place a check mark in the margin; it's not gratifying enough. You should draw a line through the task instead.

Transfer unfinished items and consolidate the pages of your Master List

The key to making your Master List work for you is to transfer and consolidate the unfinished items of business from the older pages to the newest ones. As a general rule, when 50 percent of the items on a particular page have been completed, transfer the unfinished items — one at a time — to the newest page. Then cross them off the old page. After you've rewritten the unfinished items onto the newest page, take one last look at the old page, just to see if you've missed anything, before you throw it away.

If you feel that it's important to keep your old Master Lists so that you've got a record of what you've accomplished, make a file and label it "Old Lists."

Getting your work done

Scan the items on your Master List throughout the day to determine which item of business is the most important. This helps you to identify the next task you should tackle. If you have a project that will take 30, 60, or 90 minutes, or longer, schedule a block of uninterrupted time on your calendar. Think of it as an appointment with the boss or your most important client — because it is!

If you've only got 15 minutes between meetings, use this time to make or return a few phone calls. Or pick off a few of the smaller, less time-consuming tasks so that you can get rid of them.

Review your Master List before you go home

Before you go home at night, take a few minutes to review your Master List to determine which items of business are most important. Plan to do them as soon as you arrive in the morning. You can also use this time as an opportunity to plan your work for the future. What do you have to do during the next few days? Next week? Next month? Your objective is to produce the highest quality work that you're capable of.

When you give yourself more time to do your work, you don't have to worry about whether the first draft is good enough because you've got the time to revise it. And in the end, the finished product will be great.

Give yourself plenty of time to think about and plan your work, and doing the work is much easier.

Use your Master List as a planning tool so that you can start on all of your work, tasks, and projects while you've got sufficient lead time.

Schedule your important work for the first thing in the morning

When you schedule your work, try to tackle your most important tasks as soon as you arrive in the morning, when you're fresh, alert, and energetic. You'll be amazed at how much you can accomplish when you get into the habit of working on your most important projects early in the day before the inevitable fires flare up.

If you give *yourself* the first two hours of the workday — no meetings, no phone calls, and no interruptions — you'll find that you're able to complete twice as much work, in half the time, with half the effort.

Don't rewrite your Master List every day

Some people make it a point to rewrite their things-to-do list every morning so that the most important items are at the top of the list. I think that this is not only a waste of time but also a waste of effort. You're in the business of doing your work, not rewriting your lists.

You're not going to get everything done

You must also realize that you're not going to complete each and every item on your Master List every day. Your reason for writing items on your Master List is so that you won't forget them.

Your goal is to get to your important work, do it well, and get it done on time. Your Master List is the tool that helps you stay focused on your most important tasks and projects and keeps you in complete and total control.

Unfortunately, Your Master List Can't Do Everything

The Master List is great for initially getting organized, but as you use it, you'll find that it has some shortcomings, the biggest of which is that it doesn't integrate with a calendar. Let me give you a few examples.

It's not easy to keep track of future follow-ups

Let's say that you have an item on your list to call Jim Smith. So you make the call and are told that Jim is not going to be in the office until Wednesday of next week. The Master List doesn't offer an efficient way to keep track of when you need to make this next call.

You can write down the date on which you plan to make this call in the margin next to the original entry (or somewhere else on the line which notes the item), perhaps using a red pen. But things get more complicated when you call again and are told that Jim will be out of town for another ten days.

Now you've got to cross out the original follow-up date and replace it with a new one. Or maybe you rewrite the entire entry, or perhaps you just forget about it and hope that you'll remember to call Jim at some future date.

As you can see, the more times that you have to reschedule the follow-up date of a call or to-do item, the more complicated the process becomes. Your Master List gets messier and messier. A daily planner is better suited to dealing with this type of situation because you can write a person's name on the day of the calendar that you plan to call.

How do you remember to call someone six months from now?

Another ticklish problem arises when a person asks you to follow up in six or eight months or, for that matter, any time in the future. Your Master List is designed to help you stay on top of your daily work, not the things you may need to do in the coming months.

One possible way to deal with this situation is to create a Master List that's designed solely for your long-range projects, tasks, and calls. On this Master List, you keep track of things by date.

But for most people, this follow-up process can become rather cumbersome, and in the end, some important things will probably slip through the cracks. A daily planner can also solve this problem because you can write information down on any future date in the book.

How do you remember to start on a project two weeks from now?

Here's another problem that highlights the shortcomings of using a Master List: You've got a task or project that needs to be completed at some point in the not-so-distant future, but you don't plan to start working on it for several days, or even several weeks.

Once again, a daily planner solves this problem. You just write down when you want to start on the project on a specific future date in the daily planner.

What about names, addresses, and phone numbers?

And finally, what do you do with the names, addresses, phone numbers, and notes of conversations that may have become part of your Master List? How do you keep this valuable information if you're in the habit of throwing the pages of your Master List away after the list of unfinished tasks has been transferred to another page?

A daily planner gives you the ability to maintain access to this valuable information because you don't throw the old pages away. They're still in the book and are available for future reference.

Always write a person's name and phone number in your name and address book or Rolodex file so that you can find it when you need it.

It is for these, and many other, reasons that many people have found daily planners to be so useful when it comes to helping them take control of their daily activities and affairs. A daily planner is designed to integrate your calendar, things-to-do list, list of people to call, and your meetings and appointments into one book that can help you to stay on top of all of your unfinished work, tasks, and projects.

So What Now?

Using a Master List is a great way to keep track of your daily work, but as the preceding section illustrates, you need to supplement your Master List with a daily planner, which just happens to be the topic I cover in the next chapter.

Chapter 4

Taking Control: Using Your Daily Planner

● ●

In This Chapter

▶ Taking control of your schedule

▶ Putting your Master List inside your daily planner

▶ Making your daily planner work for you

▶ Recognizing the limitations of daily planners

● ●

*F*or years, people have been keeping track of meetings, appointments, telephone calls, and unfinished work by using daily planning books — Day Timers, Day Runners, Filofaxes, and Franklin Planners. These leather-bound personal organizers are wonderful productivity-improvement tools.

They help us set our priorities, organize and coordinate our important long-term projects, keep track of our delegated work, and establish and set our goals. We also use them to jot down notes or background information about our business meetings and phone conversations, keep track of miscellaneous ideas and thoughts, and record our tax-deductible or reimbursable expenses.

In addition to helping us keep track of what we need to do and when we need to do it, we use the phone book section to store the names, addresses, and phone numbers of our family, friends, customers, clients, and other important people in our lives.

We use these books to not only keep track of our daily activities but to keep our lives in order. For some of us, these books play such an important part of our lives that we won't go any place without them. We even use them to carry our checkbooks and credit cards.

It's a To-Do List, a Calendar, and a Dessert Topping

The basic concept behind the daily planner is that you use it to coordinate your list of things to do (your Master List), your list of people to call, and your meetings and appointments with your calendar. You're no longer writing these lists of your unfinished work, tasks, and projects on a things-to-do list; you're writing them on a specific date in the daily planning book — a date when you think you can get to them.

The integration of your things-to-do list with your calendar gives you the flexibility to schedule future tasks on a date when you plan to start working on them. In many cases, this date will not be the date on which you wrote the item down in the book.

You can schedule to-do items on future days

Have you ever been given an assignment by your boss that was due in, let's say, two weeks? The boss walks into your office on Monday morning, hands you a piece of paper that outlines the project, and tells you that it has to be completed by a week from Friday.

As you look at your calendar, you realize that this week is shot because of all of the other appointments and commitments you made. So you look at your calendar and block out two hours of your day — from 9 a.m. to 11 a.m. — on Tuesday of next week. Now you've worked it into your schedule and can start, and finish, it without being rushed. That's what the daily planner is designed to do.

I used a guy named Jim Smith as an example in Chapter 3, so I might as well use him again for another example here. Let's say that on Monday of this week you decide that you want to call Jim to discuss the benefits of the new product that your company's about to introduce. But in looking at your calendar, you realize that you're all booked up until Thursday, which will be your first full day in the office. So instead of writing your note to call Jim on Monday's page, you enter it in your book on the day you actually will be able to make the call, which would be Thursday.

You have more control of your scheduling

In scheduling your daily activities, you need to have some flexibility. With a daily planner, you've got a lot of flexibility because you're able to associate specific tasks with certain days of the week.

So when someone asks you to call him, or her, a week from Thursday, all you've got to do is write it down on Thursday's page, and it's done. And if you're asked to follow up with someone in six months, you just select a date six months in the future and write down the person's name and the purpose or nature of the call on that page. When that date arrives, six months from now, you'll find that person's name with your note to give him or her a call.

A daily planner also gives you flexibility in planning your schedule and work flow. With a Master List, you're always looking at a list of everything you need to do — things that need to be done today, as well as those tasks that need to be done in the future. When you're using a daily planner, you don't need to list all of your to-do's, calls, and other tasks on a single day. You can spread them out. You'll do some of the work today, some tomorrow, and the rest on the following day. And when you find that you're not able to get to certain tasks because of your other commitments, just write down those tasks on a day you know you can get to them.

When you use your daily planner, rather than a piece of paper, to list all of your tasks, then you have much more control of your day. You have control because you're able to associate an unfinished task or other item of business with a specific date on the calendar.

Making Your Daily Planner Work for You

If you've been keeping track of all of your unfinished work, tasks, calls, and projects on a Master List, the first thing you'll have to do is transfer the items onto the pages of your daily planner.

If you haven't been keeping track of things with a Master List, it's about time you started writing everything down and getting yourself organized. So if you haven't done so already, please read Chapter 2, which explains how to get your office cleaned up, and Chapter 3, which discusses how to develop a Master List.

Transfer your to-do items to your daily planner

As you review your Master List, ask yourself when you plan to get to each specific task. Write the task in your planner on the day you *expect* to get to it, start it, or complete it.

Don't write down things to do on a day when you already know that you're going to be tied up in meetings or out of town.

As you transfer each item to your daily planner, draw a line through it to ensure that you don't miss anything. When each item on your Master List has been transferred, you can throw the list away.

Add new items of business to your daily planner

Throughout the day, new items of business will come up. When they do, enter them immediately in your book on the day that you plan to do them. Just because you were assigned a project this morning doesn't mean that it has to be entered on today's page of your daily planner. Maybe it should be entered on tomorrow's page, or one day next week. By writing things down immediately, they won't get buried in a pile and easily lost or forgotten.

Cross off completed items of business

As you complete a task or project, draw a line through it. (A check just isn't gratifying enough.) The line is your way of knowing that the task was in fact completed.

Move each unfinished piece of business to a future day, one item at a time

The single most important part of keeping your daily planner up-to-date comes when you move the unfinished work from one day to another. Many times, when a day has ended, a person just turns the page of his or her daily planner without checking to make sure that everything that had been entered on that day had actually been done. In most cases, there are at least one or two items, sometimes many more, that remain undone.

If you haven't moved these items forward, you'll soon find yourself flipping through your daily planner to see which items of business weren't completed. This method of organization guarantees that something will slip through the cracks.

Draw a line through each item as you transfer it and then draw a big X across the page

To guarantee that nothing slips through the cracks, at the end of each day, go through the to-do items, one at a time, and move them to a future day. You can move them to tomorrow, later in the week, or some other date in the future.

After you move each item, draw a line through it. When all of the items have been moved, draw a big **X** across the page. By drawing a line from one corner of the page to the other, you know that everything on that page has either been completed or moved forward. And when you see that **X**, you know that you never have to refer to that page again.

Use a pencil to schedule appointments

When you schedule your meetings or appointments, write them into your daily planner with a pencil because half of all the appointments that you schedule will be rescheduled or postponed. By using a pencil, you can erase the meeting from your daily planner. If you use a pen, you have to scratch it out.

Write your to-do and call items with pen

Use a pen to write your to-do items and follow-ups into your book. Pencils tend to smudge, and since you won't be erasing these items, you'll have a more permanent record of the things that you did or need to do.

Write your phone numbers in your Rolodex file or in your name and address book

If you're in the habit of writing people's names, phone numbers, or other information on the pages of your daily planner, you *must* transfer that information to your name and address book, Rolodex file, or database. Otherwise, you may not be able to find a piece of information when you need it, or at the very least, it won't be at your fingertips.

If you don't transfer important phone numbers and addresses to an address book or Rolodex file, you may never be able to locate that information after the end of the current calendar year, when you start using your new daily planner.

Block out vacation time for yourself

Most of us are spending too many hours at the office and not enough time with our family and friends. So go through your daily planner and decide when you want to take a vacation. If you don't block out time for yourself, there won't be any.

At the beginning of each year, a friend of mine, who is the vice-chairman and chief financial officer of a Fortune 500 company and on the board of directors of several public companies, asks for a list of all the various meetings that he is expected to attend during the coming year. After he enters these meetings into his daily planner, he then decides when he wants to take his vacations and also enters those dates. He knows that if he doesn't block out some time for himself, and his family, there wouldn't be any.

Add birthdays and anniversaries

Add the birthdays and anniversaries of your family, friends, relatives, and important customers or clients to your daily planner so that you'll remember to send them a card, buy them a present, or invite them out to celebrate that special day.

Enter birthdays and anniversaries in your daily planner at least two weeks in advance of that special day so that you'll have plenty of time to go out and buy a card or gift.

Daily Planners Do Have Limitations

You will find that there are some limitations to using a daily planner, based upon the simple fact that you're using a pencil and paper. I'm going to point out these shortcomings now because, in the next chapter, I'm going to explain why I think you should replace your paper-based personal organizer with a computerized contact manager.

Today, it's easy to harness the power of your computer to help you stay on top of every task and project that crosses your desk. With a computerized contact manager, it's no longer necessary to write and rewrite the same information over and over again. You can spend your time doing your work, instead of *planning* to do your work. The rest of this section shows some examples of what I mean.

It's not easy to keep your to-do list up-to-date

It takes a lot of work to keep a list of things to do up-to-date. You meticulously write down the names of various tasks, projects, or other items of business that need to be done on a specific day's page in your daily planning book. But if that item isn't done on the day it was entered, it must be moved to a future day. And if the item is not moved, you run the risk of forgetting about it.

A computerized contact manager solves this problem because an unfinished task is automatically moved forward at the beginning of each day.

Moving or changing to-do items can be a lot of work

For example, suppose you have a to-do item that says: **Call Jim Smith to set up a luncheon appointment.**

In all likelihood, you'll have to move this item around several times before you're able to schedule the appointment. On Monday, you call and learn that he's out until Friday. When you call on Friday, you're told that he's in meetings all day and won't be in the office again until the following Thursday. And when you call on Thursday, you finally get through and set up your luncheon meeting for the following Wednesday.

Now look at what you did physically to schedule this appointment:

1. First you wrote down the item: "Call Jim Smith to set up luncheon appointment."

2. Then you wrote it a second time when you moved it to Friday.

3. You wrote it a third time when you moved it to the following Thursday.

4. You wrote the item a fourth time when you scheduled the luncheon appointment for Wednesday.

And if you weren't in the habit of moving items of business from one page to another in your daily planner, it's quite likely that you would never have gotten around to scheduling the appointment in the first place because you would have forgotten about it. (This scenario is a perfect example of how easy it is for a person to lose track of things by not continually writing them down.)

A computerized contact manager, on the other hand, automates this task for you. For starters, you only have to enter the item on your to-do list once. Thereafter, you only have to change the date.

When you were told on Monday that Jim was out till Friday, you just clicked on the pop-up calendar and selected Friday's date. The item was moved electronically.

When you called on Friday and were told that he was out until Thursday, you clicked on the pop-up calendar again and selected Thursday's date. The to-do item was once again moved electronically.

When you turned on your computer on Thursday morning, the item that said "Call Jim Smith to set up luncheon appointment" was at the top of your list of things to do. And when you spoke to Jim on Thursday and scheduled the luncheon appointment for Wednesday, all you had to do was change the to-do item to a meeting, change the date to Wednesday, and select the time.

With a contact manager, it's easy to move items from your to-do list to your appointment calendar and back again because it's all done electronically. With just a few clicks of the mouse, you have complete control of everything that's going on in your business life.

Do you like to carry your calendar around with you?

Many people have more than one calendar. They keep a calendar on their desk and carry a pocket calendar with them when they travel or are out of the office. And secretaries or administrative assistants often keep a third calendar so that additional appointments can be scheduled while people are away from the office. But when people keep more than one calendar, eventually they're going to experience scheduling problems.

"He who has two calendars never knows his true appointment schedule." And the same goes for the "she's" out there.

A computerized calendar guarantees that you'll always have a true picture of your daily activities — appointments, calls, and to-dos — because it's always up-to-date. Your assistant can have a printed copy of it on his or her desk, and when you leave the office, you take a printed copy with you. If your assistant has access to your computer, he or she can make changes to your calendar. If you're on a network, your assistant can access your calendar from another computer.

It takes a lot of effort to keep track of the important people in your life

In today's fast-paced world, keeping a person's vital information up-to-date isn't easy. Everybody has a direct phone number and fax number. Then there's a number for the beeper, car phone, mobile telephone, and home phone and fax. And let's not forget about e-mail addresses and their company's Web site.

To make this record keeping more complicated, most people change jobs or positions or relocate to a new city every few years. Each time a person makes a change, you've got to update your records. How do you do it?

You have three real choices:

- ✔ Rolodex cards
- ✔ A name and address book
- ✔ A computerized contact manager

You also have a fourth choice, which is to not bother trying to keep track of any of these people. But if you go this route, your career will be brief.

Let's look at the shortcomings of using either a Rolodex card file or a name and address book.

- ✔ **Rolodex cards quickly become unreadable.** How much information can you really store on a 2-x-4-inch or 3-x-5-inch card? If you're writing the names, addresses, and phone numbers by hand, it doesn't take very long before the cards become beat up, dog-eared, and dirty, especially if you're using them every day. And what happens to a card when you learn that something has changed in a person's life? You scratch out the old information and start scribbling the person's new company, address, and phone number on the card. To say the least, it soon becomes unreadable.

- ✔ **Name and address books quickly get beat up.** Keeping a name and address book can cause you even bigger problems. For starters, you must write each name, address, and phone number by hand, which is an enormous waste of time. And after a couple of months of continuous use, a name and address book can get pretty beat up and messy — because old numbers have been scratched out and replaced with the current numbers. It doesn't take very long before you've got a really big mess.

One day my wife, Mitzi, and I were at a nearby park with our daughter DeLaine. While we were there, we watched a woman who was sitting on a park bench rewrite the list of names that were in her old address book into the new address book she had just purchased. As Mitzi and I watched her, we said to each other, "Doesn't she have something more important to do?"

Put your names and addresses inside your computer

When you keep your list of name and addresses inside your computer, it's easy to keep everything up-to-date. Whenever a number changes, you just make the change to the person's record. And with just a few clicks of the mouse, you can add additional people to your contact manager or remove them from the program.

Once the names are inside your computer, you can use them for your mailing lists, phone lists, or even your Rolodex cards. You can also use your computerized list to send these people e-mail and faxes. Chapter 5 tells you all about it.

Chapter 5

ACT!ing Lessons, or Learn How to Put Your Daily Planner Inside Your Computer

. . . .

In This Chapter

▶ Improving your business relationships

▶ Storing and finding names, addresses, and phone numbers

▶ Scheduling your activities

▶ Viewing your meetings and appointments in a calendar view

▶ Putting your Master List inside ACT!

▶ Storing and dialing phone numbers

▶ Sending and receiving e-mail

▶ Writing letters, memos, and faxes

▶ Creating reports

. . . .

*I*f you don't have a computer, you may not want to spend too much time reading this chapter. You should skim it and consider investing in a computer, which, as this chapter explains, can be a great time management tool. There is more to come for you non-computer users.

However, if you would *really* like to improve your daily productivity and take control of all of your daily activities — your telephone calls, to-dos, meetings, and appointments — start using a contact manager and put your daily planner inside your computer. The whole idea of using a computer is to help you get more work done in less time. And with a contact manager, you can coordinate the basic components of your planner with a single software program.

Not just an *everyday* user!

By the way, I would like to mention that I don't work for Symantec, and I don't own stock in the company. I'm just an everyday user who thinks ACT! is a very good productivity improving tool. Well, to be honest, I'm no longer just an everyday user. I've written three ACT! books in the past four years, the newest being *ACT! 4 For Windows For Dummies*.

I'm also the publisher of the leading ACT! newsletter, *ACT! in ACTion*. If you would like a free trial subscription, you can fill out the online form at my Web site, www.ACTnews.com, or fill out the response card at the back of this book.

These components include your

- ✔ Calendar
- ✔ Appointment book
- ✔ To-do list
- ✔ Name and address book

There are many good contact management programs available today — Goldmine, Maximizer, and Sharkware to name a few — but I've found the Symantec ACT! contact management program to be the best at keeping me on top of everything that's going on in both my business and personal life.

On the following pages, I'm going to tell you how ACT! can help you to organize your day, and your life. If you're not presently using a contact management program, it's my suggestion that you go out and purchase a copy of ACT! today. If you're using a different contact manager, I still think it would be worth your while to take a look at ACT!

ACT! is made by Symantec Corporation, 10201 Torre Avenue, Cupertino, CA 95014; phone 800-441-7234. The Web site is www.symantec.com/act. (The suggested retail price is about $200. If you shop around, you should be able to purchase it for less.) It's available in Windows and Macintosh versions.

Why I Chose ACT! for My Contact Management Program

When I wrote my third book, *Winning the Fight Between You and Your Desk* — I've just completed my ninth book, *Success is a Journey* — I reviewed several dozen contact management programs. I found the majority of them to be very powerful, and most were easy to use, but when I had finished writing my manuscript, I found myself faced with an unusual dilemma: Which contact management program should I use for myself? There were so many good ones to choose from.

One of the programs I had previously evaluated was ACT!, which was, and still is, one of the most popular contact managers available. Today, ACT! commands a 70 percent market share, and has about 2 million users. I decided to reinstall it on my computer and give it another try.

After I played around with it for a few days, I discovered that it had the majority of the features that I would want in a computerized appointment book/calendar/to-do list program if I, as a time management expert, were to write such a program myself.

Today, I use ACT! all day long — and I *still* believe it's the best contact management program available! It's the main reason why I turn on my computer early in the morning, and ACT! is the last thing I turn off at the end of the day. ACT! does a wonderful job of keeping me on time and on top of everything that's going on in my life, both personally and professionally.

ACT! has a feature that enables you to import all of the names, addresses, and phone numbers that you've already entered into your current contact manager, personal information manager, computerized name and address book, or word processing merge file. This feature saves you the time and effort of reentering the same information a second time.

What ACT! Can Do for You

If you're like most people, I'm sure that you do several different things during the course of a normal business day:

- You schedule appointments with many different people.
- You have follow-up work to do.
- You have joint projects that you're working on with other people.
- You keep detailed notes of your telephone conversations and/or face-to-face meetings (or at least you're supposed to).
- You spend a lot of time on the phone.
- You send out letters, faxes, proposals, and other correspondence throughout the day.
- You send, and receive, e-mail all day long.
- You surf the Internet.

With ACT! you can manage all of these activities and tasks, and more, from inside your computer. You no longer need a Master List, a daily planner, and a calendar to stay organized. Any piece of information about a person, project, or task that you used to keep as a note in a file folder, as a scrap of paper on your desk, or as a mental note in your head can now be kept in one place, inside ACT!

This is what ACT! does for you:

- ✔ ACT! gives you a place to store the names, addresses, phone numbers, fax numbers, e-mail and Web site addresses, and lots of other information about your business and personal contacts.

- ✔ ACT! integrates that information with your list of things to do, your list of people to call, and your appointment calendar.

Once you start using ACT!, you'll find that fewer things slip through the cracks because everything's at your fingertips. Figure 5-1 shows you the ACT! Contact window.

Additional information can be stored on the different Tabs — Phone/Home, Alt Contacts, and Status — located at the bottom of the Contact window. ACT!'s Layout Designer enables you to create your own customized layouts, and you can have an unlimited number of ACT! fields.

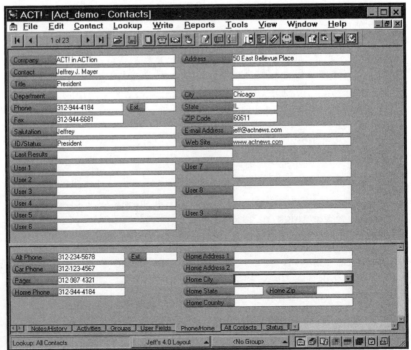

Figure 5-1:
ACT!'s
Contact
window.

Improve your business relationships, lose weight, make friends, and influence people

Day in and day out, you're working and interacting with many people — customers, clients, prospects, as well as your coworkers and colleagues — and you need to be able to stay on top of everything that's going on between you and them. With ACT!, you've got the tools you need to do a more thorough job of keeping track of all of the information that's associated with those projects, tasks, and your other daily activities.

ACT! will also help you to develop and strengthen your long-term relationships — which is the key to being successful in business — because it's designed to help a person get to know the important people in his or her life. ACT! gives you a place to store a lot of important information about a person and have it available at your fingertips.

You can use ACT! to store such pieces of information as the names of a person's spouse and children and the dates of their birthdays and anniversaries. In ACT!'s notepad you can record notes of each person's hobbies, outside interests, favorite restaurants, and most recent vacations. And ACT! gives you a place to store each person's work and/or home address(es), and phone numbers (work, home, fax, car, and mobile), as well as the names and phone numbers of the assistants.

With ACT! you've a place to routinely store little tidbits of miscellaneous information that you would otherwise forget.

Store and find names, addresses, and phone numbers

Whenever you speak with people, either on the phone or in person, you should always add their names to ACT!. Over time you'll create an electronic Rolodex file that enables you to keep in touch with hundreds, or thousands, of people easily and effortlessly.

With ACT!'s very powerful Lookup feature, you're able to find any person's name and/or phone number in a fraction of a second because the information is stored in your computer, not on a piece of paper. ACT!'s Lookup feature is shown in Figure 5-2.

How a beer can collection helped me sell some life insurance

When I started my business career as the Special Agent with Northwestern Mutual twenty-some years ago, I was taught to ask people a lot of questions about their personal, business, and financial situations. And during these interviews, I always made it a point to inquire about their outside interests and hobbies.

One day, I was meeting with the treasurer of a large public company, and during the course of the conversation, he mentioned that his son had a beer can collection. I dutifully noted this tidbit of information on my fact-finding form. When I came back a week later with my estate planning presentation, Lee was so moved by the fact that I had remembered to make mention of the beer can collection that he bought a very large life insurance policy from me.

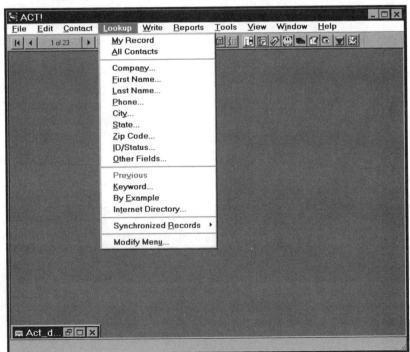

Figure 5-2:
ACT!'s
Lookup
feature.

You'll find ACT!'s Lookup feature one of its most important features. All you have to do is click Lookup with your mouse, select which criteria you want to look up (company, first name, last name, and so on), type the first few letters of the name, and the results of the search are displayed before you can blink your eyes. This sure beats trying to find someone's name in an ancient Rolodex file or an old, beat-up name and address book.

So go through those business cards that have been gathering dust in the lap drawer of your desk and put the information inside ACT!. Now you'll have a way to find these people when you need them.

You can also use the Lookup feature to help you plan your business trips. When traveling, do a lookup for the names of people you know in the cities you're visiting so that you can schedule some additional meetings. You can also use ACT! to store the names of your favorite hotels and restaurants.

With all of this information at your fingertips, what could be easier? Needless to say, trying to find all of this information in your Rolodex file or name and address book is such a boring, laborious, and time-consuming process that you probably wouldn't do it.

With Seiko's Smart Business Card Reader, you can scan your business cards directly into ACT!, thus eliminating the biggest hurdle you have for getting this important information into your computer: typing it. Seiko Instruments, 1130 Ringwood Court, San Jose, CA 95131-1726; phone 800-688-0817. Seiko's Web site is www.seikosmart.com.

If you've got mailing lists, business cards, or Rolodex files that you would like to have typed into your computer, contact Contact Data Entry. Send them your lists, and they'll type the names into their computer and send them back to you. Within minutes, you'll have your list of names inside ACT!. Contact Data Entry, P.O. Box 3998, Bartlesville, OK 74006; phone 918-335-0252; Web site www.contactentry.com.

Keep detailed notes of all of your conversations with the notepad

Each person in ACT! has his or her own notepad on which you can keep detailed notes of your telephone conversations and face-to-face meetings. This eliminates the need to write notes to yourself on sticky notes or little pieces of paper.

ACT! in ACTion

As I was writing the section on ACT!'s notepad in my word processor, the phone rang. It was my friend John in Los Angeles who was returning my call from earlier in the week.

While John and I were exchanging greetings, I toggled over to ACT!, did a lookup of his last name, found his record, and opened the notepad. With the information therein, I was able to remind myself why I had called, check the date when we last spoke, and read what we spoke about. It took me no more than four seconds to do the whole process.

While we were talking, he asked me to fax him a copy of a recent article about me that had

appeared in _The New York Times_, so I clicked on ACT!'s To-Do icon, selected today's date, and typed in "Fax NYT article." When the conversation ended, I wrote a few brief notes to myself in the notepad and went back to work on this book.

Later in the day, I selected ACT!'s QuickFax command, which launched WinFax PRO. I wrote a quick cover letter, attached the _New York Times_ article, which I had scanned into the computer, and clicked the Send button. Within seconds the fax was sent.

Each time you open the notepad, the entry is automatically date and time stamped. All you have to do is type in the notes to yourself, and in just a few moments, you're on to your next task. For ease of viewing, your previous entries are displayed in reverse chronological order.

ACT!'s Notes/History tab is shown in Figure 5-3.

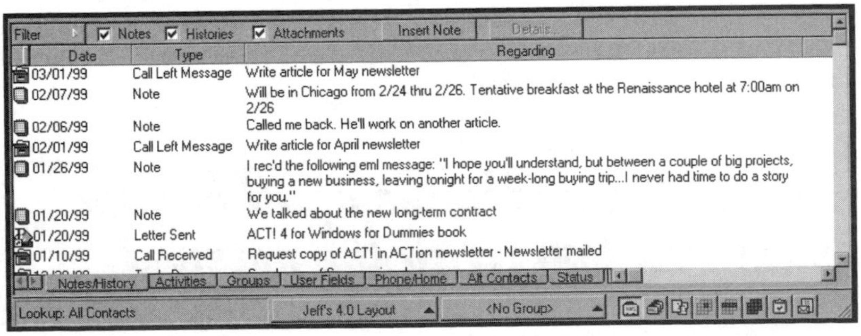

Figure 5-3:
ACT!'s
Notes/
History tab.

Scheduling activities — calls, meetings, and to-do's — is a breeze

You can use ACT! to keep track of everything you need to do. ACT! makes scheduling activities — calls, meetings, or to-do's — easy because you hardly need to use the keyboard to enter any information. With ACT!'s Schedule Activity dialog box, which is shown in Figure 5-4, you can do almost all of it with just a few clicks of the mouse.

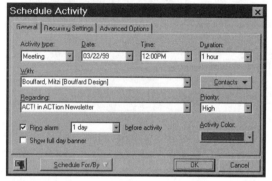

Figure 5-4:
ACT!'s
Schedule
Activity
dialog box.

Whenever you need to schedule a task, the first thing you do is find the person's contact record with ACT!'s powerful Lookup feature. (In ACT!, each task — a call, meeting, or to-do — is associated with a specific person; it's not itemized on a list.)

Then you decide which type of activity you want to schedule and click the appropriate icon on the toolbar. Once you click the icon, the Schedule Activity box opens, and a pop-up monthly calendar appears, where you select a date.

After entering the date, you press the tab key and move to the Time field where a mini-day calendar pops up. Here you select the activity's starting time and duration.

You then tab over to the Regarding field, where you enter a brief description for this activity.

You can also select an item — send proposal, send quote, send follow-up letter, confirm meeting, schedule lunch, and so on — from the drop-down menu. This list can be customized with phrases or terms that describe the specific nature of your daily business activities.

Remember to make that call

How many times have you called someone and been told: "I can't talk to you right now. Would you call me back in 20 minutes?" And what did you do?

If you're like most people, you would put this person's file aside and promptly forget about making the call.

So here's a great idea: Why not use ACT!'s alarm to remind you to make the call? Just click on the Call icon, which brings up the Schedule Activity dialog box, select the time you want to be reminded, and set the alarm.

Twenty minutes later, ACT!'s alarm will pop up, reminding you to call this person.

Additional scheduling features include

- ✔ Assigning priority levels to each activity
- ✔ Setting alarms
- ✔ Scheduling recurring activities
- ✔ Scheduling multiple activities
- ✔ Scheduling activities for other ACT! users (if you're on a network)

View your meetings and appointments in a calendar view

With a single click of the mouse, you can see your appointment calendar in a daily, weekly, or monthly format. This enables you to have a "picture" of what your future time commitments look like.

Just click an icon and you can change from one view to another. You can schedule new appointments, modify existing appointments, or clear appointments from any ACT! calendar. ACT!'s daily calendar is shown in Figure 5-5.

Put your Master List inside ACT!

In addition to viewing your activities in a calendar format, you also have the ability to view all of your tasks — your calls, meetings, and to-do's — on a single list that's conveniently called the Task List. (Creative people, those software designers.)

It was ACT!'s Task List that convinced me that ACT! was the ultimate time management tool. For the concept of the Task List is identical to my Master List.

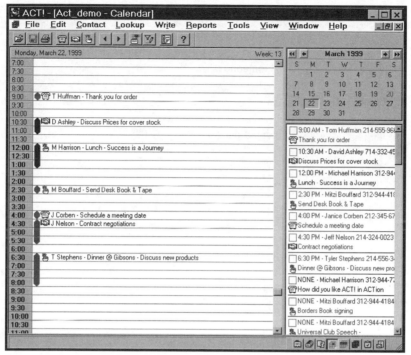

Figure 5-5:
ACT!'s daily
calendar.

With just a few mouse clicks, you can see a list of all your unfinished tasks for today, tomorrow, or any range of dates, past, present, or future. The Task List is shown in Figure 5-6.

Store and dial phone numbers

ACT! is designed to store all of a person's telephone numbers. This includes a person's phone and fax number at work, their cell phone number, a phone number at a second or third location, as well as a home number, beeper number, and home fax number. ACT! can also store the secretary's or assistant's name and phone numbers.

When you want to place a call, all you have to do is locate the person in the database, click on the Phone icon, and a list of all of the person's numbers displays in a pop-up dialog box, as shown in Figure 5-7.

If your computer and your telephone share the same line, you can have ACT! dial the phone for you. Once the call goes through, all you have to do is pick up the receiver and begin your conversation.

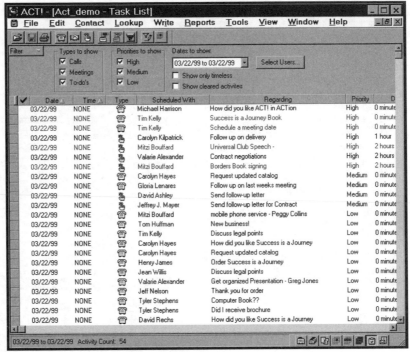

Figure 5-6:
ACT!'s Task
List.

Figure 5-7:
ACT!'s
Dialer
dialog box.

If your computer doesn't have a modem or is not connected to your voice telephone line, just click on the phone list, select the number you wish to call, and dial it manually. This sure beats trying to find a number in an old, beat-up Rolodex file.

Send your e-mail from ACT!

You can use ACT! to send and receive your e-mail. Just select the Create E-mail Message command from the menu bar, and the Create E-mail window opens. Write your e-mail message, click the Send button, and you're done.

You can also use ACT!'s mail merge features to send customized e-mail messages to an unlimited number of people.

Log on to the Web

ACT! has a special field on each contact record that is designed to store Web site addresses. Just enter a Web site address in this field and double-click on it. ACT! launches your Web browser and opens the selected Web page.

You can also add your favorite Web pages to ACT!'s Internet Links menu.

Use categories to find selected groups of people

One of the features that makes ACT! so powerful is its capability to group people in different categories based upon their business, profession, or any other criteria you might select. You can then perform a lookup, and in the blink of an eye, you have a complete listing of everybody in that particular group.

Send letters, memos, and faxes

ACT! makes it easy for you to write letters, e-mail, memos, and faxes. Just select the person to whom you want to send a letter and then click the Letter icon.

The basic format of the letter will be created in an instant. This format includes the date, the person's name and address, salutation, and your closing. All you have to do is write the text.

You can then print the letter, fax the letter (ACT! has seamless integration with WinFax Pro), or send it as electronic mail.

You can select Word, WordPerfect, or ACT!'s own word processor as your word processor.

Do you send out form letters? If so, ACT!'s mail-merge capabilities make the process fast, easy, and simple. Create your form letter template, and then merge it with the selected contacts in your ACT! database. ACT! comes with predesigned letter templates that can be easily modified so that you can create your own customized letters, memos, and faxes.

You can also print the information you've stored in ACT! as a telephone directory, mailing labels, envelopes, or Rolodex cards.

I left my Rolodex in San Francisco

I do all of my own publicity and have set up categories for newspaper, magazine, radio, television, and so on. To date, I've stored the names of several thousand newspaper, magazine, radio, television, and other media people in my database.

With the ACT!'s Lookup feature, I can do some amazing things. For example, in just a few seconds, I can create a list of the people who work for a radio station in Dallas and write for a newspaper in San Francisco.

How long would it take you to gather such information with your Rolodex file? ACT! puts the power of your computer at your fingertips.

Use ACT! to create your reports

One of ACT!'s biggest timesaving features is its capability to take any of the different pieces of information that you have about each of the people in your database and use that information to create reports.

You can generate reports of all your daily activities — your calls, meetings, and to-do's — and include any notes you may have taken about the various people in your file. You can display a history of what you've done with those people in the past and create a detailed list of the calls, meetings, and to-do's that you have scheduled with them in the future. These reports can be created for a single individual or a group of people.

Share your ACT! database with your coworkers

One of ACT!'s extremely powerful features is that it is network compatible. This enables you to share a common database and have access to another person's database.

Leaving the office? Print your calendar and take it with you

If you love your daily planner and can't live without it, you can print information from any part of ACT! onto a variety of paper sizes. Just insert the pages in your favorite daily planner, and take it with you as you walk out the door.

Use ACT!; save money

Several years ago, I was having some difficulty getting reimbursed for the telephone expenses I incurred as part of the ongoing publicity for one of my books. One day I got a letter from my publisher's publicity department stating that they would be happy to reimburse me for those expenses. There was however one requirement: I would have to provide them with the name and address of each person with whom I had spoken, the dates we spoke, and the current status of the publicity that was being generated.

They thought they were being cute. They knew that *nobody* could possibly create such a list. And even if they could, it would take them many hours trying to put it together.

Up until then, they had never heard of ACT!. I just printed a contact report for my entire "media" database — which had more than a thousand people in it. It took me more than an hour to print the 400-page report, which I promptly put in the mail. Two weeks later, I received my check for almost $2,000.

This feature enables you to have the best of both worlds: a computer program that keeps you on top of everything that's going on in your life and a paper-based program that you can take with you when you're away from your office.

Link ACT! to a palm-sized computer

You can link the information in your ACT! database with most of the popular palm-sized computers. I discuss the features of three of them — 3Com's PalmPilot, the Sharp Electronics Mobilon, and Franklin's REX PRO — in Chapter 22.

Part II
Taking Care of Business

The 5th Wave · By Rich Tennant

©RICHTENNANT

I'm still having trouble juggling my job at the snake farm and here at the day care center.

In this part . . .

*T*he chapters in this part all focus on one goal: taking control. Your workday shouldn't run you ragged; you should be the one dictating what goes on and when.

Chapter 6 helps you plan the daily routine of getting your important work done. In Chapter 7, I share some tips on making the most of your business appointments. In Chapter 8, I show how you can be a more effective speaker. And in Chapter 9, I provide you with all you need to know about getting people to make the decisions that you want them to make.

Chapter 6

Do the Right Job at the Right Time

● ●

● ●

*I*f you're like most of the people who are working in the corporate world, you've probably got too much to do and not enough time to get it all done. But as you look at your Master List, I'm sure you'll see that some jobs are more important than others, and it's usually the important ones that are going to take up most of your time. (For more information on the Master List, turn to Chapter 3.)

So if you want to get ahead in today's fast-paced world, you've got to be aware of which job you're doing and when you're doing it. It's just not enough that you're doing a particular job right. You've got to be sure that you're doing the right job at the right time, and that you're doing it right! It's not very difficult to stay focused, especially if you use your Master List or ACT! to stay organized.

✔ First off, you need to sit down and analyze all the things you've got to do — your unfinished tasks, projects, and telephone calls.

✔ Then all you have to do is make sure that you're spending your time on those activities that are of the highest priority, the ones that will have the biggest payoff for you and your company. The other tasks can wait until later.

And that's the beauty of this system. Because you're able to spend your time working on your most important tasks, you're able to take control of your work and your workday — they're no longer controlling you. You're able to see what's important, and you can set your own agenda. You're the one who is making things happen. You're no longer just reacting to events as they occur.

And after you've taken control of the tasks and projects that need your attention today, you're in a position to begin planning for tomorrow and beyond as you look at those tasks and projects that will need your attention in the days and weeks ahead.

And after you've taken control of the tasks and projects that need your attention today, you're in a position to begin planning for tomorrow and beyond as you look at those tasks and projects that will need your attention in the days and weeks ahead.

Planning Your Daily Activities

If you're not in the habit of *planning* your day, don't be alarmed — planning is really easy to do. You see, planning is nothing more than identifying, organizing, and scheduling your work. And that's what this whole book is about: helping you to take control of your day so that you can get your work done, leave the office, and spend more time with your family and friends. Common sense tells us that we should spend the majority of our time working on our high-priority work and put aside the lower-priority work until later.

But for most of us — me included — that's not what we usually do. It's just too easy to get distracted. So we end up spending the majority of our time doing things that aren't very high on the priority list, like reading the mail, answering e-mail, talking on the phone, or trying to solve someone else's problem, while our high-priority, big-ticket, big-payoff projects wait for us. Then when we finally do get around to working on them, we've got to rush through them because we've blown all of our lead time.

Now, you may be one of those people who feel that they're able to produce high-quality work under pressure. Even if that's the case, try to imagine how much better that work would be if you actually gave yourself the opportunity to put it aside for a while and then come back and make some additions, changes, or corrections. And for the rest of us, we should all be able to improve on that first draft if we leave ourselves enough time to go through it a second or a third time.

Did you know that in a recent time-management study, researchers found that most people spend only 20 percent of their time working on the handful of important tasks and projects that yield 80 percent of their positive results? This only confirms what I've long believed: Most people are spending the majority of their time — 80 percent — doing all sorts of things that keep them busy. And when they've finished doing all these miscellaneous things, they finally start working on their important and meaningful tasks and projects.

But by keeping your Master List up-to-date, you're able to keep track of all of the things you've got to do. As a result, you'll see a dramatic increase in your daily productivity. That's why it's so important for you to get organized. It's just not possible for anyone to stay on top of their unfinished work, tasks, and projects when they've so many piles of stuff lying on top of the desk that they don't even remember whether the desktop is made of wood, glass, or Formica. (If you're not familiar with the concept of how to use a Master List, you can learn about it in Chapter 3.)

Get your ACT! together

With ACT! you can always see what it is you need to do, for whom you need to do it, and when it needs to be done. All you need to do is click the Task List, shown in the following figure, and you can view a detailed list of everything you need to do today, tomorrow, or any day in the future. Then you decide which task you want to do, and you do it.

When you've completed the task, you just repeat the process and decide which item of business you want to tackle next. What could be easier?

Well, you can probably think of a lot of things that would be easier, especially if ACT! could do the work for you, but it can't. So you've got to sit down and do it yourself. Life's hard!

But there's a pot of gold at the end of this rainbow. After you start working on one of those tasks or projects that you've been putting off, you'll find that it wasn't so bad after all. And when you're finished, you'll not only have the pleasure of crossing it off your Master List or clearing it from ACT!'s Task List, which is shown in the accompanying figure, but you'll have that feeling of satisfaction that comes from knowing that you've done your job well.

For a more detailed description about how the ACT! contact management program can help you automate the process of staying organized, refer to Chapter 5.

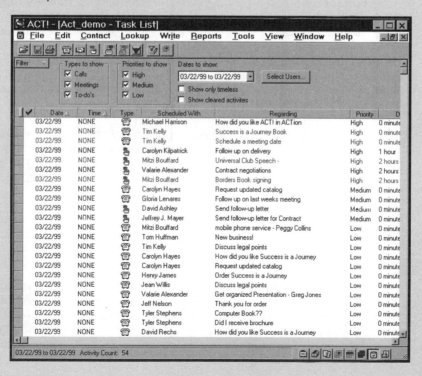

Work on your important tasks first

Have you ever come into the office with the intention of working on one specific project and then discovered that the whole day had come and gone and you never got to it? This used to happen to me on a regular basis.

Then one day I realized that my focus was wrong and that I had my priorities backwards. I was trying to complete all the unimportant tasks and projects on my to-do list — those "B," "C," "D," and "E" items that take up more of one's time than one's creative energies. I felt that once I could get them out of the way, I would be able to start working on my "A" items — the *important* work.

You see, we get paid to complete our "A," #1, big-ticket, high-priority items. And nobody really cares if, or when, the other stuff gets done. But this important stuff, if it's done right, can mean big bucks to the company, and for you, it can mean raises, bonuses, and promotions at the end of the year.

That's why I believe it's so important to focus your time and energy in the right places. If you're spending the majority of your valuable time working on unimportant tasks and projects, you won't have enough time left to work on those really important high-priority ones. And it's these projects that you need to give your time and attention to because that's where the money is.

So don't spend your time trying to complete all the easy things first, just so you can get them out of the way. If you do, you won't have enough time or energy left to work on the harder projects, the ones that will take time, thought, and consideration.

Since most of our important projects or tasks can't be completed in one sitting, you'll make your life much easier and reduce your stress level when you can start working on them while you've got plenty of lead time. You do a little bit now and a little bit later, and before you know it, you're finished.

Review your things-to-do list throughout the day

Have you ever been sitting at your desk, unable to decide what it was that you wanted to do next? You looked at one pile, then another, and then another, and the more you looked, the more depressed you got — because those piles represented an awful lot of *unfinished* work. So you shuffled some papers back and forth for a few minutes, looked at the clock, and then went out to get a cup of coffee.

If you keep your Master List on the top of your desk, you can guarantee that will never happen again! Whenever you complete a task, look at your Master List, scan it from top to bottom, and ask yourself: "What should I be working on next?" And if you're like me, you may grumble a bit because it's not a task you were looking forward to doing, but you should just stop thinking about it and do it anyway.

When I was playing ball in college, a teammate of mine would say, "Jeff, stop thinking! It hurts the ball club." It was almost 20 years before I understood what he meant. Just do what comes naturally, and don't give yourself the opportunity to talk yourself out of doing it.

This is another area where you'll find ACT! to be a tremendous productivity-improving tool. See the sidebar in this chapter, "Get your ACT! together," for more info.

Review tomorrow's agenda before you leave in the evening

I like the idea of separating thinking and planning from doing. And the more time you can spend thinking and planning your work, the easier it will be to do. So, as part of your daily planning, make it a point to review your Master List at the end of the day to see what's on your agenda. Find out whom you have to call, what projects or tasks need to be done, whom you have meetings with, and where will they be held. By reviewing your Master List in this manner, you can get an overview of all the things that need to be done and identify the most important tasks or projects that you'll need to work on.

You may even want to pull out the project's file, just to refresh your memory about what's got to be done and to put yourself in the right frame of mind so that when you arrive in the morning, you'll know exactly what you need to do. After you've taken the time to determine whichever task is most important, you may not realize it, but you've already made a commitment to start working on it. When you arrive in the morning, you'll be ready to go to work.

ACT! makes it a breeze to keep your daily plan current and up-to-date because you're able to use the power of your computer, instead of a pencil and paper, to keep you organized. This system allows you to spend your time working on your important tasks and projects — the ones that will make you money — instead of *wasting* time making up a new daily plan or rewriting your to-do list so that the highest priority items are at the top of the list.

If you work with other people, make it a point to sit down with your secretary, administrative assistant, or the other members of your organization for a few moments at the end of the day so that they know exactly what things they should be working on when they arrive in the morning.

Get the most out of the first two hours of the day

Have you ever felt like Snoopy as he's trying to write his first novel and always gets stumped after he writes, *It was a dark and stormy night . . .*? What probably happened is that you tried to start this difficult, time-consuming project and you didn't have enough mental or physical energy left to move forward. It's late in the day. You've gone from one meeting to the next. And now that you're sitting at your desk, you're so exhausted that you can't write and you can't think. Nothing's happening!

You probably never gave this much thought before, but have you ever noticed that there's a time of day when you have the most energy and enthusiasm, and your ability to concentrate is very high? I call it Prime Time, the time of day when you're at your best. And if you're like most of us, you're probably at your best the first thing in the morning. You're bright, alert, and ready to go. That's why you may even call yourself a "morning person."

Put your big rocks in first

Years ago, I was attending a time-management seminar. The speaker pulled out a one-gallon, wide-mouthed mason jar, set it on the table in front of him, and carefully placed about a dozen fist-sized rocks into the jar.

When the jar was filled to the top, he asked, "Is this jar full?"

Everyone said, "Yes."

Then he reached under the table and pulled out a bucket of gravel. He dumped a few handfuls into the jar and began shaking it. Within a few moments, the gravel had worked itself into the spaces between the big rocks. Then he asked the group once more, "Is the jar full?"

By this time, the class was onto him. "Probably not," one of the participants answered. "Good!" he replied.

Next he brought out a bucket of sand. He dumped the sand into the jar, and with a few shakes, it had filled the spaces between the rocks and the gravel.

Once more he asked the question, "Is this jar full?" "Yes!" the class shouted.

"You're wrong!" he said as he grabbed a pitcher of water and poured it in until the jar was filled to the brim.

Then he looked up and asked, "What is the point of this demonstration?"

One eager beaver raised his hand and said, "The point is, no matter how full your schedule, you can always fit some more things into it!"

No," the speaker replied. "This is the point:

Put your big rocks in first! Otherwise, you'll never get them in.

What are the big rocks in *your* life? Put those in first.

Here's a nifty idea: Tackle your most important work at the time of day that you have the most energy and enthusiasm. When you're able to complete your important work early in the day, it's much easier to deal with the inevitable fires that flare up.

If you're really adventurous and want to try something new, try this: Give yourself the first two hours of the workday and actually block it out on your calendar. Then when you come into the office, close the door, turn off the telephone, and don't allow yourself to be interrupted. You'll quickly discover that you're able to complete twice as much work in half the time with half the effort.

Schedule an appointment with yourself

Have you ever thought of scheduling an appointment with yourself? I'm serious. You schedule appointments with everybody else — your boss, your customers, your clients, your coworkers. Well, why not schedule an appointment with yourself so that you can get some of your important work done?

For instance, let's look at that big file that's been sitting on the corner of your desk for a week. If I were to guess, I'd say that it's there because you have to do some work on it.

Well, if you want to guarantee that it gets done, why don't you schedule an appointment with yourself to do the work? Yes, actually write it down on your calendar and think of it as an appointment with your boss or most important client. Because in a way, it is. Your boss gave you the assignment but doesn't want to sit at your desk and watch you do the work. Your boss has other things to do, and besides, that's why he or she hired you in the first place.

When you've got an important project or task that you need to work on, schedule an appointment with yourself and write it on the calendar. When it's time for your appointment, close the door and turn off the telephone so that you won't be disturbed. Then go to work. After you get started, you'll find that this dreadful project wasn't so bad after all. When it's done, you'll experience the feeling of satisfaction that comes from doing a job well, and you will have a big smile on your face as you cross the item off your to-do list.

Give yourself more time than you think you'll need

Have you ever started a project, and just as you were getting to the *good* stuff, you ran out of time and had to go to a meeting? Then when you got back to your office, did you find that it was difficult to get started again?

Well, this situation happens to almost everybody because most of us aren't very good at estimating time. We usually underestimate the amount of time it will take to complete a difficult project, and then we overestimate the amount of time it will take to complete an easy one.

When you start working on a task, ask yourself how long you think it will take and then expand that amount by at least 50 percent. (If you think you need an hour, give yourself 90 minutes. If you think you need two hours, give yourself three.) This strategy will help to ensure that once you start working on a project, you'll have enough time to complete it.

Solve your problems before they become problems

Someone once told me that there are three kinds of problems:

- ✔ Those that solve themselves
- ✔ Those that will wait for you
- ✔ Those that need your immediate attention and force you to drop whatever you're doing

But as I thought about what she said, I eventually came to the conclusion that most problems can be avoided in the first place if the work is done the right way the first time. And those little problems that eventually grow into BIG problems won't *become* BIG problems if they're addressed while they're still little ones. In fact, even the most insignificant things can become major headaches if they aren't addressed in a reasonable period of time.

Leave yourself some time to deal with unexpected problems

I have a friend who would plan his day as if nothing unexpected would come up. But then he would become very upset and frazzled because whenever things went wrong, he was forced to stop whatever he was doing to help solve a problem. After we talked about his scheduling system for a while, we came up with a unique idea: Plan for those unexpected problems and actually allocate time to solve them on your daily calendar.

Get your important work done early in the morning, before the inevitable fires flare up, and then you can spend the rest of the day putting out those fires. As you begin to take more control over your daily affairs, you'll find that you have fewer fires to put out because the situations that previously would have become three-alarm blazes had been dealt with long before being ignited.

And while we're on the subject of fires, you don't have to accept that putting out fires is an unavoidable part of your daily life. If you're coming into work each morning with the expectation that you're going to have to spend a major part of your day firefighting, you've got a problem: You've been putting out fires — usually started by other people — for so long that it has become a part of business as usual for you.

Someone else's fire doesn't have to be your fire. Nowhere does it say that you have to drop everything because someone else has a problem.

So the next time people walk into your office with a problem, ask them what they would do if you were on vacation — on a beach in the Caribbean would be nice — and weren't available at this very moment. Then tell them that you're too busy doing your own work and that they should figure out a way to solve their problem all by themselves. Of course, you may not be able to say it quite so tactfully.

Meet your deadlines

When you were in school, did you have any friends who never opened a book, and then when it was time to prepare for a test, they would stay up all night and try to memorize enough material to pass the exam? I had a few friends who liked to pull all-nighters, and I even tried it myself a few times, but I eventually came to the conclusion that nothing was worth losing a night's sleep over.

Well, many people in business pull the equivalent of all-nighters when they let an assignment sit, and sit, and sit. Then when they finally begin to work on the project, it's the fifty-ninth minute of the eleventh hour and they haven't left themselves enough time to even proofread their work for spelling or grammatical errors.

Maybe the work is satisfactory, but more often than not, it leaves something to be desired. If this approach isn't for you, I can show you a better way to get your work done, meet your deadlines, and get a good night's sleep. Just start on the project as soon as it's assigned. This way, you can do a little bit at a time and think about what you're doing; the more time you're able to put into it, the better it will be.

This is another way in which ACT! can help you get your work done on time. You can use it to schedule your tasks and projects as soon as they are assigned to you. Then you can start working on them long before you need to be concerned about an approaching deadline. The goal is to have a great finished product, not a great first draft.

The more time you can spend thinking about and planning what it is that you have to do — *before* you begin doing it — the easier the work becomes.

Don't use the arrival of the daily mail, an e-mail message, or voice mail as an excuse for interrupting yourself

Most of us require some motivation to get started on a project, but after we do get started, we begin to develop some momentum as we become more engrossed in the work. And after you get into the mood, the last thing you want to do is interrupt the flow of things by allowing yourself to be interrupted.

Don't use the arrival of the daily mail, e-mail messages, or a voice mail message as an excuse for taking a break. When you interrupt yourself — and lose your flow, rhythm, and momentum — it's twice as difficult to resume your work.

So don't drop everything just because the mail's arrived, the lights on your telephone are flashing, or your computer is beeping. Just ignore these interruptions and continue working. When you've completed your task, you can see what new things need your attention.

When you go through your mail, e-mail, and voice mail, look for things that need your immediate attention and add them to your Master List at once so that you won't forget about them. You can get to the other things that you need to read, look at, or review later in the day.

When you open an envelope, don't look at the contents and then place them back inside the envelope. Take the papers out, unfold the paper, use a paper clip to group the papers together, and throw the envelope away.

Just do it! But keep it short

Abe Lincoln once said, "I would have written a shorter letter, but I didn't have the time." It's easy to write a letter, memo, report, or presentation that's 5, 10, or 20 pages in length.

But it becomes much more difficult, and it takes a lot more time, as you try to make it shorter, more concise, and to the point. How many months do you think it took to come up with Nike's slogan: "Just Do It!"?

Try to give yourself plenty of time to write, rewrite, edit, and think about your work. And after you've written, rewritten, and edited something — two, three, or even five times — you will finally reach the point where you feel satisfied with the quality of the work you produced.

You can now pat yourself on the back and congratulate yourself for a job well done. Then you can move on to your next project.

Getting back to work after a marvelous vacation

I don't know about you, but when I return from a vacation, or if I've been away from the office for a few days, my desk looks like a disaster site. There are piles of letters, memos, and reports, a stack of phone messages to return, and a two-page list of people who want to see me.

So here are a few thoughts on how you can go about cleaning up the mess.

✔ First off, before you even leave town, start planning for your return by blocking out some time on your calendar to get organized.

✔ Leave your schedule open the morning of your first day back in the office. Then when you arrive, give yourself some quiet time, without any interruptions or phone calls, to go through the piles of things that have accumulated. This approach will help you to see what's important and what's not.

✔ If there's work to do, just note it on your Master List or add it to ACT!.

✔ If you need to keep something, put it into a file folder.

✔ And if you don't need something any longer, throw it away.

It's just that simple!

Planning Your Meetings, Your Appointments, and Your Day

One part of our daily planning that most of us don't spend enough time thinking about is how we go about scheduling our meetings, our appointments, and our day. So I would like to ask you a few questions. Don't worry, you're not going to be quizzed; you don't have to write your answers out on a piece of paper and mail them to me for grading. All you've got to do is ponder the enormity and importance of these questions, for perhaps five to ten seconds:

✔ How much time do you spend planning your appointment schedule?

✔ How much thought do you give to the number of appointments you schedule during the course of a normal business day?

✔ How much thought do you give to where the appointments are located geographically?

✔ How much thought do you give to the amount of time it will take to get from one appointment to another?

If you're like most people, you don't give much thought to any of these questions. In fact, you're probably so excited that you were able to schedule that appointment in the first place that you would be happy to meet the person at his or her office at 5:00 p.m. on Super Bowl Sunday.

But unless you spend more time planning your appointment schedule, you'll find that it's very easy to waste a lot of time going back and forth, and before you know it, you've completely lost control of your workday.

Don't schedule appointments for early in the morning

It's been my experience that most people are capable of doing their best work during the early-morning hours. They've got a lot of energy, and their ability to concentrate is very good.

If that's true for you, then try your best to keep the early morning hours open so that you can get some of your important work done, and then schedule your meetings and appointments for later in the day.

If, on the other hand, you find that you do your most productive work during the early afternoon, late afternoon, after dinner, or in the middle of the night, make it a point to block out that time for you, and schedule your appointments around it.

Don't be in a hurry to schedule appointments for 8:30 or 9:15 a.m. When someone asks if you're available at that time, just say that you've got a conflict and suggest that you meet later in the morning, or perhaps after lunch. Ninety-nine times out of a hundred, the other person will say OK. It's my suggestion that you try to keep the morning open until at least 10:30 or 11:00 a.m.

Actually block out the first two hours of the workday for yourself and write it on your calendar.

Give yourself breathing room between appointments

Have you ever had an appointment with your doctor and then discovered after you got there that the doctor was running two hours late? That's happened to me on one too many occasions, and now I always schedule my appointments so that I'm the first patient.

Make it a point to call the doctor's office, just before you're about to leave for your appointment, to see whether the doctor is going to be on time or is running late. This way, you won't waste too much time sitting in the waiting room.

Whoops! I don't know how I got sidetracked, but I'm the author, so I can get away with it. So let's get back to the subject at hand: keeping you from booking so many appointments that when the first one runs late, all the others run late, and your day collapses around you like a falling stack of dominos.

Let's start with a basic premise: One of the easiest ways to throw your daily schedule off track is to schedule your appointments back-to-back-to-back. Instead, you should always assume that a meeting will start late and take longer than you had anticipated.

How many times has this happened to you? The meeting that was supposed to start at 9:30 and end by 10:00 didn't start till 9:45 and didn't break up until 10:25. Once in your lifetime? Twice in your lifetime? Or several times per day?

Well, it can only happen once for the 9:30 a.m. meeting, but it can happen again and again and again to the other meetings you've scheduled. Once your 9:30 a.m. meeting runs long, what happens to the quality of the meeting that you've got scheduled with the person who has been waiting for you in the reception area since 9:55, and it's now 10:25?

As you plan your day, assume that every meeting will take at least 50 percent longer than you expect. Block out that additional time on your calendar.

✔ For a 30-minute meeting, allow 45 minutes.

✔ For an hour meeting, give yourself 90 minutes.

Always give yourself at least a 15-minute cushion between your meetings. This guarantees that you'll have at least a moment or two to catch your breath, return a few calls, and look at the mail before the next meeting starts. If this first meeting should end on time, and even if it doesn't, maybe you won't be too late for your next meeting.

Group your appointments together

I have a friend, perhaps you know her — well, you probably don't, but you've certainly seen how she goes about scheduling her meetings and appointments. She'll come into the office and go out to a meeting, and then she'll return. A little while later, she leaves the office for a second meeting.

After she returns, she sits at her desk, reads the mail, returns some phone calls, and then goes out for a third appointment. Apparently, it never dawned on her that she's wasting a lot of time — usually sitting in traffic — going back and forth from the office to meetings and then returning.

If you want to have more time during the course of your day, look for ways in which you can eliminate the wasted commuting time. I call this strategy *Addition by Subtraction.*

If you will be out of the office, try your best to group your appointments together to eliminate the time spent driving or walking from one person's office to another. You may also want to try to schedule appointments so that you can stop on your way into the office in the morning or on your way home in the afternoon.

If you need to travel through areas where traffic is heavy or the roadway is under construction, take this extra commuting time into consideration when you're setting up your appointments and meetings.

This is another way ACT! can help you to use your time more effectively. With ACT!'s Lookup feature, you can look up people by city, zip code, or even telephone number. If, for example, you find that you've got to drive a long distance for an appointment, you can search your ACT! database to see who else you may know in that community that you could set up a meeting with. As long as you have to drive out there, you may as well try to see some additional people.

If time is money, why do you spend so much of it sitting in traffic?

Have you ever thought about how much time you spend in your car? (I know that some of you may take public transportation — a bus or a train — to work, but the same thought applies here, too.) At a minimum, you go to work, and at the end of the day, you return home. And if you're in your car driving to other places during the day, that's just more time that you're going to be stuck in traffic.

But if you're spending several hours per day in your car, it may be costing you a lot more of your valuable time and money than you might think. Yes, I know that you can make or return some phone calls and may even have a fax in your car, but trying to run a business from behind the wheel of your car just isn't the same as running your business from behind your desk.

ACT! does my out-of-town meetings

ACT! helps me schedule my out-of-town meetings. I recently scheduled a trip to Los Angeles, and after I had scheduled my main appointment, I did a lookup of all the people I knew in L.A. and was able to schedule several additional appointments while I was in town. After I had scheduled these appointments, I booked my airline and hotel reservations.

I got tired of commuting, so I quit!

In the mid-'70s, when I lived in the Chicago suburb of Evanston, I discovered that if I left the house just before 7 a.m., I could cut my commuting time to my office from almost an hour to about 25 minutes.

But with the passage of time, I became more and more disenchanted with sitting in traffic, so I moved into the city and cut my commuting time to under 15 minutes. Eventually, I decided to eliminate commuting entirely and started working from home.

Before you read any further, why don't you make a few copies of the Travel Time Analysis Form (Figure 6-1) and keep track of how many hours you spend commuting for two weeks? You may discover that you're spending much more time commuting to and from work than you thought.

After you've accumulated this information, why don't you try leaving your home at a different time in the morning, or your office at a different time in the afternoon? For illustrative purposes, how much would you shorten your travel time if you were to change the time you left your home by 30 minutes? What if you were to change the time you leave your home by 60 minutes?

Now I'm not trying to get you to spend more hours working — but if the time savings were large enough, perhaps you could work out an arrangement with your employer to change the starting and ending time of your workday. But by leaving earlier in the morning and earlier or later in the afternoon — to avoid the rush-hour traffic — you may be able to convert some of the time that's wasted sitting in traffic to time that you can use more productively in the office.

And while you're taking the time to analyze how much time you spend going to and from work, you should think about how much time you spend driving from one appointment to another. Whenever you schedule an appointment, you should always ask yourself whether you could group this appointment together with any of your other appointments.

At the same time, you should see whether it would be possible to schedule your appointments for the beginning or end of your workday to combine your driving to or from work with an appointment.

Travel Time Analysis						
	Monday	Tuesday	Wednesday	Thursday	Friday	Total Travel Time
Time you leave your home						
Time you arrive at the office						
Travel time						

Time you leave the office						
Time you arrive at your home						
Travel time						

Figure 6-1:
Travel Time
Analysis
Form.

Total weekly travel time						

The next time you schedule a business meeting or appointment, ask the person to come to your office. This way, you can eliminate the need to travel. If that's not possible, perhaps you can meet somewhere in the middle to reduce your total driving time.

What does it cost to operate your car?

The time spent commuting is one thing, but what does it cost you to own and operate your car? When you add up the cost for auto insurance, gas, oil, regular maintenance, and wear and tear on your car, it may end up costing you 40 cents per mile to drive your car.

I thought it would be helpful for you to see how expensive it is to own and operate a car. So in the Annual Mileage Expense Chart (Figure 6-2), I used my super-duper spreadsheet program to work out these sophisticated mathematical calculations. It took me only four hours to write the formulas. (I would have used my calculator, but my daughter had been playing with it and I couldn't find it.)

In Your Annual Auto Expense Chart (Figure 6-3), I included the major expenses that most people incur in operating a car. You're going to have to fill in the blanks yourself.

Take a few moments and add up your total operating costs and then divide that number by the total number of miles you drive each year. If you're able to reduce your operating costs, you'll have more money left over that you can spend on yourself.

Manage your out-of-town travel

It's one thing to be losing valuable and precious time while you're sitting in traffic, but it's even easier to lose a lot of hours, if not days, sitting in airplanes. How many people do you know who brag about how much they fly? They feel important because they're flying 250,000, 500,000, or even 1 million miles per year. Apparently, they believe that the size of their frequent-flier mileage statements is a measure of their persistence, determination, and success rather than a time log of the many hours they've wasted sitting in airplanes.

Yes, laptop computers and cell phones can help you stay on top of things. But when you're traveling in an airplane and living in a hotel room, there's no way you can operate as efficiently and effectively as when you're working in your office. Today, a person has a lot of communication alternatives to choose from before having to hop on an airplane to meet with someone face-to-face.

ANNUAL MILEAGE EXPENSE CHART		
Total Miles Driven	Cost per Mile	Total Cost to Operate Your Car
10,000	$.30/mile	$3,000
10,000	$.40/mile	$4,000
10,000	$.45/mile	$4,500
15,000	$.30/mile	$4,500
15,000	$.40/mile	$6,000
15,000	$.45/mile	$6,750

Figure 6-2:
Annual
Mileage
Expense
Chart.

✔ First, why not try using the telephone? You can certainly have a conversation, or several of them, before you've got to fly off somewhere.

✔ You can send materials by fax, overnight delivery, or electronic mail. After the materials have been received, you can have another series of phone calls to discuss them.

✔ You can even utilize a videoconferencing center so that you can talk to other people face-to-face.

If you've done all of the above and you feel that it's still necessary to hop on a planc and see the person face-to-face, then do it.

YOUR ANNUAL AUTO EXPENSE	
Auto insurance	$
Gasoline	$
Oil	$
Regular	$
Emergency maintenance	$
Miscellaneous auto expenses	$
Depreciation	$
Total annual cost	$

Figure 6-3:
Your Annual
Auto
Expense
Chart.

And while you're examining the amount of your out-of-town total travel, you should analyze your visible, and *invisible,* costs. Your visible costs include

- ✔ The cost of the plane ticket
- ✔ Taxi fares to and from the airport
- ✔ Meals and hotel rooms

Your invisible costs include the cost of your time.

You need to take into consideration the cost of your time because you're not only away from the office, but you're spending an awful lot of time sitting in traffic while you're going to and from the airport in both your home city and in the city you've flown to. And you're wasting a lot of time while you're in the airport waiting for the plane to depart.

Don't waste your valuable time being an errand boy (or girl)

And while we're on the subject of wasting time, try not to waste your valuable time as an errand or delivery boy. Instead of wasting a couple of hours running something over to a client, have a messenger service or a taxi do it. You can save yourself time by not wasting it, and then you can continue working in your office. This suggestion is another example of my Addition by Subtraction advice.

Do you hate to fill out those air bills when you use an overnight delivery service? If so, here's a neat timesaving tip: Use your computer. Overnight delivery services such as Federal Express and United Parcel Service have software that enables you to print your shipping labels right off your printer. The software will even schedule the pickup for you. Best of all, the software's free.

Two hours waiting time for a 30-minute flight

One day I had to fly to Indianapolis on business. It took me 45 minutes to get to the airport, and then I waited another 20 minutes before I boarded the plane, and it was another 20 minutes before it left the gate. Then it was 15 minutes before we actually took off.

After I arrived in Indianapolis, it took me 35 minutes to get to my hotel. So I spent more than two hours sitting in a taxi or waiting for the plane to take off for a flight that was in the air for only 30 minutes.

Chapter 7

Take Control of Your Business Appointments

● ●

● ●

*E*very day, we have meetings and appointments. Some of them are internal sales or staff meetings; others are just brief meetings with your boss, colleagues, or coworkers. And other times, we'll have a meetings with someone outside our organization. These meetings may take place within our offices, at the other person's office, or somewhere else, like a restaurant.

Regardless of who you're meeting with, you need to create a strong first impression and accomplish the goals you've established for the encounter. In this chapter, I show you how you can save time in your business meetings by preparing well, starting out strong, and steering the meeting in the right direction.

Bring the Right Tools to Your Meetings

Have you ever had a business meeting and the person with whom you were meeting didn't even have a pencil or a piece of paper to write anything on? Isn't it amazing that some people can be so unprepared? And even worse, isn't it interesting that sometimes no one can recall what was accomplished during the meeting?

That said, here's a list of things you should always have with you when you go to a meeting:

- ✔ A pen or pencil.

- ✔ A letter-sized pad of paper.

- ✔ Your appointment book and calendar. If you're using a computerized calendar, always take along a printout of your scheduled activities for at least the next four weeks.

- ✔ Business cards. You never know when you might run into someone who could offer a potential customer or client, or someone who could help you in a future career move.

- ✔ Any files or papers that pertain to the subject being discussed.

Always carry a small pen in your pocket or purse and business cards in your wallet. This way, when you need to write something down, you've got the necessary tools.

Dress Appropriately

A question that I'm often asked is "How should I dress for work and for my business meetings?" The answer is rather simple: Your choice of clothing should be appropriate to the business environment. If you're working for an advertising agency, the dress may be rather casual — blue jeans and a T-shirt.

But if you're working for IBM or some big investment banking house, you've got to wear a deep blue suit, a white shirt with a "power tie," and wing-tip shoes. Flashy red braces (suspenders) would be appropriate at the investment banking firm, but not at IBM.

And when you're having a meeting with people from outside your firm, you should feel comfortable dressing in the same manner as they do. If they're wearing business suits, you should also; and if they're dressed casually, then it's okay for you to do so.

No matter what you've chosen to wear, you should always look your best. Your business suits should be freshly pressed, your shirts should be starched, and your shoes freshly polished. Your fingernails should always be clean and trimmed and your hair neatly groomed. The amount of jewelry you choose to wear is really a personal decision, but in most instances, the less jewelry you wear, the better.

Have you ever been in an elevator and thought that the "aroma" of another passenger's cologne or perfume was a bit too strong? Well, a strong fragrance may be appropriate in a social setting, but in business, you don't want your scent to arrive ahead of your handshake. I personally believe that the less fragrance you wear, the better. And under fragrance I would include everything from perfume to cologne to scented deodorant.

I could have sworn I put it in my briefcase . . .

I once knew a man who liked to schedule early-morning appointments. But he often forgot to look in his briefcase before he went home at the end of the day. Invariably, he would have to come into the office before he went to his meeting because he needed some miscellaneous form that he had forgotten to take with him. And he never realized why he always felt tired and looked like he had been run over by a train.

And while we're on the subject of scents, you should pay attention to the foods that you eat. I know that onions and garlic may be your favorite foods, but in a business situation, you're trying to draw the other person closer to you, and when people smell of onions, no one wants to come near them.

And finally, business and politics don't mix. When you're meeting someone for business purposes, your personal beliefs and opinions should be placed in the background. Avoid wearing anything that identifies you with any religious belief, political or social persuasion, or outside organization.

Always Check Your Briefcase Before You Leave the Office

I know that this probably sounds stupid because it's just common sense, but you should always check the contents of your briefcase before you leave the office for a meeting or an appointment. You just don't want to get to a meeting and discover that you left a document, a file, some miscellaneous form, or some other piece of information sitting on your desk.

This advice becomes very important when you have an appointment scheduled for early the next morning: You certainly don't have time to go into your office. Make sure that you check your briefcase before you leave at the end of the day.

Always Call Ahead to Confirm Your Appointments

When I was first starting out in business, I scheduled appointments days or weeks in advance and then just showed up at the person's office at the appointed time and on the agreed-upon date. There was only one problem.

Sometimes I found that the person I was to meet had gotten tied up with something and couldn't see me. Other times, I arrived at his office only to learn that he was out of town for the day. And worst of all, there were times that the person hadn't even put me into his calendar. To say that this was a waste of time and money is an understatement!

I learned a lesson — the hard way. Always confirm an appointment before you leave the office! You probably weren't aware of this, but almost 50 percent of the appointments that you schedule will need to be postponed.

In today's fast-paced, high-pressure business world, there are just too many things that can happen at the last minute to keep a meeting from taking place. But if you call to confirm your appointments before you leave the office, your day won't go up in flames just because a person wasn't able to see you.

When you call to confirm appointments, keep these tips in mind:

- Always confirm an appointment at least a day ahead.

- When you have a long drive to get to your appointment, you should also call the morning of the appointment so that you know that nothing unexpected has come up.

- When you have an early-morning appointment, always take the person's home phone number and give the person yours. Should something come up at the very last minute, you both have a way of reaching each other.

- When you have an early Monday morning appointment, always take the person's home phone number and call on Sunday to remind him or her of your meeting on Monday.

- When you're going out of town for a business meeting, call several days before you're scheduled to leave, and call once again on the day you're scheduled to leave.

A colleague of mine once got on an airplane for a meeting with a customer in New York. When he got to the customer's office, he learned that the person had been called out of town unexpectedly the day before. Because my colleague hadn't confirmed the appointment, he found that the entire trip was a total waste of time and money.

Whenever you schedule an appointment, always give the person the correct spelling of your name. Then ask the person to take down your phone number and write it in his or her book. Say something like, "Let me give you my phone number so that if something unexpected comes up, you can give me a call so we can reschedule it." This statement serves two purposes:

- First, it forces the other person to actually write your name down. (Yes, some people schedule appointments without writing them down.)

- Second, it lets the person know that you're very serious about your own time when you ask the person to call you if there's a conflict.

Try Your Best to Be on Time

Now, if you're going to go out of your way to thoroughly prepare for your meetings and then confirm them a day or two ahead of time, you should try your best to arrive on time. It makes a great impression when you're on time, even if you have to sit in the reception area for a few minutes while the person with whom you're meeting concludes a phone call or wraps up a meeting. It shows that you respect the person's time and lets the person know that you're there to talk business and that you take your job seriously.

 To keep yourself on time, *try* to arrive at all of your appointments at least five to ten minutes early. You'll find that when you try to get there early, it increases the odds that you'll be there on time.

 Set the time on your watch five to seven minutes fast. This way, you'll always know that you've got a few minutes as a cushion. Remember, it's far better to wait for a few minutes because you're early than to make the other person wait because you're late.

Call Ahead If You're Running Late

Have you ever gotten tied up in a meeting that just wouldn't end, and as a result, you were running 30 or 60 minutes late for your next meeting? Well, sometimes meetings do run long, or you get tied up on the phone and you can't get off. When this happens, there's nothing wrong with calling the person you're meeting to say that you're running late.

While you're speaking to this person, you want to ask two questions: ""If I can get over to your office in (15, 20, 30) minutes, would you still have enough time to meet with me?" If the person says, "Yes," then tell him or her that you're walking out the door.

If the person can't keep the appointment, say something like, "Since you're all booked up for the remainder of the afternoon, do you have some time tomorrow morning, or would the following afternoon be better?"

Calling ahead serves two useful purposes:

- ✔ The other parties will certainly appreciate receiving the call because it lets them know that you respect and value their time.
- ✔ By calling and finding out if the other parties are still available, you can avoid rushing to a meeting that isn't going to take place.

Let your fingers do the walking before you leave the office. You'll convert the time that would be wasted sitting in a reception area into time that you can use much more productively back in the office.

When you're trying to schedule an appointment with someone, always give the person two choices. "Would you prefer meeting on Tuesday at 10 a.m. or on Wednesday, right after lunch?" This way, you're changing the question from *Do you want to set up an appointment?* to *When would you like to set up an appointment?*

Make the Most of Your Waiting Room Time

If you've got to spend a few minutes sitting in someone's reception room, do something useful and constructive with this down time. You can use this time to review the information in your files one more time, or you can use this time to catch up on some of the reading — newspapers, magazines, newsletters, trade journals, or any memos and reports — that have accumulated in piles on the top of your desk.

When you're traveling, use your time in the airport and on the plane to update your expense accounts, compose memos, write letters, work on your business plans, or just catch up on your reading. Most people complain that they don't have enough time to get everything done. Look for ways to save time in small pieces. (Bring your cell phone, and you can make a lot of calls while waiting in the airport.) You've got a lot of opportunities to convert wasted, unproductive time into profitable time.

Your Meeting Starts with a Smile and a Handshake

If you're meeting with your boss, a colleague, or a coworker, your meeting actually starts the moment you get up from your desk to go to the meeting. You've got to be friendly and cordial and walk into the meeting — on time — with a smile on your face.

A smile makes a lasting impression.

Should your appointment be with someone outside your office, your meeting actually begins the moment you walk into the person's building. For all you know, the person who got into the elevator or walked into the building with you is the president or owner of the company, or he or she may be the person with whom you've got a meeting.

You never have a second chance to make a first impression, and first impressions are usually lasting ones. For those reasons, you should try your best to be friendly and personable to everyone you meet, and that includes the

"Is this the party to whom I am speaking?"

In ACT!, you have the capability to store the name of a person's secretary or administrative assistant, and you can even record the name of the receptionist who answers the phone when you call. When you walk in the door, you can ask the person behind the desk, "Are you so-and-so?," and then introduce yourself because the two of you have spoken so many times on the phone. It makes a nice and lasting impression.

receptionist, the person's secretary or administrative assistant, and anyone else you may see in the hallway. Display and use all of your social skills.

When you walk through the front door of the office, have a smile on your face — it adds warmth to your voice — as you say "Hello" to the secretary or receptionist who will inform the person you're meeting that you have arrived. Warm up to those people and try to make them your friends.

Do you like to work with, or do business with, a grouch? I sure don't! And I'm sure you don't, either. We all prefer to do business with nice, friendly people, so even if the other person's a grouch, we don't have to become grouches ourselves.

Instead, we must work hard at making and maintaining favorable impressions with everyone we come in contact with. It starts by having a smile on your face, a twinkle in your eye, and a warm and open handshake as you introduce yourself and say, "It's nice to meet you," or "It's nice to see you again."

If you're carrying a briefcase, carry it in your left hand so that when you greet the other person, your right hand will be free as the two of you shake hands. Another reason for holding your briefcase in your left hand is that it keeps your right hand drier. No one likes shaking hands with a person whose hand is moist and clammy.

Sitting in the Right Seat

It may never have occurred to you before, but where you choose to sit in a business meeting can have a dramatic effect on the outcome of the meeting. For example, let's assume that you're meeting with a client in his office. If you're sitting at his desk, there will probably be two chairs placed in front of the desk, and it's assumed that you will sit in one of these, and the other person will sit in his chair, on the other side of the desk.

But if you accept this seating arrangement, there's a barrier — the desk — separating the two of you, and during a meeting, you want to remove as many barriers as possible. If, on the other hand, you were to sit next to that person — instead of sitting on the opposite side of the desk — you would have a much greater opportunity to maintain control of the conversation and the meeting.

And because you're sitting next to each other, you have the opportunity to dramatically improve the flow of conversation between the two of you. As an additional benefit, you won't have to look at the materials you've given to the other person upside down.

Getting your chair around to the other side of the desk can be a little tricky, but once you've done it a few times, it's really easy. And besides, what's the person going to say after you've done it? Nothing. So here's what you do:

- ✔ First, you sit down in the chair that will be the easiest for you to pick up and move, and as you're exchanging pleasantries, you remove your papers from your briefcase.

- ✔ Then, as you're about to start talking business, you stand up, pick up your chair, and move it to the other side of the desk so that you're sitting next to the person.

- ✔ While you're moving your chair, you say in a soft tone of voice something like, "I'm sure you won't mind me sitting next to you. I think you'll find this material to be very interesting."

By picking up and moving your chair while simultaneously stating your intentions to do so, there's really nothing the other person can do to stop you. The whole thing happens so quickly that by the time the person has had a chance to respond, you're already sitting next to him.

Here are some tips about how you should position yourself during a meeting:

- ✔ Whenever you're sitting with another person at a table — be it in one of your offices or at a restaurant — you should always sit next to the other person instead of sitting across from each other.

- ✔ It does make a difference whether you sit on the left or the right side. If you're right-handed, you should sit on the person's right side. This way, when you're writing, the person can read your notations as you're writing them because your writing hand will not hide your pad. If you're left-handed, you should sit on the person's left side for the same reason.

- ✔ When you're making a presentation to two people and you're sitting at a table, you want the two of them to be sitting next to each other. This way, you can address both of them at the same time. If you're sitting between them, you'll find that whenever you address one person, you're no longer able to look at the other person. And when you're trying to share the same piece of printed information with two people who aren't sitting next to each other, one of them is always looking at it upside down.

✔ If you're sitting at a long table, like a conference table, you should still try to get the two people to sit next to each other. Then you should sit down on the same side of the table right next to them.

✔ The chair you choose to sit in can also contribute to the eventual outcome of your meeting. When possible, you should always sit in a straight-backed chair. This keeps you alert and focused. Try your best to avoid sitting in a soft, comfortable lounge chair or couch because it becomes too easy for you to relax and lose your competitive mental edge.

✔ Try to avoid sitting in a chair that is lower in height than the chair of the other person. The person who is sitting in the higher chair is able to look down on you and will have more power and control over the flow of the meeting. This situation usually occurs when you're sitting on a couch and the other person is sitting in a straight-backed chair.

Your important business meetings should take place in the office, not in a restaurant. Business breakfasts, lunches, and dinners are fine for getting to know a person, but they are not good places to try to conduct important business because of the lack of privacy, constant interruptions, and continuous distractions.

Managing Your Business Meetings

Meetings play a very important part in everyday business life. It's a crying shame that so many of them are unproductive. From the studies I've seen, most of the people working in corporate America are spending at least 40 percent of their time sitting in these meetings. And I would hazard a guess that this figure is understated because it probably doesn't include the time spent in unscheduled, or impromptu, meetings.

If you were to define a meeting as any time two or more people get together to talk about something pertaining to business, then we're probably spending at least 90 percent of our time in meetings. The unfortunate thing is that the majority of these meetings are so poorly run and so poorly organized that they're nothing more than a complete waste of everyone's time.

When the purpose of a meeting isn't well thought out, the participants may not know what they're supposed to be discussing, what they're trying to accomplish, or even why they're there in the first place. In the end, decisions aren't made, important issues aren't resolved, and nothing gets done.

A lot of valuable and precious time is wasted, and the only decision to come out of the meeting is the decision to hold another meeting. But it can't be scheduled because the person who called the meeting doesn't have his calendar with him.

The following sections contain some tips on how you can turn unproductive meetings into action-oriented meetings.

Distribute an agenda

If someone's scheduling a meeting, you and everyone else should know why. If the meeting doesn't have a well-defined purpose, it shouldn't be held. You also need to know what's expected of you and what you're trying to accomplish. Are you getting together for the purpose of discussing a new business opportunity, solving a business problem, or just sharing information and bringing everyone up-to-date on the status of specific projects or clients?

The best way to inform meeting participants of what the meeting's about is to prepare an agenda. In most cases, a detailed agenda should be written and distributed well in advance of the meeting. This way, everyone will be thoroughly prepared to discuss the items on the agenda.

Insisting that a written agenda be distributed in advance forces the person who is calling the meeting to think about why the meeting is necessary in the first place.

If you're the person calling the meeting, always prepare an agenda. And if you're the person who is being asked to attend a meeting, insist that an agenda be prepared so that you can properly prepare yourself for the meeting.

If you've never created an agenda, an *agenda form* can help you draw up a plan for a meeting. Figure 7-1 shows a blank agenda form.

After the agenda has been distributed, it's even possible that some of the items on the agenda can be dealt with over the phone or by written correspondence. If that's the case, then these items should be removed from the agenda.

A great question to ask at the beginning of any meeting is, "How do we know when this meeting is over?"

After the meeting starts, it's the responsibility of the meeting leader to see that everybody sticks to the items on the agenda.

Sample Agenda Form

Date of Meeting _____

Place _____

Starting Time _____

Ending Time _____

Person Calling Meeting _____

Purpose of the Meeting _____

Desired Outcome of the Meeting _____

Meeting Participants

     1. _____

     2. _____

     3. _____

     4. _____

Agenda Items/Time Allotted for Discussion on Each Item

     1. _____

     2. _____

     3. _____

     4. _____

     5. _____

(Note: The most important items should be listed at the top of the agenda and should be discussed first. The person who prepares the agenda should also include the amount of time that will be allowed for discussion of each of these points.)

Figure 7-1: A sample meeting agenda form.

You need to know the meeting's purpose and location

When you're asked to attend a meeting, you should always know the purpose of the meeting. Will you be expected to make a decision, or will everyone just be sharing information? Is the meeting being called in order to solve a problem, plan for the future, bring everyone up-to-date on the status of a project, discuss new business, or something else? When you as a meeting participant know what's expected of you, you're better able to prepare yourself for the meeting.

And to ensure that nobody comes in late with some lame excuse about going to the wrong office or conference room, always state where the meeting will be held. And if you're holding a meeting at an off-site location, be sure to give the street address of the building along with the name and location of the meeting room. In some cases, you may want to include a map so that everyone knows how to get there.

Meetings should have specific starting and ending times

It's unfortunate, but some people just don't take meetings seriously. They come in late, they leave early, and they talk during the meeting.

It's rather easy to get people to change their previous pattern of behavior, however, if you let them know that you want your meetings to become more productive and meaningful. You start by insisting that everyone arrive on time.

The next time you're in charge of an office meeting, close and lock the door so that late arrivals will have to knock to get in. You can then use their late arrival as an opportunity to inform them that they're expected to be on time in the future.

Latecomers also need to know that you're planning to stick to your agenda, that there is only a limited amount of time available for discussion of each point, and that you plan to adjourn at the designated time.

When you're asked to attend a meeting, it's okay to insist that it start on time, and it's okay to point out that the discussion has strayed too far from the items on the agenda. If the person who called the meeting isn't going to take control of it, then you should speak up and remind him or her that time's running short and you've got other things to do, or another meeting to attend, as soon as this meeting is over.

Avoid unnecessary meetings

Just because someone wants to schedule a face-to-face meeting doesn't mean that the meeting must be held. After you get the agenda, it's okay to call the person and ask about the meeting's particulars and what outcome is expected from the meeting. After you speak on the phone, you may discover that you can accumulate the necessary information without ever having the meeting.

Just because you've been invited to attend a meeting doesn't mean that you've got to attend. You just wouldn't believe how many people attend meetings where their presence isn't necessary. But they waste a lot of their valuable time sitting there anyway. So if you don't think that you'll have much to offer at a meeting, it's okay to call the person who scheduled the meeting and say so.

Why waste your valuable time sitting in a meeting discussing things that are not of direct concern to you when you could be doing important and meaningful work at your desk?

Do you have to attend the entire meeting?

Occasionally, a person's presence is needed for only a small portion of a meeting. Should that be the case, when you're asked to attend a meeting, pick up the phone and ask the person who scheduled the meeting if you can attend only the portion that applies to you. This way, you don't have to waste hours of time listening to others discuss things that aren't of immediate concern to you.

Impromptu meetings can be a Big Waste of Time. When people call and say that they want to see you, you don't have to drop everything you're doing to have that meeting. It's okay to ask why they want to get together with you, what it is that they want to discuss, and what they want to accomplish. In many instances, a face-to-face meeting can be replaced by just a few telephone calls and some correspondence between the two of you.

What should you bring to the meeting?

I know this advice sounds silly because it's just common sense, but when a meeting's called, all participants should be informed by the agenda sheet as to what materials or other information they're expected to bring.

If you're the one who is calling the meeting, try to distribute all of your handouts or other information at least 24 hours before the meeting takes place. This way, everyone will have the opportunity to read and think about the topics of discussion before the meeting starts.

I once sat on a committee where the committee head made a practice of distributing the packet of information to the committee members at the beginning of each meeting. We were then expected to read the material and make decisions based upon that material without having any time to think about the things we had just read. I thought this was a very sloppy way to run an organization. I didn't stay on this committee for very long.

What happens next?

At the conclusion of a meeting, the person who called the meeting should take a few minutes to summarize the points that were discussed and determine what is to be done next. If additional work needs to be done, those tasks should be assigned, and the people who are doing the work should be told when the tasks need to be completed.

If you're the person to whom the work is being assigned, you should ask some questions — and take detailed notes on what you're being instructed to do — so that there can be no misunderstandings about the format in which it's supposed to be done and the due date for completion. If another meeting needs to be scheduled, a date and time should be set before everyone walks out the door.

Keep minutes of the meeting

Someone's got to keep minutes of the meeting so that everyone will know what was discussed, what decisions were made, and what is to be done next, by whom, and when. These minutes should be distributed within a few days of the conclusion of the meeting.

Make the last person who arrives at the meeting take the minutes. Since no one wants to be responsible for taking the minutes, you should see people's arrival times improve.

Chapter 8

Maintain Control of Your Conversations

· ·

· ·

*H*ow many conversations do you have during a typical workday? You probably don't have the slightest idea, and frankly, I don't have any idea how many conversations I have, either. But I know that we spend a great deal of time interacting with other people each and every day.

We're talking to people on the telephone, getting together in *formal* meetings in a conference room, holding *informal* meetings in someone's office, and having many impromptu meetings as someone stops us while we're walking down the hall to get a cup of coffee.

And that's just the people we work with in our own organization. During the day, we're also interacting with people from the outside. They may be customers, clients, prospective customers, the people who supply us with goods and services, and the people who would *like* to be selling us goods and services in the future.

Before you begin asking yourself why a chapter on how to maintain control of your conversations is included in a book on time management, let me take a moment to explain. Each of us spends a lot of time interacting with other people, but we don't necessarily do a good job of *communicating* with each other. As a result, we don't get the information we need to do our jobs correctly.

This chapter is included because if you're able to improve your ability to communicate and get the information you need, then you can spend less time in meetings or on the phone and more time working on your important work, tasks, and projects.

You Get Information by Asking Questions

The easiest way to go about getting information is to ask questions. And as you get better at asking questions, it becomes easier for you to obtain the information you need to do your job. Let me give you a few examples of how you can do your job more quickly if you're good at asking questions:

- ✔ When you're given an assignment, you need to know what you're expected to do, how you're supposed to do it, and when it's got to be done. You obtain this information by asking questions.

- ✔ When you're trying to sell someone a product, service, or idea — and we're all selling *something* — you've got to find out what it is that the other person wants, needs, or desires before you can show how your product, service, or idea can fill that want, need, or desire. You obtain this information by asking questions.

- ✔ When you want to get information about what's happening within your company or organization, you sit down with a colleague or coworker and ask some questions.

- ✔ When you want to find out what one of your competitors is up to, you ask some questions.

- ✔ When you meet someone of the opposite sex and you want to find out if he or she is free for a date on Saturday night, you've got to ask some questions. (Time management is one thing, but this *really* is important!)

The better you are at asking questions, the easier it will be for you to obtain the information you need to get your work done, to help your company prosper, to further your career, and maybe even to better your social life.

Encourage the Other Person to Talk

People love to talk about themselves, so let them. And by asking a series of questions — sometimes over an extended period of time — you'll end up learning a great deal about their business affairs, their business activities, their ongoing business relationships, your competition, and almost anything else that's going on in their lives.

Questions enable you to tune into other people and learn what they are thinking; and questions can help you to identify their real needs and real motives. And it's by asking questions that you can identify existing problems that you can help solve, discover potential business, or even find new career opportunities for yourself.

Here are three things to remember:

✔ There's often a big difference between what people say and what they think and feel deep down inside. Getting someone to talk by asking questions gives you an opportunity to discover what someone is really thinking.

✔ When you talk about yourself, you're a bore. When you encourage the other person to talk, you're a brilliant conversationalist.

✔ During your business meetings, listen more than you speak. As a general rule, you should listen at least 60 percent of the time. If you find that you're talking too much, it's time to ask another question.

Keeping a Tight Lip Yourself

Now I know that you probably love to talk, especially about yourself and your accomplishments (I can talk about *me* for hours). But you'll go much further in business and your career if you encourage the other people to keep talking and you just sit there asking questions and listening attentively. Besides, you can't learn very much when you're the one who's talking.

If you're asked a question during a conversation, give a brief answer and then follow up your answer with another question.

Talk about being tight-lipped. Several years ago, I read a newspaper story about the late Bill Casey, the former director of the Central Intelligence Agency. He was so tight-lipped that if your jacket had caught on fire, he would tell you so only if you asked him the question: "Is my jacket on fire?" And then his reply would be: "Yes."

He (Or She) Who Asks the Questions Controls the Conversation

When you're able to ask a person a series of questions, you're able to maintain control over a conversation. It's easy to ask that first question, but it takes some work and effort to be able to ask a second, a third, and a fourth question. By doing so, however, you place yourself in the desirable position of being able to control the flow of the conversation.

Would you like to say a few words?

You've probably never realized this, but when you're able to keep another person talking during a conversation, you give yourself a competitive edge. You see, people can think at a rate of about 1,200 words per minute but only talk at a rate of about 250 words per minute.

So when people are talking at 250 words per minute and trying to focus on what they're saying, you can be thinking — at 1,200 words per minute — about what you want to say in response. You're thinking more than five times faster than they are talking.

Your objective in asking these questions is to keep the other person talking so that you can get some useful information. (Such as: Where do you live? What's your telephone number? Do you have plans this weekend? Never mind. . . .) The more information you have available to you, the easier it is for you to do your job.

Whenever you're talking to people who appear to be losing interest, beginning to daydream, or falling asleep, just ask a question, and you'll bring them back to life. Now they not only have to wake up and clear the cobwebs from their brains, but also have to listen because they know that they're expected to give you some kind of response.

Try to discover the hot button

Many people in sales use a phrase that defines their reason for asking a lot of questions: They want to discover a person's *hot button.*

What's a hot button? When you know what someone likes or dislikes, when you know what excites or concerns a person, when you know what a person's problems are, then you've discovered his or her hot buttons.

And when you know what to say and when to say it, it becomes much easier for you to get people to say "Yes" to whatever you're proposing or suggesting. (And when you know what not to say and when *not* to say it, you can keep yourself out of an awful lot of hot water.)

Get to know the hot buttons of your boss, your colleagues and coworkers, your largest customers and clients, and your significant other, and you'll dramatically improve your relationships with all of them.

The Art of Asking Questions

Asking questions is an art. It's easy to just ask one or two questions, but it takes a lot of hard work to be able to ask a person a series of them. You'll find that it takes a little bit of practice to learn how to ask the right questions in the right way at the right time; but after you get the hang of it, you'll be amazed at how much information people are willing to volunteer just because you asked.

To keep a conversation going, always ask open-ended questions

When you ask open-ended questions, it not only encourages people to continue speaking, thus keeping the conversation going, but also gives them the opportunity to fully explain their thoughts, opinions, or comments. With an open-ended question, you're asking people to give you an informative and descriptive answer.

To ask an open-ended question, all you've got to do is phrase your question in such a way that it includes one of the five "W" words or the "H" word. These words are

- Who
- What
- When
- Where
- Why
- How

Now, how can a person give a "Yes" or "No" answer to a question that includes a Who, What, Where, Why, When, or How without appearing evasive?

When I was in high school, I would often have the following conversation with my mother:

>Mom: *Jeff, where are you going?*
>
>Me: *Out.*
>
>Mom: *When will you be back?*
>
>Me: *Later.*
>
>Mom: *Who are you going with?*
>
>Me: *Friends.*

(Just like Marlon Brando in *The Wild Bunch*, right?)

Avoid asking close-ended questions

The flip side to an open-ended question is a close-ended question, which is a question that can be answered with a simple "Yes" or "No." When you give someone the opportunity to answer a question with just a "Yes" or "No," you've created a situation where the flow of conversation can easily die. You just can't have a meaningful conversation when all you're getting is yes or no answers.

Calvin Coolidge, the 30th president of the United States, had the nickname "Silent Cal" because he didn't say very much. One day, a reporter said to the President, "I'll bet you ten bucks that I can get you to say more than two words." And Silent Cal replied, "Nope!"

Don't ask questions in a negative way

When a question is asked in a negative way, it can change the course, mood, tone, and flow of a conversation and take it in the wrong direction. You always want to talk about things from a positive perspective.

For example, instead of saying, "What don't you like about . . . ," you could say, "What would you like to see improved?" Or rather than ask, "What did I do wrong?" you could ask, "What should I have done differently? How could I have done it better?"

When you don't understand, ask for clarification

If, during your conversation, you ask someone a question but you're not completely sure what the answer means, it's okay to ask for clarification. This is another way to show your interest in what's being said. You can say something like the following:

> *Can you go into a bit more detail?*
>
> *What does that mean to you?*
>
> *How did you arrive at that conclusion?*

By asking for more detail, you'll get some additional information.

Paraphrase, summarize, or simonize

During a discussion, your conversation partners always need some positive feedback — be it a smile, a nod of the head, or a twinkle in your eye — as encouragement to continue talking. And by paraphrasing or summarizing what was just said, you can encourage your partners to continue speaking. It also provides reassurance that you're trying your best to understand what it is that they are saying.

To paraphrase a person's previous statement, you can start your sentence with one of the following phrases:

> *If I understand you correctly, you're saying . . .*
>
> *It seems to me . . .*

By summarizing all the things that were just said — and feeding it back — you can pull everything together so that you can confirm that you fully understand what's been discussed.

Other techniques to keep a conversation going

In addition to asking direct questions, there are several other techniques that you can use to encourage people to continue talking and to show them that you're interested in what they are saying.

Echo the speaker's words

The *Echo* technique is an easy way for you to keep someone talking, and when you use it effectively, you don't have to do too much thinking or talking yourself. This technique is especially useful if you're stuck and can't think of anything more to say, because it can buy a few moments of time so that you can think about what you want to say next.

To use the Echo technique, just take the last few words of the sentence that the person just said and repeat them as if you were asking a question. Here's an example:

> *"I just came back from a meeting with my boss."*
>
> *"Your boss?"*
>
> *"Yes. She just gave me another project that she says she needs tomorrow."*
>
> *"Tomorrow?"*
>
> *"Yeah. It's for Pepperdine Manufacturing. You know, the new account she landed last week."*

"Last week?"

"Yeah. She was on a plane coming back from Toledo, and she started talk-ing with this guy who was in the next seat. . . ."

You get the idea. In theory, you can use the Echo technique to keep someone talking for hours at a time. In reality, you can't use it for more than a few moments because it won't take too long for the other party to catch on to what you're doing.

So, for a little variety, you can throw in an occasional "Oh?," "Uh huh," or "Hmmmm." Don't stop reading just yet. In the following section, I describe this marvelous conversational technique in more detail.

Just say "Oh?," "Uh huh," or "Hmmmm" and nod your head

As an alternative to echoing each and every statement during a conversation, you can throw in an occasional "Oh?," "Uh Huh!," or "Hmmmm," just for vari-ety. No matter what the person says, you simply respond with "Oh?," "Uh huh!," or "Hmmmm," and the person will continue talking.

This technique is another easy way for you to signal to other people that you're still listening. You also let them know that you would like them to con-tinue speaking. It's especially effective when you nod your head, as a sign of agreement, at the same time. Let's go back to the last conversation:

"I just came back from a meeting with my boss."

"Oh?"

"She just gave me another project that she says she needs tomorrow."

"Tomorrow?"

"Yeah. It's for Pepperdine Manufacturing. You know, the new account she landed last week."

"Oh?"

"Yeah. She was on a plane coming back from Toledo, and she started talking with this guy who was in the next seat. . . ."

If you would like to have some fun and improve your relationship with your spouse or significant other, try using the Echo technique and these other related techniques when you come home from work this evening. Lead off with a question like

How was your day today?

See how long you can keep the conversation going. You'll quickly see his or her eyes begin to light up with the realization that you're *really* paying attention. At the conclusion of the conversation, you'll know *everything* that happened during the day, and he or she will think that you're a brilliant conversationalist.

Mirror the person's feelings and emotions

When your partner in conversation is expressing emotions or articulating feelings about something, you should reflect — mirror — those emotions or feelings. As a part of your response, make eye contact, show concern, and nod in agreement, or disbelief, as the situation may dictate.

This way, you acknowledge to the other person that you heard what was just said and you offer an emotional response. You can usually pick up the emotion or feeling from the tone of voice, the choice of words, or a look in the eyes. Someone looking for emotional support may say something like:

> *Do you think that's fair?*
>
> *Do you think I did the right thing?*

But when someone's asking an emotional question, you don't necessarily need to offer an answer or response. Instead, it may be entirely appropriate to respond to the question by asking a question. You can say something like this in response:

> *What do you think?*

Listen more and talk less

Asking questions is just the first part of being a good conversationalist. If you're going to be good at asking questions, you've got to be good at listening to the answers. You must listen closely to what the other individual is saying so that you can give positive feedback and, when appropriate, ask another question. In this way, you're able to guide the flow of a conversation in the direction you want it to go.

He who talks *dominates* the conversation. He who listens *controls* the conversation. The same thing applies to "*shes*."

Tips for Being a Brilliant Conversationalist

Here's a quick list of conversation do's and don'ts:

- ✔ Do show interest in what the other person is saying.
- ✔ Do make an effort to understand what the other individual is trying to say.
- ✔ Do make an effort to understand the other person's point of view, even if you don't agree with it.
- ✔ Do let the other person know that you disagree with his or her point of view at the appropriate time.

✔ Do remain quiet when silence is the best answer to a question.

✔ Don't enter the conversation with preconceived ideas.

✔ Don't argue, even if you disagree.

✔ Don't interrupt unless you have a very good reason.

✔ Don't pass judgment too quickly.

✔ Don't offer your opinion unless you're asked.

✔ Don't give advice or behavioral feedback (tell the person how his or her behavior affects you) unless you're asked.

✔ Don't allow yourself to react emotionally to a statement; keep your cool and don't get angry.

✔ Don't cut other people off. Let them finish their thoughts before you offer yours or ask another question.

Winning in a conversation means using active listening techniques to control and guide the flow of the conversation so that you and your partners have the opportunity to fully express yourselves.

Chapter 9

Helping People Make Decisions . . . Faster

● ●

In This Chapter

▶ Getting someone to say "Yes"

▶ Finding the decision maker

▶ Handling objections effectively

▶ Mastering the art of negotiating

● ●

*I*f you thought that the biggest time waster in business today was time wasted in meetings, you're mistaken. The biggest time waster in business today is the inability of people to make decisions. In the corporate world, we all spend hours of time in meetings, but when it comes to making a decision and actually doing something, the only decision that's made is to schedule another meeting. And when decisions are not made in a timely manner, windows of opportunity open and close very quickly, usually before anything gets done.

One day Mitzi and I (Mitzi's my wife) were trying to decide which movie we wanted to see, and because neither of us could make a decision, we missed the starting times of *all* the movies.

Now why do so many people find it difficult to make a decision? Because they're afraid that they're going to make a mistake. They're not confident that they're making the *right* decision. As a result, they become paralyzed.

And when someone avoids making a decision, nothing gets done. So if you want to get ahead in this world, you've got to be good at making decisions yourself and at helping other people make decisions.

There's a common tool that an individual or an organization uses to put off, delay, or postpone the making of a decision. It's called *The Objection!* But dealing with and overcoming objections is a daily part of our business and personal lives. Every day, we're selling our thoughts, ideas, and concepts, as well as our products and services, to others — be it trying to get the company's

Management Information Services Department to order a new piece of computer software, trying to close a multimillion-dollar deal, or getting a date for Saturday night.

When you're able to compress the time it takes for someone to make a decision, you're able to get your work done more quickly.

Your Objective Is to Get the Person to Say "Yes"

I don't know what you do for a living — hey, I'm just the author — but if you're like almost everyone else, you've got to be selling something. And you're selling something to someone every day. It may be a product or a service to a new corporate account, or a new idea to your boss. Or maybe you're trying to convince a new employer that you're the best candidate for the job. Or maybe you're trying to persuade your new neighbor down the hall to have dinner with you tomorrow night.

But no matter what it is that you're selling, you've got to be able to get the other person to say "Yes." People make decisions for their reasons, not yours or mine (I know that fact may be hard for you to accept), so when you're able to discover what those reasons are — their *hot buttons* — then the process of getting someone to say "Yes" isn't quite so daunting.

People make decisions for their reasons, not yours, and when they can feel, touch, and see something, it's much easier to get them to say "Yes."

The ABCs of selling

When you're trying to convince someone to say "Yes" to whatever you're selling, you should always remember selling's ABCs:

✔ **Advantage:** Always promote the *advantages* of the features of your product, service, or idea.

✔ **Benefit:** Talk about how these features will be of value and provide *benefit* to the person you're trying to convince. Describe how these features will help solve problems or improve the quality of life.

✔ **Commitment:** Get the other person to make a *commitment,* to indicate that he or she wants to own the product, service, or idea you're selling.

Don't take "No" for an answer

The only way you can get people to say "Yes" is by asking them to say "Yes." If you don't ask, you don't get! Now the first time you ask a person to say "Yes," he or she will probably say "No" and at the same time give you a reason for saying no — it's called an *objection*. (And you'll probably be scared to death, but you shouldn't let that fear stop you from asking the person to say "Yes.") An objection isn't the end; it's the beginning. You just need to talk a bit more and discuss why the answer was no.

To get someone to say "Yes," you've got to be persistent. I saw these interesting statistics one day in a magazine article. Of those who asked the other person to say "Yes," look what happened to them after they were told "No."

- ✔ After they got their first "No," 44 percent called it quits and went back to the office.

- ✔ After they got their second "No," an additional 22 percent quit and went back to the office.

- ✔ After they got their third "No," another 14 percent quit and went back to the office.

- ✔ After they got their fourth "No," another 12 percent quit and went back to the office.

These statistics tell me that 66 percent of the people called it quits after they heard their second "No"; 80 percent called it quits after hearing a third "No"; and after hearing the fourth "No," 92 percent packed up their bags and went home, without having made any money.

So if you want someone to say "Yes" to whatever product, service, or idea you're selling, you had better be prepared to stick around for a while. You should plan to ask the person to say "Yes" at least five, six, or seven times before you decide to call it quits. Just because a person says "No" once or twice doesn't mean that he or she won't say "Yes" if you continue to ask a third, fourth, or fifth time.

If you're not being rejected, you're not trying hard enough. (My editor wrote this query: "Jeff: I think that applies to my writing career. I've been rejected a number of times, but not for quite a long time — mostly because I haven't sent out any of my articles for quite a long time. I need to get back to doing that.")

You build on agreement

The process of getting people to say "Yes" is the process of building on agreement. As you successfully deal with each objection, you eventually change people's opinions about your product, service, or idea. Your goal is to move people from feeling indifferent to feeling positive about what you have to offer.

A treatise on seafood

There was a barracuda swimming in a tank of water with another fish that just happened to be the barracuda's favorite meal. There was only one little problem for the barracuda: His meal was enclosed in a glass container.

Every time the barracuda tried to eat this fish, he crashed into the glass and bumped his nose.

He did this over and over and over and over again, and his nose became very, very, very sore. After a few days of this, the fish was taken out of the glass container and was free to swim wherever he wanted to.

And the barracuda starved to death.

You can't overcome indifference

When people say, "I want to think it over," or "I'm in no real hurry," that's usually an indication that they aren't really sold on the idea. Either your proposal or presentation hasn't convinced them that your product, service, or idea will help solve a problem, or they are not sufficiently uncomfortable with their present situation to want to do something about it. This indifference often stems from the four basic *No*s.

- ✔ **No Trust:** I really don't trust you.

- ✔ **No Need:** I'm not aware of a need for your product, service, or idea.

- ✔ **No Help:** I'm aware of a need, but you haven't convinced me that your product, service, or idea will satisfy it.

- ✔ **No Hurry:** Okay, you can satisfy my need, but my problem doesn't really bother me enough yet for me to pay to make it go away.

In order to convince people to say "Yes," these four *No*s first have to be identified and then dealt with one at a time.

When you perceive that a person's attitude is one of indifference, it's time to start probing. You probe for areas of discomfort or areas of dissatisfaction with the person's present situation. (For more information about asking questions, see Chapter 8.) You do this by asking open-ended questions, questions that can't be answered with a "yes" or "no."

Your goal is to help people become aware of a problem, or to help them realize that they aren't entirely satisfied with something. After you've done so, you have the opportunity to point out that the product, service, or idea you're offering provides a solution to that problem.

People are always more comfortable when they identify a problem and then discover its solution all by themselves. You're just there to help them along.

Look for that magic moment

In every successful sale, there is a *magic moment* when the buyer is most likely to agree with you and say "Yes." And you've got to watch for and pick up those signals.

It could be just a simple physical gesture, such as leaning forward slightly, that indicates "I'm ready to say yes," or there could be a twinkle in the eye or a slight smile. When you hear, feel, or see such a signal, you must stop your presentation and try to get a commitment immediately.

Your objective is to close the sale by getting your potential customer to say "Yes," not to complete the presentation.

Ask "How?"

One of the most effective closing methods is getting people to discuss how, not if, they are going to buy. Make a request for action. To close the sale, you've got to ask for the order. If you don't ask, you probably won't get it.

Who Makes the Decisions?

In every organization — be it a large multinational corporation or a sole proprietor who works out of his or her home — there is a method or a process set up for making decisions. And if you're going to be successful in getting someone to say "Yes," you've got to know how the organization goes about making decisions.

If the decision is to be made by more than one person, you need to know who the other people are, how they fit into the organization, and what their overall level of involvement in the decision-making process is.

After you know who the decision makers are, you should meet with them individually or speak with them on the phone, if that's appropriate, in order to try to win them over and sell them on the benefits of your product, service, or idea.

Who has the authority to say "Yes"?

When you're trying to get someone — or an organization — to make a decision, you've first got to learn who has the authority to make that decision. Who has the authority to say "Yes"? After you learn who that person is — because he or she may not be your initial contact — then you've got to sell him or her on the merits of whatever you're proposing.

If you're unable to deal directly with the decision maker, there's a pretty good chance that you're going to waste a lot of time, energy, and money.

Who has the authority to say "No"?

Within every organization there may be a number of people who don't have enough authority to say "Yes," but they *do* have the power to say "No" and can effectively kill whatever you're proposing. You must discover who those people are and get them to support you.

A "No" is a "No" until it's a "Yes"

No matter how nice and friendly and courteous a person is, a "No" is a "No" until it becomes a "Yes." Occasionally, you'll come into contact with people who give you every indication that they're going to say "Yes," but you can never get them to make a commitment. They'll talk to you at length, both on the phone and in person. But you can't get a commitment. They lead you on. They raise your expectations. But still, they don't say "Yes." Instead, they just leave you hanging because they don't say "No."

Beware of these kinds of people. They're dangerous. They don't have the courage to tell you the truth: They're not interested. Or even worse, they don't have the authority to say "Yes." And the really infuriating part is that they couldn't care less that you've invested a lot of time, effort, and money on them, and it was all done at their encouragement.

Are you dealing with a decision influencer?

Sometimes you'll find yourself dealing with a person who is in a position to influence the final decision but is not in a position to make the final decision. For example, if you're dealing with the president of the company, this person may need to get the final approval from the board of directors before he or she can say "Yes."

Or someone may need to get the okay from a supervisor or manager before giving the go-ahead. Or, on an individual level, a person may not be able to give you a final answer until he or she has had an opportunity to discuss it with his or her spouse.

In situations like these, you've got to be sure that you've "sold" the decision influencer. If you haven't, he or she won't be very enthusiastic about presenting it to the other people who will participate in the final decision.

To find out whether the person with whom you're dealing has the authority to make a decision, or whether he or she needs to consult with someone else, you should always ask this type of question somewhere along the way:

> *Before you make your final decision, is there anyone else whom you want or need to consult?*

Court your champions

A *champion* is a person inside the organization who stands to gain something — prestige, recognition, or some other benefit — by supporting your program and defending your cause. As you meet the people who are part of the decision-making process, try to identify those people who will work on your behalf and help promote your product, service, or idea within the organization. You should always keep them advised of your progress.

Beware of blockers

There are also people who, for one reason or another, will go out of their way to try to block or sabotage your activities and put a halt to whatever you're trying to accomplish. Maybe these people have an axe to grind, maybe they're against change, or maybe they aren't happy that a new idea is being promoted by someone else rather than them.

To neutralize these individuals, you need to find a way to work around them so that other people will become more involved in the decision-making process and the blockers' involvement will be minimized. If these people are your only contacts within the organization, then you've got to find someone else to talk with because otherwise you're dead in the water. This situation is where a champion can be of help, and it's always helpful to have a coach available to give you some tips.

Get yourself a coach

Every once in a while, you may find yourself in a situation in which you're not sure what you should do next. You may not be sure who the decision makers are or how the organization goes about making decisions, and you need some help in navigating through these unfamiliar and uncharted waters. In this situation, you should look for someone who has done it before, a person who can give you some ideas, tips, techniques, and strategies on how to deal with this situation. This person could coach you through each step in the decision-making process.

Your coach can help you prepare your proposal or presentation, give you suggestions as to what you should say and how you should say it, and assist you in creating an overall strategy so that you can get the other person, or the organization, to say "Yes."

Handle Objections Effectively

The meat and potatoes of getting someone to say "Yes" is your ability to handle objections effectively. This is the main course. You asked all those questions so that you could get people to give you all the reasons that they don't like the product, service, or idea that you're trying to sell them. You encouraged them to be honest and open with you about what it is that they want and don't want, like and don't like, need and don't need. And now that you've been given a list of all the reasons that they're going to say "No," you're in a position to deal with each objection, one by one, and convince them that it's in their best interest to say "Yes."

Objections are like a minefield: If you don't locate, uncover, and remove all of them, one at a time, they'll blow you away.

Here are some tips on dealing with objections:

✔ When you prepare for a presentation, put yourself in the other people's shoes and make a list of every possible objection that you think they could give you. Then write down an appropriate answer or response to each of these possible objections.

✔ Don't be afraid of objections. An objection often indicates a sincere interest by people, and it merely means that they aren't in agreement with you at this particular moment.

✔ Don't deal with each objection at the moment it's given to you. By responding to each of them, you'll certainly be giving more weight and importance to some of them than they deserve, and at the very least, you'll be wasting some of your valuable time doing it. Get the people to give you *all* their objections, and then you can begin discussing the most important ones first.

✔ In the absence of a response, most objections simply go away. The important ones will be brought up again.

There are two kinds of objections

Objections can be classified into two categories: factual and emotional. One is valid; the other may or may not be.

> ✔ **Factual objections are based on logic.** A valid objection is based on logical and factual reasoning. It's valid because this is the way the person perceives the facts to be. And even if the person's facts may be incorrect, based on unsubstantiated information, or even on a rumor or false innuendo, it's still a valid objection.
>
> Factual objections can be discussed in detail because you're analyzing the "facts" of a situation, or at least someone's perceptions of the facts. Incorrect information can be corrected, and there can be a complete flow of conversation.
>
> ✔ **Emotional objections are neither logical nor factual.** These objections are based on an emotional response and would often be considered an excuse or a smoke screen. Emotional objections sound logical, but when you take the time to think about and analyze them, they don't make any sense.

When a person is giving you one objection after another after another and none of them seems to make any sense to you, then you're probably dealing with a person who is making a decision based on an emotional reaction. No amount of factual information or logic will turn around an emotional objection. The person is saying "No" but won't explain the real reason for saying "No."

If your instincts tell you that you're getting emotional objections, it's your cue to attempt to change the flow of the conversation back to a discussion of the basic facts. If you're unable to do so, it's time to pack up and move on.

People often make the decision to say "Yes" based on an emotional reaction or response, and then they often justify that decision with factual information.

Techniques for overcoming objections

During your conversation with your potential customers, they are going to be making statements — offering objections — that indicate that they don't want or aren't ready to buy the product, service, or idea you're selling. After you have flushed out all of their possible objections, you can begin to tackle the objections one by one, starting with the most important ones, using the techniques in the following sections.

Answer a question with a question

When you're asked a question, you don't necessarily have to give a direct answer. Use your answer as an opportunity to ask the person another question so that you can learn more about what he or she is thinking. Remember: Whoever asks the questions controls the conversation.

Let people speak

Encourage people to talk about what they want or don't want, like and don't like, or need and don't need. Resist the temptation to respond to each statement. And don't interrupt while they're talking.

Agree that the point is a good one

It's okay to say, "The point that was raised is a good point." Making this statement doesn't mean that you agree; it only means that you agree that the point raised was a good one. To indicate that you think the point is a good one, you can say something like:

> *I can see why that would be of concern to you.*
>
> *I can understand your feelings.*
>
> *That's an interesting observation that you just made.*
>
> *You've brought up a good point.*

And even though you may not agree with what the person has to say, you should try your best to express yourself in a positive way. Instead of saying "No," you can replace it with

> *Yes, but. . . .*

This way, it *appears* that you're always in agreement with the other person when in fact you may not be.

Clarify those statements

If you would like the people with whom you're talking to give you a little more background information regarding a specific statement, you can ask them to clarify by saying something like:

> *How did you happen to arrive at that conclusion?*
>
> *What is it that makes you feel that way?*
>
> *It seems to me that you have a very strong reason for saying that. Would you mind telling me what the reason is?*

Identify all the important points

The more you're able to get other people to talk, the easier it will be for you to identify and isolate their most important points. To encourage people to talk, you may want to ask these kinds of questions:

Is there anything else you're concerned about?

Are there any other points you feel need to be addressed?

One of the reasons you ask questions is to try to discover what it is people really want, not what you think they want. After you've done that, it's much easier to get them to say "Yes."

Feed back statements

To confirm that what you heard is what was meant, you should feed back statements by saying something like:

If I understand you correctly, you said. . . .

If I understand you correctly, you're concerned about. . . .

If I understand you correctly, you believe. . . .

Soften the objection by eliminating confrontation

No matter what someone says — especially when he or she gets excited — try your best not to get into an argument. You may win the argument, but you'll never get that person to say "Yes." Instead, you can respond in this manner:

I can understand why you feel that way; however. . . .

The phrase "I understand," when said in a quiet, sympathetic tone of voice, can be very helpful in defusing a potentially explosive or confrontational situation. Using this phrase doesn't require you to state whether you agree or disagree with the statement.

Isolate the most important objection

Try to isolate the most important objection to whatever you are selling or proposing. In a way, the person is telling you that this objection is the *only* reason for not making a decision now. And if you can deal with this one objection, then the person is ready to say "Yes." To isolate the objection, you can say something like:

Other than (insert objection), is there any additional reason that you can think of for not giving your approval to go ahead with this right now?"

If I understand you correctly, (insert name), if I could show you (convince you, display to you) that this (product, service, concept, or idea) will in fact save you (time, money), would you be prepared to give us the go-ahead this very moment?

Picking on an insurance salesman for fun and profit

A friend, who was a life insurance salesman, once told me with great pride how he had effectively overcome each and every objection that one of his prospects had given him. He was so proud because he thought that he had done a great job of answering every question.

So I asked him: "How much life insurance did the man purchase?" With that, Bob gave me a strange look and began to stammer as he looked away from me and down at the papers on his desk.

"Well," he said sheepishly, "he didn't buy any life insurance."

"But you just said that you did an absolutely marvelous job of overcoming his objections."

"Well I did, but. . . ."

Then I said, "But Bob, if he didn't buy any life insurance from you, then you didn't overcome his objections!" With that, Bob gave me that "It's about time for you to get out of my office" look, so I left.

Always take a deep breath before you begin speaking. Before you respond to an objection, always take a deep breath. This does two things for you: It gives you the opportunity to fill your lungs with air so that your voice will sound deeper and more powerful, and it will buy you a few moments of time to collect your thoughts.

To stress a point, hand over your pencil

Whenever you want to stress a point, give your customers a pencil and a piece of paper and ask them to write something down. This technique guarantees that they will not only pay attention to you but they will also listen to what you're saying as they write stuff down.

When you've got to add a column of numbers or multiply several numbers, give your customers-to-be a pencil and a piece of paper and let them do the calculations. (If there are a lot of numbers to add, subtract, multiply, or divide, give them a calculator.)

When you allow people to participate in this manner, they can actually see and understand how you arrive at the final results. If they are the ones who do the calculations and write down the numbers, they are much more likely to believe that the results are correct. The final calculations are not *your* numbers — they're the numbers of your customer-to-be.

When you want to emphasize the many benefits of the product, service, or idea that you're selling, ask people to write down the key points, one at a time, as you say what to write.

The balance sheet is a great selling tool

When you want your customers to create a list of reasons to buy whatever you're selling, have them create a *balance sheet*. You hand over your pen and a blank sheet of paper and ask them to draw a line across the top of the page and a line down the middle. Have them write "For" above the left column and "Against" above the right column, as shown in Figure 9-1.

Then ask your customers to start listing the advantages of your product, service, or idea, one item at a time. If they are having trouble coming up with these items, you dictate them as they write them down. While your customers are writing, take advantage of this opportunity to emphasize every detail. Don't stop until the list contains at least 20 items.

Now, here's where you get to the fun part. When you and your customers have gotten to the point where you've run out of additional reasons for a "Yes" response, you then say:

> *Now let's list all the disadvantages of not (using, buying, doing) my (product, service, idea).*

And now you become invisible. You don't say anything. You just sit there quietly and watch them *attempt* to fill in the Against column.

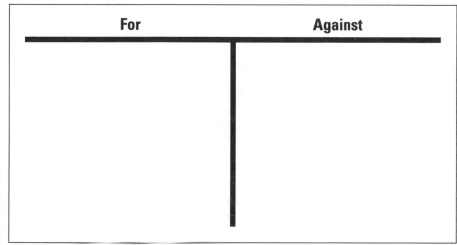

Figure 9-1:
A balance
sheet.

When they finish, you ask for a "Yes" response by counting the *For*s one at a time. As you count off each item, you read each item aloud. When you're finished, you disappear again and don't say another word until they do something.

Just stop talking!

Has someone ever asked you a question, and when you didn't respond to it, the other person didn't say anything further either . . . and there was just silence? Wasn't the silence deafening? And the longer the silence lasted, the louder it got.

Well, you can use silence as a very subtle but dramatic selling tool. When it comes down to the final question of whether or not your customers will say "Yes," you ask your question, and you stop talking. You don't say anything more; you sit; you wait! You don't say another word!

Silence creates tension, and the longer it lasts, the more tension it creates. The silence can last for 10 seconds, 15 seconds, or what seems to be an eternity, and it keeps getting longer. Still, you don't say one single word! You just sit there. You take a deep breath; you try to sit still in your chair; you clasp your hands together and squeeze your fingers tightly so that you won't fidget; and you try not to perspire too much. And you wait.

And your mind is racing. You're asking yourself, "What are they going to say? What are they going to do? What's going to happen next?" You don't know, but you keep waiting, silently. And you keep reminding yourself: *Whoever speaks first has lost.*

If you can wait until they speak, they will usually say "Yes." They'll buy whatever you're selling.

Create a sense of urgency

People are motivated to make a decision when they feel that their opportunity to do so may be lost. If you're dealing with a procrastinator, it's important to demonstrate not only the benefits of your product, service, or idea but also the importance of making a decision NOW! And to do that, you must make that individual feel that there's a sense of urgency. Help your procrastinator seize the moment.

Ten ways to avoid killing a sale

After you've worked so hard to get people to the point of saying "Yes," you don't want to blow it at the very last moment by saying or doing the wrong thing. People become very nervous when it comes time to make a decision or sign a piece of paper, so you've got to make it easy for them to say "Yes."

The following are some key phrases that can kill a conversation or a sale. In their place, you should use words and phrases that will make the process of coming to a decision less threatening.

- ✔ You don't ask someone if he or she is ready to say "Yes"; you just assume so.

- ✔ You don't ask a person to buy something. Instead, you say, "Let's give it the go-ahead," or "Let's get the ball rolling," or "Why don't we give it a try?" Meanwhile, you're pulling out your order pad, form, or application. Then you ask, "Now, what is the correct spelling of your first name?"

- ✔ You never sign a contract; you initial an agreement or ask for approval.

- ✔ Contracts become paperwork.

- ✔ You don't talk about costs or expenses; they become investments, gains, or benefits.

- ✔ When you're talking about costs, speak of them on a daily or monthly basis, and you should state the profits as an annual return. Use little numbers for expenses and big numbers for profits or returns.

- ✔ Talk in terms people understand and relate to. People buy with dollars down and dollars per month, but the returns are annualized.

ANECDOTE

And after your meeting's over, keep detailed notes of what happened

Over the years, I've found it to be extremely helpful to keep detailed and meticulous notes of all of my meetings and conversations so that I wouldn't forget what was important to the other person.

These notes were then placed in that person's file for easy reference. They became a permanent record of what was discussed, what decisions were made, who was supposed to do what, and when it was supposed to be done.

Included in the notes would be my personal comments, thoughts, and opinions.

Keeping meeting notes is another reason that you'll really enjoy using a program like ACT!, as Chapter 5 explains. With ACT!, you can keep all your notes electronically — inside your computer — and you'll eliminate the need to write notes on small pieces of paper that get lost on the top of your desk and add to the overall clutter of your office.

> ✔ You don't buy something; you own it.
>
> ✔ You don't sell products or services; you sell benefits and solutions to problems.
>
> ✔ There are no problems, only points to be addressed.

After "Yes," the Fun Begins: You Start Negotiating

Just because a person has said "Yes" doesn't mean that you're out of the woods yet. In fact, the good stuff is just beginning. You now get to negotiate the terms of the transaction, preferably without giving away the company.

You see, you want to *negotiate* the terms of your transaction; you don't want to make compromises or concessions. Your ultimate goal is to achieve a mutually satisfactory agreement where both of you think that you got the majority of the things you wanted. If you think that you were taken to the cleaners, then you gave away too much.

When you're negotiating, you never want to give something up without always getting something in return.

Negotiate from a position of strength

Every negotiation starts with the respective parties having a general impression of their own strength and the strength of the person sitting across the table. When you begin discussing the individual items that will make up the terms and conditions of your agreement, you want to start out strong, show confidence, and convey the impression that you're negotiating from a position of strength.

When you have a strong opening, you can make the other party think that your bargaining position is a bit stronger than he or she thought it was, and you'll probably do better in your overall negotiations.

Get all the issues on the table

Effective negotiation can begin only after all the issues — major and minor — have been put on the table. That means you've first got to take the time to create a complete list of all the points of concern, *before* you start negotiating each of the various items. The greater the number of variables, the more opportunities you have for negotiating an agreement that everyone will be comfortable with.

In any negotiations, you and the other party will feel that some items are more important than are others. Your objective is to create a situation where you can make a small concession, yet receive something that is of substantial benefit in return. When both you and the other party have been able to make small concessions — while getting large benefits in return — you've had effective and successful negotiations, and you both have won.

A fundamental basis of effective negotiating is that whenever you make a concession, you always get something in return — you never want to make unilateral concessions. And getting something in return is always much easier to do when you're able to provide the other person with a large number of alternatives, all of which are equally acceptable to you.

That's what makes negotiating such a fun game to play — both of you can walk away feeling that you've won. So, while you're negotiating the terms of your agreement, you should keep searching for new variables that you can discuss. The more items you have on the table, the better your chances of assembling a package that will be acceptable to both of you.

A word or two about concessions

I would like to add a word or two on the subject of agreeing to make concessions:

- **Don't make concessions too readily.** Even if you're chomping at the bit to say "Yes," take a moment or two — or a few days — to ponder your decision.
- **Make it look like giving in to this concession hurts.** If you give in too quickly, the other party will decide that they could have done better if they had tried a bit harder. So on the next item of business, they probably will try harder. When this happens, no matter how good a deal they got, they won't be happy, and the deal itself may start to unravel.

The best way to keep a deal together is not to agree to demands or to make concessions. Always demand at least something in return, or refuse to go any further. This strategy will generally be the most effective way to tie the whole package together.

Don't negotiate one item at a time

When you're negotiating the terms of a deal, there could be just a handful, or several hundred, issues that need to be discussed and agreed upon. But when you're negotiating each one of them in isolation — one at a time — the final results are often unsatisfactory.

When you're trying to negotiate one item at a time, you've created a situation where you can have only one of three outcomes, none of which will be satisfactory to either of you:

  ✔ If you win, the other party loses.

  ✔ If the other party wins, you lose.

  ✔ If the two of you were to cut it down the middle, then you both lose.

And the only thing you will have gotten is the opportunity to move on to another point and continue the win-lose process.

If you're the seller, negotiating one item at a time is a prescription for disaster. However, if you're the buyer, negotiating one item at a time can be a very effective negotiating tactic because it can coerce the other party into making unilateral concessions.

Let me give you an example of what happens to you, the seller, if you negotiate each item one at a time:

A prospective buyer says to you that he would like to buy 10,000 of your widgets but feels that your price is too high. So he tells you that if you were to cut your cost by 10 percent, he'd be happy to place the order, and you say okay.

Now that he's gotten you to cut your price, you start discussing shipping dates. You tell him that you can deliver the complete order in 60 days. But he wants it in 15, so you agree on 30. You've lost again.

And finally, it's time to talk about payment terms. Your normal terms are a 50 percent deposit with the order. The balance will be shipped COD. He explains that his company couldn't possibly do that. His company's policy is to pay 50 percent on receipt of the order and the balance in 30 days. After the two of you talk, he finally agrees to give you a 25 percent payment now, pay 50 percent on delivery, and submit the balance within 30 days.

Because the terms of this sale were negotiated one at a time, you lost on every item of discussion, even though you were so excited because he told you that he wanted to buy 10,000 of your widgets.

But look at how you could have negotiated the terms of this sale if you had talked about all three points — price, delivery date, and payment terms — together. Here are a few different scenarios:

  ✔ When he asked you to lower your price, you could have asked him then how he planned to pay for the widgets by saying, "I can cut 10 percent off the price, but I'll need a deposit of 75 percent now, with the balance on delivery, which will be in 60 days."

> ✔ If he had first said that he needed delivery in 15 days, you could have responded by saying, "Our normal delivery is within 60 days. However, we can get you a delivery in 15 days, but not at this price. I'll have to charge you 10 percent more, and our normal terms are 50 percent now and the balance on delivery."

I'm sure that you're beginning to get the picture.

By discussing all three points at the same time, there are a lot of different variables that can come into play. Maybe the final terms are: delivery within 21 days, at an 8 percent increase in price, with a 30 percent payment today, 50 percent on delivery, and the balance payable in 30 days. Since these are all terms that the parties can live with and they feel good about the results of the negotiation, everyone walks away feeling like a winner.

Negotiating one item at a time is not a satisfactory method of negotiating the terms of any agreement because these individual items don't exist in isolation. They're all part of an overall package, the details of which have to be worked out.

Before you start negotiating, take the time to ask a lot of questions so that you can identify all the different issues and points of discussion that need to be laid on the top of the table. This approach helps you get a sense of the other party's real needs and objectives. And during your conversations, let the other party know that you're willing to discuss anything, but don't make any commitments until you've gotten a complete list of all the points that need to be addressed.

Part III

Improve Your Ability to Communicate Information

The 5th Wave   By Rich Tennant

Cell Phones

"This model comes with a particularly useful function—the simulated static button for breaking out of long-winded meaningless conversations."

In this part . . .

In the next few chapters I'm going to give you a lot of tips, ideas, techniques, and strategies that you can use to make it easier for you to communicate information to all of the important people in your business life.

First, I'm going to show you how you can use the telephone more effectively. Then in Chapter 11, I'm going to help you get more mileage out of your voice mail system. In Chapter 12, I'm going to show you how you can write better letters, memos, and reports. And finally, in Chapter 13, I'm going to give you some tips on how you can spend less time dealing with your e-mail.

Chapter 10

Make the Telephone Your Friend

● ●

In This Chapter

▶ Making a good impression on the phone

▶ Determining the purpose of a call

▶ Dialing for dollars

▶ Selecting a cell phone

▶ Getting more out of your telephone

● ●

*I*f you were to look at your daily activities, there are two certainties, in addition to death and taxes:

✔ You're going to spend a lot of time in meetings.

✔ When you're not in meetings, you're going to be on the telephone.

Chapter 7 discusses things you can do to make your meetings shorter and more productive. And now that we're tackling the telephone, let's take a step back and look at its basic purpose: to allow us to communicate information with other people.

Look at how far we've come with the telephone in just the last 40 years. We've gone from phones you had to dial (we still say "dial the phone," but when was the last time you *dialed* a phone?), to Touch-Tone phones, to having the computer dial the phone for us, to cell phones we carry around in our pockets.

When I was a kid, we had two phones in the house. There was a phone for the downstairs and another one upstairs; today we've got wireless phones that we can use anywhere in the house or yard and cell phones that we install in our cars or carry in our pockets, purses, or briefcases. And at this moment, I can't even imagine what's in store for us as we enter the 21st century.

But putting all this fancy, high-tech stuff aside for a moment, the phone is still a device that you and I use so that we can communicate with each other.

How Do You Come Across on the Phone?

I know you've been using the phone since you were about 4 years old, but have you ever thought about how you come across on the phone? And no matter how good you are on the phone, you can still work on improving your telephone techniques.

Your feelings and emotions come across loud and clear

Have you ever been really angry about something and then got on the phone to call someone else — who had nothing to do with the source of your anger — and then let this poor unsuspecting soul have it? I know that I have, and usually I felt so bad about it afterwards that I often called to apologize for my rude behavior.

Well, whatever your feeling is inside — happy, sad, joyful, depressed — it will be reflected in your voice as soon as you pick up the receiver and start talking to someone. If you were speaking with an individual face-to-face, he or she would see — and respond to — your nonverbal messages, such as your facial expressions, eye movements, and posture, as well as the gestures you make with your hands, arms, and legs.

And when you're on the telephone, even though the party at the other end of the phone can't see these nonverbal gestures, your attitudes, feelings, thoughts, and opinions are immediately transmitted by the tone of your voice, its pitch, the speed with which you talk, and even your choice of words.

So whenever you're speaking on the phone, you're going to be conveying a message. It may be one that indicates that you're happy to talk and want the conversation to continue. Or the message could be one that indicates that you're bored and disinterested, and have a desire to be doing something else at this very moment.

Keep a smile on your face

You may find this hard to believe, but you'll come across much better on the phone if you can keep a smile on your face and project that smile onto the other person while you're talking on the phone. People warm up to you when you meet them face-to-face and smile, and they'll do the same thing when you smile at them through the phone.

For many years, I've kept a picture of a smiling face in front of me as a reminder to smile when I'm on the phone. It helps me sound more friendly and open. My suggestion to you: Put a small mirror on your desk so that you can watch yourself smile when you're on the phone.

Be enthusiastic

Have you ever had conversations with people who sound as if they've just come back from a funeral or a wake? They're talking in a very dull and dreary monotone. The tone of voice is completely void of life and energy, and this is when they're calling to tell you *good* news! I don't know about you, but when I get these kinds of calls I want to crawl under the desk and hide.

So when you get on the phone, put some life, energy, and emotion in your voice. Don't be afraid to express yourself verbally and emotionally. Make your voice so interesting that the person at the other end of the phone wants to hear what it is that you've got to say. (In Chapter 14, I've a section, "Make your voice sound interesting," that talks about how you can expand the range of your voice when you're speaking in front of an audience.)

Have fun when you're on the phone. Be yourself. Let your sense of humor show through and don't forget to laugh. Laughter can be a great ice breaker.

Always take a deep breath before you begin to speak. When you have air in your lungs, your voice has more depth and power. (And if there's no air in your lungs, you're very likely dead.)

Hear how others hear you

I know that up until now, you've probably never given a moment's thought to your telephone technique, but it can be a real ear-opener when you record some of your calls and hear yourself as others hear you.

You would be amazed at how many times you said things such as "you know," "and," and "um," during each sentence. Then there are the sentences that you start but never complete. And finally, there's your voice itself. What does it sound like? Is it energetic and enthusiastic, or does it come across like a limp wash-rag?

But no matter what your voice sounds like today, with just a little bit of practice on your part, it's very easy to improve your ability to express yourself and communicate with other people over the phone. When you play back a tape of yourself speaking on the phone and hear what you're saying and how you're saying it, you become much more aware of the speech habits you've picked up.

Breaking those habits so that you speak with more clarity is easy. The first thing you'll become aware of is how many times you say such things as "you know" or "um." In no time at all, you'll be able to stop yourself from saying these things.

For just a few dollars, you can go to an electronics store — like Radio Shack — and get a microphone that's designed to record telephone calls. The microphone attaches to the handset of your phone with a tiny suction cup and plugs into the microphone jack of your tape recorder. But before you run to the electronics store, see if your telephone answering machine has the capability to record conversations. In many machines, this is a built-in feature. (Before you start recording your calls, however, you should find out if you have any legal responsibility to inform the other party that the call is being recorded.)

The first few times I recorded myself on the phone, I was appalled at how I *thought* my voice sounded, and to this day, I still don't like hearing my voice on tape. But as I thought about it, I realized that I had been speaking with people for years, and most of them enjoyed talking with me, some for even hours at a time. So the concern that I had about the tone of my voice was my problem, and nobody else's.

What Is the Purpose of the Call?

Being aware of how you sound and come across on the phone is one thing, but why are you making a call in the first place? In today's high-pressure business world, we don't have the luxury of wasting time. Yet one of the biggest time wasters of all is the phone call that has no apparent purpose. Whenever you're about to make a call, always ask yourself these questions:

- ✔ Why am I making this call?
- ✔ What information do I want?
- ✔ What information do I wish to convey?
- ✔ How much of the other person's time do I need?
- ✔ What do I do if the other person is not there and I get his or her secretary, assistant, or the receptionist? (I'll talk about this later in the chapter.)
- ✔ What do I do if I get the other person's voice mail? (I'll be discussing voice mail in the next chapter.)

Beating the odds

Because everyone's so busy, it's almost impossible to reach a person on the phone the first time you call. As a result, everyone ends up playing telephone tag. You know how the game's played: I call you and leave a message, and then you call me and leave a message; and this goes on and on. Eventually we talk, or we get tied up with other things and forget about it.

But there are a few facts about the telephone that you should be aware of. The chance of actually reaching a person on the first try is less than 20 percent. What I mean by this is that there's only a one in five chance that when you call a specific person, he or she will be available to take your call. And there's an 80 percent probability that the person you hope to talk to will be out of the office, tied up in a meeting, or on the phone. So, if you want to reach an individual on the phone, you've got to be persistent and should expect to call at least five times.

Here are some tips that can help you to prepare for your phone calls:

✔ Make a list of the items that you want to discuss with the person.

✔ Arrange the sequence of the items so that the most important items will be discussed first.

✔ Have the files or other papers to which you'll need to refer at your fingertips.

✔ If you are planning an important or difficult call and you're not sure exactly what you want to say or how you want to say it, write everything out on a piece of paper. A word of caution here: When you get the other person on the phone, have your notes available for reference, but don't read them.

Spend a few moments thinking about and preparing yourself for each call before you make it. Treat each call as if it were a face-to-face business meeting.

If you think your call will take more than a few minutes, you may want to say something like this:

> *Jim, I'm glad that I was finally able to reach you. I've got a handful of things I would like to talk to you about that could take five or ten minutes (insert other lengths of times). Do you have some time now, or should we schedule a conference call for later this afternoon or tomorrow morning?*

When you know that it's going to take you a half-hour to an hour to go through all the things that you've got to talk with a person about, schedule a conference call. This way the two of you can block out the time on your calendars. Let the other person know, in advance of that call, what you're going to be talking about so that he or she can be thoroughly prepared. You should also exchange telephone numbers and decide who will initiate the call.

If you're calling to schedule an appointment, always offer people two different times on different days. You could say something like, "Are you free on Monday afternoon, or would Tuesday morning be better?" This changes the flow of the conversation from if they will see you to *when* they will see you.

Knowing When to Call

If you're in a business where it's important for you to spend time on the phone, you should know that there are certain times during the day when you're most likely to find the person sitting at his or her desk and available to take your call. As a general rule, people are usually in their offices from 9 a.m. to 11 a.m. and from about 2 p.m. to 4 p.m. You should always block out those times on your calendar so that you can get on the telephone and make your calls.

Don't waste your valuable telephone time doing tasks that can be done at another time, can be done by someone else, or don't need to be done at all.

Getting through to Your Party

If there's someone you want to speak to, it's your job to track him or her down. And just because you left a message doesn't mean that you'll be called back — your call may be much more important to you than it is to the other person — and even if you are called back, the odds aren't very good that you'll be there to take that return call.

So, when you need to speak to someone, here are some techniques you can use to increase your odds of getting through.

- ✔ **Work with the secretary.** If the person you're trying to reach is in meetings, try to find out when the person will be available to take a call. If the person is on the phone, ask the secretary if he or she has any idea how long the call will last. Then ask whether it would be better for you to be put on hold for a few moments or call back in 15 minutes. When the secretary says, "Let me take your number, and I'll have So'n'so call you back." Just say, "Thank you. I'll call back later," because So'n'so probably won't be calling you back.

- ✔ **Get a direct number.** Try to get the person's direct number so that you can bypass the secretary, administrative assistant, or switchboard entirely.

- ✔ **Call early in the morning.** Many business people are at their desks as early as 7 a.m. each morning. So ask the secretary if the person you're trying to reach comes in early in the morning.

> ✔ **Call after work.** Many people are also working long after 5 p.m., so perhaps you can get through if you call after 5:30 p.m.

> ✔ **Call during lunch.** Many people work through lunch — or eat at their desks. So give it a shot and try your luck by calling at 12:30 p.m.

ACT! can really improve your productivity when you're trying to reach someone by phone. (See Chapter 5 to read about ACT! basics.) First off, you can't lose track of a call if you use ACT!. If you don't reach an individual today, ACT! automatically rolls it over to tomorrow. Second, when you're told that someone's out of town for two weeks, you just click the pop-up calendar and change the date of the call. In two weeks, that person's name appears again. And third, you'll love ACT!'s alarm. When you're told that someone's tied up in a meeting for about another 20 minutes, just set the alarm. In 20 minutes, you'll be reminded to make the call.

Take Notes of the Conversation

I know that I've said it before, and I'll probably say it again before this book is finished, but when you speak to a person on the phone, you should keep notes of your conversation and place them in the file you keep for that person. Though you may be blessed with a phenomenal memory, with the passage of time, it becomes difficult to remember exactly what a person said and when he or she said it.

When you get off the phone, you should write a brief note to summarize what was said, who's got to do what, and when it's supposed to be done. This note should be put in the appropriate file. And if there's work to do, it should be added to your Master List. (See Chapter 3 for more information on using a Master List.)

Taking notes is another area where ACT! excels. After the call, you enter your notes in the person's notepad, and if there's work to do, you schedule a to-do. The whole thing takes just a few moments. No muss. No fuss. And no pieces of paper to file.

How to Call a Stranger

Every once in a while, you may need to call someone who is a complete and total stranger. If you're in sales, you're doing this kind of thing almost every day, but if you're not, calling a stranger can be an absolutely terrifying experience.

Now, I don't have the slightest idea why you may be calling a stranger. Maybe you're doing some fund-raising for your favorite charity. Or perhaps it's time to explore new career opportunities and you're looking for a new job. Whatever the reason, here are some tips on how to call a stranger:

✓ **Get the person's name.** The first thing you need to do is get the name of the person to whom you would want to speak. To do this, you should place an *exploratory* call to the company's main number. Then you ask the person who answers the phone (probably a receptionist, operator, or secretary), "What is the name of the person who is the . . . [president of the company, head of human resources, and so on]?"

✓ **How is it spelled?** Then you ask for the correct spelling of the person's name.

Why do you want this info? If the person who is giving you this information starts to ask you lots of questions like "Who are you?" and "What do you want?" just say "I want to send Ms. Such'n'such a letter." Then say, "Thank you so very much for your help," and hang up the phone.

✓ **Call later in the day or tomorrow.** Now that you've got the person's name, call later in the day or the following morning, and ask whether he or she is available.

✓ **Does the person have a direct phone?** As you're asking whether Ms. Such'n'such is in, you can ask in an offhanded way, "Oh, by the way, what is her direct phone number?"

Now that someone has put your call through, one of several things is going to happen:

✓ The person is at his or her desk and will actually take your call.

✓ You get the voice mail system.

✓ The secretary will answer and screen the call.

Let's explore each situation.

Your call goes through

Let's say your call is put through, and you find that the person actually answers her own phone. She says, "Hello," and you start to panic. Just take a deep breath and say, "Is Ms. Such'n'such available?" (You ask this question because you want to try to get Ms. Such'n'such to say, "Yes.")

She says, "Yes, this is Ms. Such'n'such." And you say, "Ms. Such'n'such, my name is So'n'so, of (company name or other affiliation), and I was wondering whether you had a moment?" (You ask this question because you want to know whether she's available to talk at this moment or whether it would be better to call back later.) If she says that she's got a moment, you start delivering your spiel.

If she's tied up, just ask, "May I call you back later this afternoon, or would tomorrow morning be better?" At this point, she may ask you why you're calling, so you should give her a short answer and then say, "Thank you for your time. I'll call back when you have more time to talk."

You get voice mail

Take another example. If you are trying to call someone and get his or her voice mail, you may or may not decide to leave a message. However, if you do leave a message, you shouldn't expect to receive a return call. (I'll be discussing voice mail in the next chapter.)

You get the secretary

A good secretary is trained to screen the boss's calls, so you should be prepared to answer a few questions, but you don't want to volunteer much information.

When the secretary says, "Hello, this is Ms. So'n'so's office," you ask, "Is Ms. So'n'so available?" (With this question, you want to try to learn whether she's in the office, on the phone, in a meeting, or away from her desk.)

The secretary then asks, "Who's calling?" to which you reply, "This is Ms. This'n'that. (If you're a man, you should say, "This is Mr. This'n'that.") Is she available?" (You repeat the question because you want the secretary to give you information without volunteering any information yourself.)

At this point, the secretary *may* put your call through or possibly put you on hold to tell the boss that you're on the phone. (If the secretary comes back and asks you the name of your company and why you're calling and then puts you on hold again, it's a pretty good indication that the boss is having calls screened.) Another possibility is that the secretary may start to ask you more questions. It's at this point that you want to try to make the secretary your friend.

Most secretaries feel that it's their job to protect the boss from unwanted telephone calls, and they're trained to say "No" to whoever is calling.

Make the secretary your friend

Now you have to make the secretary your friend. When the secretary starts asking you questions, the first thing you should say — in a nice and friendly voice — is, "To whom am I speaking? Are you Ms. So'n'so's secretary or assistant?" (Write down the name so you won't forget it.)

If you're speaking to a temporary secretary or someone who's just filling in, just say, "Thank you very much. I'll call back later." (You don't want to waste your time talking with someone who can't be of much help to you, so get off the phone as fast as you can.)

If you are speaking with the secretary, he or she will probably begin by asking you questions as to who you are and why you're calling. To these questions you should give short, concise answers and once again ask, "Is Ms. So'n'so available?" At this point, the secretary probably will say that this person is in a meeting and ask if you would like to leave a message.

Now you've got two choices: To leave or not to leave a message, that is the question. What you choose to do depends on the situation and how comfortable you feel in talking with the secretary.

You may want to go into detail as to why you're calling and see whether the secretary can be of help to you — perhaps refer you to someone else within the company. Or you may just want to say, "Thank you very much for your help. I'll just call back later. Will Ms. So'n'so be available later this afternoon, or would tomorrow morning be a better time to call? And by the way, does Ms. So'n'so come in early in the morning?" (Again, you want to try to discover when the person may be available to receive a call.)

Remember these tips:

- ✔ Don't try to sell your product, service, or idea to the secretary. The boss is the decision maker, not the secretary. Your job is to sell the secretary on putting your call through to the person you want to talk to.

- ✔ If you aren't having any luck getting past the secretary, try calling another department to see whether you can get someone to give you the boss's direct number.

- ✔ Call the office of someone who is higher than the person you're trying to reach and use that person's name as your referral. Then you can say something like, "I was speaking with Ms. Bigfoot's office and she suggested that I speak with Mr. Littlefoot. Is he available?"

Dealing with Incoming Calls

Up until now, I've been discussing how you can get through to people when you're calling them. But what do you do when *your* phone rings? You need some techniques that will help you with your incoming calls, and that's what you're going to get in the following section.

TIP

Improve your productivity by using a telephone headset

Does your neck ever get stiff from cradling the telephone handset between your ear, chin, and shoulder? Do you find it difficult to take notes while you're on the phone — because you just can't find an easy way to hold the phone to your left ear, use your left elbow to keep the pad of paper from moving, write with your right hand, and remain comfortable, all at the same time?

Do you experience increased muscle tension as you try to enter information into the computer while speaking with someone on the telephone?

If you answered "Yes" to any of these questions, you should be using a telephone headset instead of the traditional handset. In fact, if you spend any time at all on the phone, you should be using a telephone headset. I've been using a Plantronics headset for years and have found that it's not only comfortable, but it has greatly improved my productivity and efficiency as well.

Today's headsets are so light and comfortable that after you put one on, you'll quickly forget that you're even wearing it. And when you're on the phone, you'll have the use of both your hands, so you can concentrate on the conversation instead of the pain in your neck or the tenderness in your ear.

Plantronics makes a full line of headsets for people who work in an office — corporate or SOHO, and for those on the go. They include:

✔ **Encore Headset.** The Encore headset is lightweight, comfortable, and convenient. It's available in monaural (one earpiece) or binaural (two earpieces), and has a noise-canceling microphone.

✔ **FreeHand Headset.** The FreeHand headset fits into your ear and is extremely light, weighing 8.5 grams, 0.3 ounces.

✔ **PC Headset.** The PC Headset CAT-132 (Computer Audio and Telephony) headset can be used instead of your PC's microphone and speakers. It enables you to work with computer telephony integration, voice recognition, personal conferencing, and Internet telephony applications.

✔ **Hands-Free Mobile Headset.** The Hands-Free Mobile Headset enables you to speak on your car or cell phone without holding it to your ear or using the speaker phone. (If your cell phone does not have a 2.5mm headset jack, you'll need an adapter.)

For a catalog and a current price list, you can reach Plantronics at 345 Encinal Street, Santa Cruz, CA 95060. Phone: 800-544-4660 or 831-458-7700. You can also visit their Web site at www.plantronics.com.

You don't have to answer every call

Just because the phone rings doesn't mean that you have to answer it. Whenever the phone rings, it's an interruption. And if you're in the midst of doing something important, the last thing you want to do is allow yourself to be interrupted.

It's OK to let your voice mail system, answering machine, secretary, or receptionist take the call. If you answer the phone every time it rings, you'll never get any work done.

Use the screening feature of your voice mail system to see who is calling. You can let the machine answer the phone, and if it's important, then you can pick up the receiver. And if it isn't important? Keep working!

Who's calling?

When you do answer the phone, you need to know the answers to two questions:

- ✔ Who's calling?
- ✔ What do they want?

If a caller doesn't identify himself or herself or is very vague about the purpose of the call, it's OK to say, "Good-bye!" and hang up the phone.

If you do want to talk to the caller, you should ask, "How much time is this going to take?" If the call will just take a few minutes, you may wish to have the conversation now; otherwise, you should schedule a time to talk later in the day. Most important, you want to avoid spending 30 minutes on a call when you should be completing your important work.

Get rid of cold callers

It seems that whenever I pick up the phone, there's someone at the other end trying to sell me medical insurance, penny stocks on the Vancouver Stock Exchange, a new long-distance phone service, or something else that I don't need or want. You can always tell who these people are because they all start their calls in the same way:

Caller: *Is Mr. Mayer there?*

Me: *Yes, this is he.*

Caller: *How are you today?*

And when callers say, "How are you today?" you know that they're trying to sell you something.

If you let these people get started with their sales pitch, it's difficult to get rid of them — you don't want to be rude — because they're always asking you to answer questions that are impossible to disagree with, such as, "How would you like an investment that has a very high rate of return with no risk?" The best thing you can do is to cut them short and just say, "I'm not interested!" and hang up the phone.

Now, the two or three minutes that it takes to answer an unsolicited call may not sound like much. But if you multiply that amount of time by several dozen calls each day, you've eaten up a huge chunk of time that you should have spent working on your high-priority projects. (And you wonder why you never get anything done.)

The next time you get an unsolicited call, try this: Just press the hold button on your phone and see how long it takes for the salesperson to realize that you're not there any longer.

Don't say to salespeople, "I can't talk to you now; just send me something in the mail." First of all, you don't need any more junk mail. And second, after they send you their materials, they're going to start calling again to ask whether you've had a chance to look at it.

Cutting off a long-winded speaker

Do you ever get calls from people who are happy to talk forever? (Don't they have work to do?) If so, here are a couple of tips on how you can regain control of the conversation:

- Listen to the person and wait patiently for the first opening that he or she gives you so that you can take control of the conversation. When the caller pauses to take a breath, just jump right into the conversation and say, "Now, what can I do for you?"

- Tell the caller at the start of the conversation that you were just walking out the door and only have a minute.

- Tell the caller that you have someone in your office, so the conversation will have to be short.

- Say that you've got a long-distance call on hold on the other line.

- When the conversation begins to drag, put the caller on hold for a moment. When you come back on the line, tell the caller that you have a long-distance call that you've got to take.

Watch your socializing

I know that it's nice to chat with friends, but if you do it throughout the day, it's a very easy way to lose track of a lot of time. Just add five minutes of socializing to each of your calls, and by the end of the day, you could easily lose an hour or two. And let's not forget about those five-minute calls that end up lasting an hour. So try to keep the number of your social calls at a reasonable level, and be aware of how much time you're spending on each of them.

No one has enough time during the course of the workday, and one of the ways you can give yourself more time is to minimize the number and length of your social calls. As an alternative to talking over the phone, perhaps you should meet for lunch or dinner.

Dealing with angry callers

Every once in a while, you're going to have to talk to people who are very angry and upset. Unless you've done something to anger these people, you must remember that they are not angry with you, but rather with a situation or a problem. Don't take personally any of the things that they say about you, your company, or your products.

Just let such callers vent their feelings and blow off some steam. Within a few minutes, they will wear themselves out, the fury and rage will subside, and they will regain their composure. When angry callers calm down, you can try to help solve their problems.

While a caller is ranting and raving, you can say, "I understand how you feel . . ." or, "I can see that you're very angry. . . ." (The statements don't mean that you agree with any of the things being said.) Try your best not to get sucked into an argument with an angry caller because that will only get you upset, making an already intense situation more explosive.

Thank the caller for complaining

A person who takes the time to complain is a person who wants to continue doing business with you. By complaining, people are telling you what it is they want or need from you.

When people call to complain, don't become defensive or argumentative. Just thank them for telling you what it is that they're unhappy with, and then say something like, "Thank you for taking the time to call. I'm glad you brought that to my attention. We'll do our best to solve this problem for you."

Don't pick up someone else's phone

Have you ever walked by someone's desk when the phone was ringing and decided that you would be a nice person and answer the phone? But after you picked up the phone, you found yourself with a big headache instead.

The caller had a problem and he or she wanted you to help solve it. (Well, you did pick up the phone, didn't you?). Or the caller wanted to leave a detailed message for someone, but you couldn't find a pencil or a piece of paper, so you tried to commit the message to memory, and then you forgot to tell the intended recipient about the call.

So the next time you hear someone else's phone ringing, just let it ring and go back to work.

After so many rings, the call will be transferred to the person's voice mail or to the receptionist. And if no one picks up the phone, the caller will call again.

You don't have to tolerate crude or obscene language. If a caller is being abusive, it's OK to say something like, "Mr./Ms. Foul Mouth, I'm willing to deal with your complaint, but I'm not willing to take this kind of verbal abuse. If you don't stop, I will terminate this call." If the caller doesn't stop immediately, hang up.

Coping with difficult telephone conversations

I don't know how often this happens to you, but now and then I find that I've gotten myself into a difficult phone conversation, and I'm having a hard time trying to get myself out of it.

Sometimes things just aren't going my way, and other times my mind's coming up blank. So here are a few tips for dealing with these types of situations:

> ✔ **Put the caller on hold.** When you need a moment to regroup yourself or to get the other person to calm down, just put the caller on hold for a few moments. When you get back on the line, you'll be better prepared to continue your verbal jousting.

Improving your telephone techniques

Andrew Wetzler and Art Sobczak are two valuable resources for improving telephone techniques.

Andrew Wetzler & Associates, Inc. Andrew Wetzler & Associates, Inc. has been providing telemarketing consultation and training since 1989. They've been providing their clients with methods to increase their telemarketing unit's performance and provide results-oriented strategies that improve their bottom line. Their dedicated staff of professional consultants assist organizations with their tele-sales and lead generation programs. They can help you develop an Overall Department Strategy, create scripts, test programs, analyze data, develop compensation plans and much more.

Andrew Wetzler & Associates, Inc. is located at 5030 Champion Blvd., Suite 6299, Boca Raton, FL 33496. Their phone is 800-688-8353, e-mail:

awetzler@telesales.com. You can visit their Web site at www.telesales.com.

Art Sobczak's Business By Phone. Art Sobczak is your one-stop resource for telesales, telemarketing, telephone prospecting, and telephone sales resources to help you get more business using the phone. Whether you use the phone to just cold call and set up appointments, or completely sell and service customers by phone, Art Sobczak shows you how through his many books, tapes, special reports, customized and public seminars and workshops, and his Telephone Selling Report sales tips newsletter.

Art Sobczak's Business By Phone is located at 13254 Stevens St., Omaha, NE 68137. Their phone is 800-326-7721 or 402-895-9399, e-mail: arts@businessbyphone.com. You can visit his Web site at www.businessbyphone.com.

✔ **Hang up on yourself.** If things aren't going well during a phone conversation, just hang up — in mid-sentence — on yourself. The other person will think that there was just a glitch in the line. Here's how you do it: While you're saying something important, just hang up on yourself, right in the middle of your sentence. By the time the conversation resumes, you will have given yourself a few minutes to think about the topic of your conversation. (Depending upon the dynamics of the situation, you'll have to decide whether you want to call back immediately, wait a few minutes and then call back, or wait for the other person to call you.)

Picking Out the Right Cell Phone

Almost everybody I know has a cell phone. How about you? Doesn't it seem like every time you get into an elevator, someone is talking on the phone?

In today's fast-paced world, the cell phone has become the road warrior's major means of communication, because it enables you to be in constant contact with your customers, clients, and your office. This saves you time and makes you much more productive. So when you're purchasing a cell phone, here are some things to think about.

Ask about the phone's warranty. Most phones are covered for a year, although a few manufacturers offer long-term protection.

Select the right size

You've lots of different makes and models to choose from. But before you make a purchase, think of how you plan to use your cell phone.

If you plan to keep your cell phone in your briefcase or a purse, you may not notice the size and weight difference between a small 3.1-ounce featherweight model, and a larger 8- to 10-ounce average-sized phone. On the other hand, if you plan to carry the phone in a belt holster or in a shirt or jacket pocket, the phone's size and weight become a much bigger issue.

The smaller and lighter the phone, the more it costs.

Consider a phone with a retractable antenna; it's easier to store.

Get a phone that feels right

Each cell phone has a distinctive ergonomic profile. If you've large hands, you may not find a small phone easy to use. Conversely, if you've small hands, you may find it uncomfortable to hold a larger and heavier phone.

The size and shape of the cell phone's earpiece also varies. Most people have become accustomed to the concave earpieces that are used in an old-fashioned *traditional* telephone — the kind you cradle between your ear and shoulder. Many cellular and PCS phones also offer that design element, but others have flat or convex earpieces.

Try out the phone's earpiece to see whether it's comfortable in your hand and against your face.

Control the earpiece volume

The ability to control the earpiece volume is very important. Make sure that the range of volume from low to high meets your needs. Many people find that separate up-and-down volume-control keys are easier to use than a single key that requires a special sequence of presses to increase or decrease the volume.

Side-mounted volume-control keys are a plus because they are easier to operate during a conversation. Volume controls located on the front of the phone may require you to move the phone away from your face to adjust the volume.

A headset jack, available on some models, offers added flexibility. This port typically enables the use of an earpiece and microphone; users can then carry on a conversation without holding the phone up to their ear. (See the sidebar about Plantronics headsets, earlier in this chapter.)

Examine the keypad and display

Check out a phone's keypad before you make a purchase. The keypad should have well-spaced keys that are easy to push. It should be easy to toggle between alphabetical (A through Z) and numeric (0 through 9) entries, and there should be a lock to prevent accidental use. (The ability to dial an emergency number even when the phone is locked is a plus.)

Try dialing some numbers and see what phone number was actually dialed. Make sure the keys are large enough, and spaced far enough apart, for accurate dialing.

In addition to the cell phone's keypad, you should also try each of the phone's features to see how much information is shown on the display. You should be able to view a full phone number, including area code, on the phone display. Also, check the glare on the display and keypad under bright outdoor lighting conditions.

Commonly used functions should be easily accessible

The phone's most commonly used functions should be easily accessible. Menu-driven phones make it easy to select features without memorizing commands.

Try accessing the phone's functions without using the manual.

How does it ring and does it vibrate?

If you spend a lot of time in crowded areas, such as airport terminals or train stations, you may want to select a cell phone that offers a choice of several ringer tones. This feature will help you to distinguish the sound of an incoming call to your phone from calls to the phones of other people.

Select a phone that vibrates if you want the phone to alert you to an incoming call when you're in a meeting and have turned off the ringer.

What kind of battery do you want?

Batteries vary widely, and you should choose a battery for your phone with as much consideration as you choose the phone itself. Some types of batteries hold a charge for a longer period of time than others, and often batteries can weigh as much or more than the handset itself.

A cell phone only operates as long as its battery lasts.

The amount of use that the power source delivers to the phone is measured in talk time (the amount of time, estimated by the manufacturer, that a battery will last while a phone call is in progress) and standby time (the number of hours a battery will last while a phone is on and awaiting calls). Using any of the talk time reduces the standby time, and vice versa.

You've three choices for batteries:

✔ **Nickel Cadmium (NiCd):** These batteries are generally the least expensive type of battery. They are, however, subject to the *memory effect,* which occurs when a battery is recharged before being fully discharged, dramatically reducing its lifespan. These batteries are OK, but don't last as long as the other types of batteries.

✔ **Nickel Metal Hydride (NiMH):** These batteries hold more charge for their weight than NiCd batteries, but they are more expensive and often take longer to recharge. NiMH batteries do not appear to exhibit memory effect. They also provide more talk time than a NiCd battery of the same size. NiMH batteries are a better choice than a NiCd battery.

✔ **Lithium ion (Li-ion):** These batteries provide very long talk and standby times, are impervious to the memory effect, and are much lighter than the other batteries. Li-ion batteries are the best choice but are the most expensive.

When selecting a phone, check out not only the type of battery that comes with the phone, but also the types of spare batteries that are available. A wide selection of optional batteries can expand the phone's capabilities.

Make your battery last

Have you ever lost your call because your cell phone's battery ran out of power? If you have, you're not alone, because this rates high on the list of cell phone frustrations. Here are some tips for getting the most from your cell phone's battery:

- Always keep your antenna fully extended to optimize signal strength. A weak signal strains your battery and consumes more power than necessary.

- Turn the ringing volume to the lowest setting.

- Switch off the key-pad tones.

- Program numbers you dial regularly into memory and make use of the one-key dialing feature. Remember: The more keys you have to press, the more power you use.

- Keep your phone in a cool, shaded place. Direct sunlight is bad for your battery and cell phone.

- Don't overcharge your cell phone's battery. Overcharging could damage the phone. Remember: If your handset does not indicate when your battery is charged, check your manual for the suggested maximum charge time.

- Carry a spare charged battery when you're traveling or when you think you're likely to run out of battery power. As a last resort, purchase a second — longer-life — battery.

Using your cell phone with your computer

If you will be using your cell phone with your computer or fax machine, you must make sure the phone is data-capable. If you plan to hook your notebook, fax, or other peripheral to your cell phone, verify that the phone is capable of sending and receiving data.

Check out the cost and availability of any accessories you may need to use your cell phone with your computer.

Safeguarding your phone against theft or loss

It is common knowledge that your phone can be PIN-code protected. (PIN stands for personal identification number.) As a new subscriber, you should change the default, network-supplied pin code 00000 (five zeroes) immediately after purchase.

Your new PIN should be seven digits or less. To change your PIN, refer to your phone manual or enter the following GSM short codes directly into your handset: **04* old pin number * new pin number * new pin number (again).

Here's how the above instructions would look using real numbers:
**04*00000*8372*8372

Less well-known is the fact that every GSM phone is manufactured with a unique ID number, much the same as those used in credit cards. In GSM, this is known as the International Mobile Equipment Identity (IMEI) and is most commonly located inside the battery compartment of your handset.

You can also key in the GSM short codes *#06# to get the ID number displayed on your handset. GSM Network operators maintain a registry of all phones active on the network and can render a stolen or lost phone inoperable if you report it together with its IMEI.

Treat your phone with as much caution as you do your credit cards. Write down the IMEI number and keep it in a safe place.

Getting More Out of Your Telephone

While we're on the subject of making the telephone your friend, I thought it would be a good idea to include some information about additional services you can get from your local phone company. These services can help you save time and make your life easier.

Contact your local phone company for an up-to-date list of all of its services and their costs.

Here are some phone services that will save you time:

- ✔ **Voice mail:** As an alternative to keeping your own voice mail machine, you can have your local phone company maintain your voice mail for you. It takes your voice mail messages while you're on the phone, receiving a fax, or surfing the Internet.

- ✔ **Call waiting:** Call waiting lets you answer a second call while you're already speaking to a person. It's like having two separate telephone lines. With call waiting, you won't have to worry about missing an important or emergency call. You can even switch-hook between calls.

  In some areas, call waiting works with caller ID. This service is called Wait & See. It enables you to see the name and number behind the call-waiting beep.

✔ **Caller ID With Name:** Caller ID With Name tells you who's calling before you pick up the phone. (A display device must be purchased. Telephones with Caller ID screens are also available.) Just imagine how many unnecessary conversations you can avoid.

✔ **Call Forwarding:** Call Forwarding transfers your incoming calls to another telephone number. So when you're away from your desk, or away from home, you won't miss any calls.

✔ **Multi-Ring Service:** Multi-Ring Service enables you to have up to three different telephone numbers, each with a separate listing and its own distinctive ring on a single telephone line. You could, for example, have separate lines for you and your children. With Multi-Ring Service, you always know which number is being called.

Chapter 11

Increase Your Productivity with Voice Mail

Sometimes I long for the "good old days" when everyone had a secretary who was always available to take messages. But times have changed. The secretaries are gone, we're typing all of our own letters, and we've got machines that answer our phones for us when we aren't there.

Now, if these machines are used properly, they can really improve a person's productivity. But when they aren't, they can be a real nightmare.

Why Use Voice Mail?

The telephone has one terrible shortcoming: Both the caller and the callee must be present at each end of the telephone connection for a conversation to take place. But statistics tell us that almost 80 percent of all business calls are not completed on the first attempt.

Of these calls, at least half of them are one-way transfers of information, and almost two-thirds of all phone calls are less important than the work they interrupt. So here are some reasons that you should be using voice mail:

▶ Voice mail enables you to share information without actually speaking to the other person.

Would you rather leave a message with a person or a machine?

A recent survey conducted by the Voice Messaging Educational Committee of Morris Plains, New Jersey, found that 58 percent of the callers surveyed would rather leave a message on voice mail than with a secretary or receptionist. Of these:

✔ Nearly half feared that a secretary or receptionist would lose some of the details while taking down the message.

✔ Eighteen percent felt that more detail could be conveyed through voice mail.

✔ Sixteen percent preferred delivering the information in their own speaking style.

✔ Voice mail lets you communicate in non-real time. You don't have to wait until noon, rise at 6 a.m., or stay awake until midnight to call someone on the other coast, in the Far East, or in Europe.

✔ Voice mail messages are usually much shorter than the actual telephone call.

✔ Voice mail is available 24 hours a day, seven days a week. (Some systems are designed so that when a voice mail message is received, it automatically sends a message to the recipient's pager. And when a call is received after normal business hours, or on the weekend, the system calls the recipient at home to inform him or her that a voice mail message has been received.)

✔ Voice mail can reduce the length of time you're stuck on hold.

And voice mail's biggest asset is that it takes your calls. So you don't have to answer each and every call as it comes in. This enables you to better manage your time and get your important work done.

Don't Leave Your Callers in Voice Mail Jail

Have you ever called someone and gotten a prerecorded voice mail message that said something like: "The party you have reached at extension 1234 is not in. Please leave your message at the beep." And you weren't given any other choices?

You didn't know how to get an operator! You didn't know how to get the person's assistant! And you were reluctant to leave a message because you weren't sure that the person at extension 1234 was the person you wanted to be speaking to in the first place!

So you hung up the telephone, feeling angry and frustrated. As you looked at the timer on your phone, it told you that this call took 58 seconds, and nothing happened. You were placed in Voice Mail Jail.

Or maybe you have called someone, and when the message came on, it said something like, "Hi, this is Phyllis, and I'm not in at the moment. If you would like to speak to my assistant, press 0; otherwise, leave a message at the beep."

So you press 0, and a few moments later, you're transferred to Phyllis's assistant, Tim, whose message says, "Hi, this is Tim, and I'm not available right now, so if you would like to leave me a message, I'll call you when I return. If you would like to speak to a receptionist, press 0."

So you press 0, and you're transferred to the receptionist, and no one picks up the phone. So you hang up, feeling angry and frustrated, and as you look at the timer on the phone, it tells you that this call took 2 minutes and 25 seconds, and nothing happened. Once again, you've been placed in Voice Mail Jail.

In the first instance, the person who recorded the message just didn't include any options so you could get out of, or exit, the voice mail system. There's no excuse for this.

In the second example, detailed exit instructions were given; unfortunately, no live person was available to take the call.

The biggest complaint that callers have about voice mail systems is the inability to reach a live person on demand.

Here are some tips about what you should include in your voice mail messages:

✔ Always leave instructions so that the caller can be transferred to someone else. ("Press #48, and you'll be transferred to my assistant, Jim; press 0, and you'll be transferred to the operator.")

✔ Leave instructions so that callers can leave messages without having to listen to your message each time they call. ("If you would like to skip this message in the future, press the star (*) key.")

Personalize Your Greeting

Some people like to record a basic message once and never make any changes to it. Others like to record a new message every day so that they can leave a detailed schedule of their activities for the caller.

An updated daily message is very helpful to both the caller and the callee because it helps improve the odds of their being able to reach each other. The caller knows when the callee is expected to be in the office and behind the desk.

Your message should be informative, courteous, and brief, and it should always encourage the caller to leave a message. Create your own greeting and change it frequently. When you know you are going to be out of your office all day, don't let your greeting tell your callers that you are away for a few minutes.

Let me give you a few examples of very good voice mail messages:

> ✔ *Hello, this is Fred Smith. It's Friday, January 20, and I'll be out of the office all day today and all day on Monday. Please leave me your name, number, and a brief message. I will be checking in for messages throughout the day. If you need to speak to someone immediately, press 0.*

> ✔ *Hello, this is Carol Collins of the Building Managers Association. It's Tuesday, August 22. I'm sorry I missed your call. I am out of the office today. If you're calling in regard to completion of the US Industrial survey and you need some extra time, please leave me a message as to when you think you can send it to me. If you have any questions that you need answered today, please call Sherry Ackerman in Dallas. Her number is 123-456-7890. If this call is in regard to other matters, please leave me a message, and I'll get back to you as soon as I can. If you need help immediately, please press 0.*

> ✔ *Hello, this is Kelly Green. It's Monday, October 17, and I'm in the office today; however, I'm going to be tied up in meetings for most of it. I will check in later, though, so please leave a message, and I'll get back to you as soon as I possibly can. If you need immediate assistance, press 0.*

Here are some things you should remember when you record your voice mail message:

> ✔ Smile before you start speaking. You'll leave a friendlier greeting because the warmth of your smile will come through in your voice.

> ✔ Get up from your chair, stretch for a moment, get the blood in your body circulating, and then record your message. This will put some *life*, *energy*, and *enthusiasm* into your voice mail message. You don't want your message to sound as if you recorded it just before you had to go to a funeral.

Is your telephone system user-friendly?

Many companies have phone systems that aren't easy to use. How does your system measure up? The best way to find out is to call your main number and see for yourself.

Here are some questions to ask when judging your company's phone system:

- How long (how many rings) does it take before your voice mail system answers the phone?

- How easy is it for callers to get transferred to the person with whom they wish to speak?

- Can callers reach an operator?

- Is an operator always available, or do callers get someone else's voice mail?

- If you give callers the option of selecting from a menu, how long does it take for them to make their selection and get transferred?

- How many menus do callers have to go through before they get to the desired menu? How long does this take?

- Once callers have selected a person or department from the menu, how long does it take for callers to reach the selected person or department?

- After you've tested your system, call your competitors and see how their phone systems operate.

- And finally, what are your callers listening to while they are waiting to be connected? Why not record a commercial for your company or product and play it as your *hold* music. You have a captive audience.

- When you record your voice mail message, hold the telephone mouthpiece about 3 to 5 inches from your mouth and speak slowly, distinctly, and clearly. Be comfortable, conversational, and enthusiastic. Vary your rate of delivery, pitch, and tone for best results.

- When you're asking people to leave you messages, remember to check your messages throughout the day, and be diligent about returning your calls.

- After you have recorded your voice mail message, call yourself up to listen to how it sounds. Does it have enough energy and enthusiasm? Is it short and concise? Does it say what you want it to say? If not, record it again.

Tips for Leaving Voice Mail Messages

Recording a voice mail message is one thing, but leaving messages is an entirely different subject. It is also very important. In today's business world, almost everyone has voice mail, so whenever you make a call, *always* be prepared to leave a message.

Here are some tips on how to leave better voice mail messages:

- Think about what you want to say and how you want to say it — before you make the call.

- Don't start leaving your message until you hear the machine beep. (I know that almost everybody should know this, but you would be surprised at the number of people who start talking before the outgoing message is finished.)

- Before you start speaking, take a deep breath so that your lungs are full of air. This gives your voice more depth and power.

- When you speak, speak slowly, clearly, and distinctly so that the person will understand what you're saying. Don't swallow your words.

- Make your voice sound interesting. Speak with enthusiasm. Put some energy into your voice.

- Always give your phone number twice, once at the beginning of the call and again at the end of the call. While many of the people you call may already have your number, they may be calling in for their messages and may not have your number with them.

- When you leave your message, state the most important points first, with the lesser points following.

- When you leave your name, in addition to saying it, spell it out. ("This is Jeffrey Mayer, M-A-Y-E-R.")

- If you're including your mailing address, speak slowly and spell out the name of your street and city after you say the address. ("50 East Bellevue Place, B-E-L-L-E-V-U-E, Chicago, Illinois.")

- Leave a specific time, or a window of time, when you'll be available for the person to call you back. For example: "I'll be in my office and available tomorrow morning." Or "I'm always in my office every afternoon after 2:00."

- When you're requesting information, make sure your message is complete and concise.

Be energetic and enthusiastic. Let your personality brighten the other person's day.

If you leave voice mail messages several times for a person and they aren't returned, try to talk with the person's assistant, someone else in the department, or the receptionist to find out if the person you're calling is in town and available. If you're unable to reach this person, try to get the name of someone else with whom you can speak. Don't sit around waiting for a return call that won't be forthcoming.

Dealing with Message Overload

One of the biggest complaints I get about voice mail is that people get too many messages, and it takes too long to listen to them. Here are some tips that can help you deal with this problem:

✓ **Increase the playback speed of your calls.** When you listen to your messages, speed them up so that you can get through them quicker. (This feature may not be available on all voice mail systems or home answering machines.)

✓ **Limit the length of time for each message.** If you've got long-winded people, limit the length of time that a person can leave a message to 60, 90, or 120 seconds at most. (When you record your message, tell callers that they have only 60 seconds to leave their messages.)

✓ **Limit the number of calls your voice mail box can hold.** I know this advice may sound like it's defeating the purpose of the voice mail system, but if you're getting too many calls, try limiting the number of calls that your voice mail box can hold. When your box is full, the caller will be told something like: "This voice mail box is full." Now the caller will have to call someone else, call back later, or send a letter or e-mail message.

✓ **Transfer unnecessary messages.** When you get a message about something that doesn't pertain to you, transfer the message to the person who is responsible.

✓ **Erase all messages after you've listened to them.** If there's work to do, note it on your Master List or put it into ACT!. If the information is important, take notes on a big piece of paper — one note per page — and put it in the appropriate file. (Don't forget to date your papers.)

You can reduce the number of incoming messages when you leave the *right* kind of message on the other person's voice mail.

Chapter 12

Write More Effective Correspondence

*I*t wasn't all that long ago that computers were a novelty, and we still used adding machines and pocket calculators. But times have changed.

Today, almost every business person in America — or at least it *seems* that way — has a PC sitting on the top of the desk, a notebook computer in their briefcase, and a palmtop computer in their pocket.

And what are we doing with all of this high-powered hardware? We're writing letters, memos, and reports; we're creating presentations; and sending and replying to e-mail messages. With this in mind, I thought it would be appropriate to include a chapter on how to improve your writing skills because so much of our communication is done by the written word.

Who Is Your Audience?

Good writing makes it easy for you to communicate your ideas to other people, and it helps them make better business decisions. In today's busy world, no one has time to read, so the people who are responsible for making business decisions want to get the information they need from their letters, memos, reports, and e-mail messages and then make a decision without wasting a lot of time.

To make everybody's life easier, you've got to be good at putting your thoughts and ideas on paper, using words that the reader understands, and then arranging this information in a concise and thorough way that's easy to comprehend.

In addition, give consideration to the people who will be reading your letter, memo, or report. For example, a report for your company's president, chairman, or board of directors would be written in a different manner than a weekly status report to your supervisor or manager. Likewise, a letter to a customer or client wouldn't be written as if it were an e-mail message.

Your goal is to not only communicate information to other people but also to obtain a favorable response from them.

Good Writing Isn't Easy

Good writing requires hard work. It is a laborious and slow process because we can think much more quickly than we can write. And that's why it's so much easier to write today, using high-speed computers and high-powered word processors; than it was a century ago, using a pen and inkwell; twenty years ago, with an IBM Selectric typewriter; or even ten years ago, with a dedicated word processor or a 386 computer with WordPerfect 5.2 for DOS.

Today, the computer gives you the opportunity to spend your time thinking about what it is you want to write, instead of worrying about the proper spelling of each word. Furthermore, today's word processors — like WordPerfect and Word — make the process of formatting text or moving words, sentences, paragraphs, or several pages of text from one part of a document to another a breeze.

Studies have shown that most computer users use less than 15 percent of the features in each piece of software that is loaded on their computer. Learn how to get the most out of your word processor, spreadsheet program, and every other piece of software that's loaded on your computer. You'll save yourself hours of time and complete much more work with much less effort.

Give yourself plenty of time

After you get started in the writing process, more ideas will begin to flow, and this will help you to focus on what you're *really* trying to say. That's why it's so important that you give yourself plenty of lead time when you're writing. After you write something, put it aside for a little while and then come back to it. When you resume your writing, you'll see new ways in which you can improve upon what you put down on paper.

When you're writing a letter, memo, or report, make sure that the content of the document says what you want it to say in the way you want to say it. Your goal is to write well, not necessarily quickly.

Here are some more writing tips:

✔ Whenever you write something, even if it's just a short letter, fax, or memo, always print it out, read it, and put it aside for a little while. When you come back to it, you'll usually find that it doesn't say exactly what you wanted it to say. Do some more editing, make some changes, and then send it out.

✔ When you're writing something and you seem to be stuck, just put it aside for a little while and then come back to it. By taking a break and giving yourself a little bit of time to think about your problem, you can usually solve it without much additional effort.

✔ Print out a copy of your document. Hard copies of a document often look and read a bit differently than they do when viewed on the computer screen. So when you're editing a document, print a copy of it, and you'll probably see things that you didn't notice while you were looking at it on-screen.

Use familiar words and phrases

Have you ever gotten a letter from someone and, after reading it, didn't have the slightest idea what it said? So you read it a second or a third time, and it still didn't make sense to you? It's frustrating, isn't it?

When you're composing your letters, memos, or reports, make it easy for the reader to understand what you're saying, so write short sentences, brief paragraphs, and use words that are familiar to your reader.

In today's fast-paced and hectic world, most of us don't have the time to pull out a dictionary to look up the meaning of a word we're not familiar with.

When you select your words, challenge yourself. Keep a dictionary and the-saurus at your fingertips so you can search for better, more descriptive words to express your thoughts and ideas. But don't use words that you've never seen before or that are unlikely to be familiar to your readers.

Write in a conversational style

Writing isn't much more than putting the spoken word down on paper. And you can make writing a lot easier if you just imagine that you're having a face-to-face conversation — like two friends sitting around a coffee table having a nice friendly chat — with the person you're writing for. Here are some writing tips:

- Before you start writing, always ask yourself: "What is the most important piece of information that I want the reader to know?"

- Get to the important points quickly. State the purpose of your letter, memo, or report in the first sentence of the first paragraph. The reader doesn't have the time to wade through three paragraphs or three pages of text to learn why you're writing a letter in the first place.

- Short sentences are easier to read. Present your thoughts and ideas to your reader in short bursts and keep the length of your sentences to no more than 15 to 20 words. However, you do need to add a little variety in your writing. So write some very short sentences and some longer ones every once in a while.

- Tie your thoughts together. Make your writing clear, concise, and to the point.

- Include charts, graphs, illustrations, or pictures in your letters, memos, and reports. This adds variety. The visuals can often eliminate the need to write many words of text.

- If you're having a bit of difficulty putting your ideas on paper, read the sentence aloud. When you get to the part that's giving you trouble, just imagine that you were looking at someone and ask yourself, "What would I say next?"

- When using abbreviations — such as the features of your company's newest product — explain what the abbreviations mean to your reader.

- When using initials for the names of organizations, you should first write out the name in full and then show the abbreviation in parentheses. From that point forward, you can use the organization's initials. (Use your word processor's search-and-replace feature to make the insertion of long names into a document much easier. You type in an abbreviation for the long name in your text, and when you're finished, you search for the abbreviations and replace them with the long name.)

- The more white space, the better: The more white space you have on a printed page, the easier it is to read. When writing, your goal is to give the reader the most information in the fewest number of words. And that takes some work. Abraham Lincoln once said, "I would have written a shorter letter, but I didn't have the time."

Run your spell checker

Run your spell checker and your grammar checker before you print the final version of your document. With today's powerful word processing programs, there's just no excuse for misspelled words and typographical errors. They make you look sloppy, and they make it more difficult for the reader to get through the document.

But don't put all of your trust in these newfangled devices. Your spelling may be perfectly fine, but you might just use the wrong word (for example, *two, too, to*). And a grammar checker isn't going to help you at all if you don't actually know the rules of grammar. There is no substitute for rereading everything before you present it.

*I have a spelling checker,
it came with my PC,
it plainly marx four my revue
Miss- takes eye cannot sea.
I've run this poem threw it,
I'm sure your please two no,
It's letter perfect in it's weight—
My checker tolled me sew.
—Anonymous*

✔ Have another pair of eyes read your documents. Sometimes we become blind to spelling, punctuation, or other grammatical errors, errors that are easily discovered when we have another person proofread our documents.

✔ Listen to the sound of your written words. What sounds good usually reads that way. To check the smoothness of your writing, read it out loud.

✔ Set artificial deadlines for yourself. If you have a report that's due on the 15th of the month, set your deadline for the 10th. This will motivate you to get started early, and it will give you plenty of time to think about and edit your work after you've finished. Your goal is to have a great final draft, not a great first draft.

Grab the reader's attention

No one has time to read long letters, memos, reports, or other documents. We're all just too busy. So, if you want someone to read the things you write, you've got to make it easy for them. One of the ways you can do this is by putting the most important information at the beginning of your document.

To grab your readers' attention, you've got to start with the first word in the first sentence of the first paragraph. If you don't *grab* their attention, they'll put your document down and may never pick it up again.

Don't waste your time standing in line

Purchasing stamps at the post office is a huge time-waster. You've got to drive to the post office, stand in line, and then drive back to your office. Here are some alternatives:

Purchase your stamps by mail

You can purchase your stamps by mail (Form 3227) and pay for them with a check. You can also order you stamps by phone (1-800-782-6724), 24 hours a day, 7 days a week, and charge them to a credit card.

Use a PitneyBowes Postal Meter

If you're working from home or in a small office, you should look into getting a PitneyBowes postage meter. Depending upon your postal usage, they have many different types to choose from.

PitneyBowes does however have one model that's geared to the SOHO (small office, home office) market: their Personal Post Office. The Personal Post Office enables you to stamp your letters easily and effortlessly.

It has these advantages:

- ✔ No more trips to the post office for stamps.
- ✔ No lines to stand in.
- ✔ No stamps to buy.
- ✔ No multiple stamp denominations to figure out and keep on hand. (How much does it cost for the first ounce, and how much for each additional ounce?)

The Personal Post Office gives you the postage you need right when you need it.

And best of all, the meter refills itself. When you need additional postage, you enter the amount of postage you need to purchase, and the meter makes the phone call. In less than a minute, your meter is refilled.

Use Postage by Phone. For other PitneyBowes meters, you can refill the meter by dialing into a toll-free number and resetting the machine yourself. The process takes about two minutes.

For more information, contact PitneyBowes Inc., 1 Elmcroft Rd., Stamford, CT 06926-0700; phone 800-243-7824; Web site www.pb.com.

Get your postage over the Internet with a Digital Postage Meter

E-Stamp Corporation's E-Stamp Internet Postage was the first online postage solution approved by the U.S. Postal Service for testing. (At the time this book went to press, it was still being tested and had not been formally approved.) With E-Stamp Internet Postage, you can print postage on envelopes or labels or directly onto your documents. This is what you do:

1. Install E-Stamp Internet Postage.
2. Connect to the Internet to purchase postage.
3. Point and click to print postage.

   The postage is printed on your envelope as it goes through your printer.

For more information, contact E-Stamp Corporation, 4009 Miranda Ave., Suite 225, Palo Alto, CA 94304-1218; phone 650-843-8000; Web site www.estamp.com.

Edit your letters, presentations, and reports

Revising, rewriting, and editing your work are all a part of good writing. Good writing consists of a constant effort to find and eliminate the unnecessary word, no matter how small. As you're editing your work, you should ask yourself these questions:

✔ Is each sentence complete?

✔ Is each paragraph complete?

✔ Is each section complete?

✔ Is my punctuation correct?

✔ Does my text read smoothly?

✔ Are my arguments, ideas, and relationships thoroughly developed?

✔ Have I spelled the names of persons and organizations correctly? (My editor thought this was an extraordinarily important point.)

✔ Are my telephone numbers and/or Web site addresses correct? (Call each phone number and visit each Web site.)

Put your most important information in the first sentence of the first paragraph and all of your supporting facts and other information in the sentences and paragraphs that follow. When you write in this manner, you can shorten your readers' reading time because they don't have to dig into each paragraph to try to find out what you're trying to say.

When you write the first draft of your document, your most important points probably will be at the end, and all of your supporting information will be at the beginning. So, when you start editing your work, just move your major points and conclusions from the end of the document to the beginning.

When you need to send a long document, write a one-page cover letter that summarizes the information in the document, in addition to sending the document.

Write Better Letters

Everyday we're writing letters. It's an everyday part of our business lives. And in the following section, I'm going to provide you with some great tips that will help you improve the chances that your letter will be opened and read.

Get your letters opened

When you send a letter, you want the person who receives it to not only open your envelope but then to take the time to read it and respond to it. Here are some tips on getting people to open your letters:

✔ Type your return address directly on the envelope. Don't use an address label. If possible, write the name and address of the recipient in long-hand. A handwritten address always gets someone's attention. (When an envelope bearing an almost illegible scrawl appears on my desk, I always open it first.)

✔ Hand stamp your letters. Big, colorful commemorative stamps make your mail look more interesting.

✔ Mail all your letters first-class.

✔ Write "Personal — Please" with a red pen on the bottom-left corner of the envelope. (I've been doing this for years, and it works! It's much more effective than typing "Important" or "Personal" across the bottom of the letter.)

Get your letters read

After you've been successful in getting someone to open your envelope, you want that person to read your letter. Here are some tips:

✔ The first sentence of your letter should jump out and capture your reader's interest and attention so that he or she will want to read the rest of it.

✔ Add a postscript. The postscript is usually the first or second thing that a person reads, so include a postscript that grabs the reader's attention and generates enough interest to get your entire letter read.

✔ Always try to start a letter with the word *"You"*; it makes the reader want to continue reading.

✔ Mention the person's name and the name of his or her company throughout the letter. This makes your letters more personal and friendly, and it is a powerful way of getting the reader's attention.

✔ Stress the benefits to the person reading the letter. Say what's in it for the reader. "You get this. . . ." "You get that. . . ."

✔ Eliminate the word *"I"* from your letters. *"I"* is the least important word in the English language.

Make your letters easy to read

After you've gotten someone to open your envelope, read the opening sentence, and read the postscript, you then want that person to go back and read the entire letter. Here are some tips:

- ✔ Indent your paragraphs. They're easier to read this way. And skip a line between paragraphs.

- ✔ Use a serif typeface (this book is printed in a serif typeface — except for the sidebars and running heads — and so is your daily newspaper). The typeface you use should be at least 12 points in size. This improves readability.

- ✔ Use a ragged right margin. A justified right margin makes your letters look as if they were mass-produced.

- ✔ Keep your letters short and concise and not more than one page in length. (If you're sending a handwritten note, keep it under three sentences in length. Think about what you want to say, say it, and sign it.)

- ✔ At the end of the letter, indicate that you will be doing something: "I'll be calling you within a few days to get your thoughts on this."

- ✔ Hand sign your letters.

Remember the three magic phrases: "Thank You," "Congratulations," and "Thinking of You."

How does your document look on the printed page?

If you're looking to create some interesting and attention-grabbing letters, memos, presentations, and reports, why not use a different typeface? Yes, your computer probably has dozens of fonts loaded onto it. (These are the same fonts that are also on a hundred million other computers.) So try something different and look for some new fonts.

Chris MacGregor's Internet Type Foundry Index (ITFI) — www.typeindex.com — has links to just about every computer typeface you've ever seen. And plenty that you haven't.

Save yourself the trouble of typing

Dictating letters and other correspondence is one thing. Typing them is something else again.

MobileWord offers a number of office support services over the Internet. Two of their services include TalkText and TapeText.

✔ Imagine producing documents while you're riding in a taxi to the airport, relaxing at the beach or playing golf, or working in your backyard. MobileWord's TalkText service gives you the ability to compose letters, memos, and notes anywhere, anytime.

Just call into MobileWord's dictation system from any standard touch-tone telephone and dictate your letter, memo, note, or anything else. MobileWord transcribes your text into a word processing file and places it in your very own MobileWord Mailbox within 24 hours. Guaranteed. Proof the document, spruce up the formatting, and you're done!

✔ MobileWord's TapeText service converts recorded tapes (or other recording media) into word processing text files. Send them your recording in virtually any format — VHS and beta (½- and ¾-inch) videotapes, audiocassette, mini-cassette, micro-cassette, compact discs, mini-compact discs — and they'll transcribe your tape and send it back to you as a word processing text file within 72 hours (for recordings of two hours or less).

With MobileWord's TapeText Acoustic Coupler, you can play your tape through any standard analog telephone, thereby eliminating the need to physically deliver tapes.

For more information about MobileWord's TalkText, TapeText, and other products and services, you can contact them at 145 Huguenot St., Suite 406, New Rochelle, NY 10801; phone 888-286-6245 or 914-235-7500. You can also visit their Web site at www.mobileword.com.

Chapter 13

The Ins and Outs of E-Mail (Or Is It the Ups and Downs?)

● ●

In This Chapter

▶ Writing your e-mail message

▶ Handling e-mail overload

▶ Playing it safe with e-mail freedom

▶ Guarding against e-mail break-ins

▶ Saving important information

▶ Using your e-mail software

▶ Accessing e-mail when you're away from your computer

▶ Receiving free e-mail

▶ Distributing mass e-mail messages

▶ Avoiding spam

● ●

E-mail is an electronic medium that hundreds of millions of people — all over the world — use to share information. It's become extremely popular because it's more efficient than using the telephone, less formal than writing a letter, and much faster than snail mail (the United States Postal Service).

The U.S. Postal Service maintains a very informative Web site. So when you've snail mail questions about such things as zip codes, consumer information, address changes (MoversNet), or passport information, visit www.usps.gov.

When e-mail is used properly, it's a huge time-saver because it enables you to share information with someone down the hall, or halfway across the world, in just a moment's time. But if you're spending one, two, or even three hours per day responding to your e-mail messages, it has become an enormous time waster. It's taking away from the time you should be spending on your other work.

Why is the @ symbol in an e-mail address?

Today, the @ symbol is a mandatory part of every Internet e-mail address, but it wasn't always this way. Back in 1972, a computer engineer at BBN named Ray Tomlinson had a problem. He wanted to send an electronic mail message and was trying to figure out how to make his computer differentiate between the name of the intended recipient and the address of the person's computer. He came to the conclusion that he needed to insert something — a punctuation mark or symbol — between the recipient's name and computer address. He looked at his keyboard, noticed the @ symbol, and an Internet standard was born.

Writing Your E-Mail Message

Here are some ways you can write better e-mail messages.

Maintain good writing standards

For most people, electronic mail is a very informal method of communication. The whole concept behind using e-mail is that it's fast, short, and sweet. The majority of messages you receive will have typos, utilize poor grammar, and have other mistakes you would never see in a normal letter.

For many people, that's OK. But when you are creating your e-mail messages, ask yourself this question: Do you want to be writing this e-mail message in such an informal style?

When you're drafting an e-mail message, think about how you want the recipient to react to your message. With that thought in mind, it's my suggestion that you take a moment to run your spell checker and proofread your e-mail message for punctuation and grammatical errors before you click the Send button.

Always re-read your e-mail message before sending it. Oftentimes, a bit of editing will be in order because what you wrote isn't exactly what you wanted to say.

Use the subject line

The subject line is the most important part of your e-mail message. It's the first thing the recipient sees when he or she opens the inbox. Here are some tips:

- ✔ Always write a subject line that is short, concise, descriptive, and informative.

- ✔ If action is required on the part of the reader, put it in the subject line — for example, "attend Tues. meeting at 9:30 in Jim's office" or "Attend Fri. meeting to discuss ABC project. 10:15 my office. Yes/No?" or "Need Reply by Wed. morning."

Make your subject line so descriptive that it grabs your readers' attention, and they'll probably read your message first.

You often have room for 60 or even 80 characters on a subject line, so make the most of them.

Put your most important information in the first line of the first paragraph

Today, most people receive so many e-mail messages that they don't ever get around to reading them. With this in mind, here are a few tips that will help to get your e-mail messages read:

- ✔ Put your most important information in the first sentence of the first paragraph and your background or supporting information in the following paragraphs.

- ✔ Keep the length of the e-mail message to less than three paragraphs.

- ✔ For messages that are more than three paragraphs, make it an attachment, and write a one paragraph message summary. Better yet, rewrite your message so that it's less than three paragraphs.

Keep the message simple

When you write your e-mail message, write short, easy-to-read sentences and paragraphs. Put the most important information in the first few sentences of the first paragraph. Here are some tips:

- ✔ Try to keep your e-mail messages on one screen so the reader doesn't have to scroll through the message. If a message takes more than one screen, try to shorten it.

- ✔ If you're including a list of items, use a bulleted or numbered list. It's easier to read (like this list).

- ✔ If you must send a long message, attach the file as an enclosure. Write a brief description of the message in the subject line. The e-mail message itself should be a more detailed description of the enclosed file.

Write e-mail messages that are easy to respond to

Make it easy for people to respond to your e-mail messages. When you write your message, be sure to include enough information so the recipient(s) can give you a quick answer or response. Phrase your messages so that readers can reply with a "Yes" or "No," and if you're going to ask for a reply, mention it in your subject line.

Attaching documents

When you attach a document to an e-mail message, do the following:

- ✔ Write a brief but thorough description about the document you're sending.
- ✔ Explain the purpose of the document.
- ✔ Include detailed instructions regarding what the recipient is supposed to do with the document.
- ✔ State the date you need a response.

This item of business should then be added to your Master List or added as an activity in ACT!.

E-mail do's and don'ts

Here are some additional things to keep in mind when you're sending e-mail to your colleagues and coworkers:

- ✔ Be careful about the message's *tone* of voice. It's easy for someone to misinterpret it. (See the sidebar on smileys and e-mail acronyms later in this chapter.)
- ✔ Don't send copies (cc) of messages to people who don't need to see the message.
- ✔ Don't send out blind copies (bcc) casually; they can imply that you're going behind someone's back.
- ✔ Don't ask for a receipt unless it's *really* necessary. If you do, you may be insulting the recipients by implying that they don't read their mail.
- ✔ Beware of crying wolf. Use the Urgent Message notation sparingly. If you use that option too often, your future messages may be ignored.

E-mail messages are not private!

Never write anything in your e-mail message that you wouldn't want to become public. Your message can be easily forwarded to others and could reappear months or years after you wrote it.

Don't send confidential information by e-mail.

When replying to an e-mail message, check to see who received copies of the original message. The message header usually displays a list of all the e-mail addresses that received the message. You may choose to reply only to the sender of the message or to all recipients.

And when you receive an e-mail message, don't assume that it is private. It may have been copied, or blind copied, to others.

✔ Don't write e-mail messages using all capital letters! WHEN YOU TYPE YOUR MESSAGE IN ALL CAPS, IT'S KNOWN AS SHOUTING, and people don't like to be shouted at. Use uppercase and lowercase letters just as you would when you type an old-fashioned letter.

✔ Put addresses in the To, Copies (cc), and Blind Copies (bcc) lines in alphabetical order by the recipients' last names. Doing so keeps you from accidentally insulting people — such as your boss, supervisor, or manager — because you listed them in the wrong place. (If you're going to go out of your way to insult someone, do it on purpose!)

✔ Don't overuse your mailing list. Only send your messages to people who need to receive your message.

✔ Limit your list of recipients, and you build your credibility as an e-mail sender. The fewer messages you send, the greater the attention they receive.

✔ Send only those messages that are work-related to your colleagues and coworkers.

✔ Be very careful with jokes or sarcasm. What you may perceive as being funny may be taken as obnoxious and offensive. Subtle sarcasm is almost impossible to use on e-mail and usually comes across as annoying or irritating.

Messages such as jokes or invitations to non-work-related events are best handled outside of the corporate e-mail system.

✔ Type positive messages so that the recipient will look forward to reading them.

✔ When you must communicate a negative message, try your best to say it in a positive way. Better yet, pick up the telephone or schedule a face-to-face meeting.

 ✔ If your message is very important, controversial, confidential, or could easily be misunderstood, use the telephone or set up a face-to-face meeting.

 ✔ And finally, delete e-mail messages you no longer need.

But I Get Too Much E-Mail

If you're getting too much e-mail or it's taking too many hours of your day to respond to it, maybe somebody isn't using the e-mail system in the manner in which it was intended. So let me ask you a question: How much time would you spend reading and responding to these messages if they had been sent to you the old-fashioned way, on paper?

Would you be in such a hurry to respond to them and get them off your desk? Would you drop everything and deal with them immediately? Of course not! In the old days, these types of paper memos could sit in your in-box for days, if not weeks, before you got around to them, and the world didn't come to an end.

But because the same message is now being sent to you electronically, you feel this primal urge to read and respond to it immediately. But are you in such a hurry to read your e-mail messages because they're so very important, or because you know that if you don't get to them regularly, they will just back up on you and eventually overwhelm you?

Here are some tips on how to cope with the e-mail onslaught:

 ✔ Set aside specific times during the day to go through your e-mail to see what's arrived and what's important. Don't interrupt yourself every time an e-mail message arrives.

 ✔ If it's not necessary for you to respond to each and every e-mail message that you receive, don't!

 ✔ When you must respond to an e-mail message, make your response short and sweet. Give "Yes" and "No" answers when possible. If you have to write a few sentences or paragraphs, make them concise and to the point.

 ✔ If you're getting copied (cc) or blind copied (bcc) e-mail messages that don't specifically apply to your job or daily responsibilities, ask the people who have been sending these messages to take you off their lists.

 ✔ Delete unnecessary e-mail immediately.

 ✔ If an e-mail message becomes a to-do item, immediately note it on your Master List.

✔ Don't allow the arrival of e-mail to interrupt your important work. If your computer beeps or sounds a trumpet to announce the arrival of each new e-mail message, then turn this feature off. And if your computer's hard drive starts making all sorts of whirring noises whenever you get an e-mail message, you may want to turn off your e-mail as well.

Check your e-mail box regularly. If you don't, you lose the major advantage of using e-mail over snail mail.

Be Careful with the Freedom of E-Mail

Just because e-mail's supposed to be an unstructured environment, you shouldn't allow yourself to get carried away. There's just too big a difference between writing e-mail messages to your boss, colleagues, and coworkers, and writing anonymous messages on the Internet.

When writing e-mail messages to the people within your own company or organization, use the same diction and common sense that you would use if you were writing a letter, having a conversation on the phone, or having a face-to-face meeting.

Don't flame out

If you're feeling hurt, angry, or insulted about something, don't write out your thoughts as an e-mail message and send it off, especially if you're upset with your boss, manager, or supervisor. In e-mail lingo, there is a term for this use of e-mail; it's called *flaming*.

When people let their emotions flare up and then send blistering e-mail messages, they're flaming. (It's sort of like throwing a temper tantrum.) And when the person who received the message fires off a fiery response, you've got yourself a flame war. (We used to have these kinds of fights — food fights — in the high school cafeteria, but this is the 21st century and we're more civilized now. Right?)

Try your best not to become a participant in a flame war, especially at the office. You've certainly got more important things to do. In most instances, the sender just sent a message that you misinterpreted, or vice versa. Or maybe the sender wrote something stupid, or vice versa. If you have a problem with someone, pick up the phone or schedule a face-to-face meeting so that you can talk things out.

And when you receive an e-mail message that is offensive or makes you feel angry, resist the temptation to respond immediately. If you do feel a need for an instant response, wait a day or two before sending your message. Read it later that day or the next day and then determine if you want to send it as-is or to make changes.

Smileys and other e-mail acronyms improve e-mail communication :-)

Because e-mail messages can easily be misunderstood or misinterpreted, e-mail junkies often use smileys and other e-mail acronyms to convey feelings, moods, or emotions. To see a smiley, you must put your left ear to your left shoulder and look at the computer screen sideways. Today, there are hundreds of smileys. Here's a sampling of some smileys and their meanings:

:->	Sarcastic smile
;^)	Smirking smile
>:-)	Devilish smile
0:-)	Angelic
:-P	Sticking tongue out

Over the years, e-mail writers have come up with many shortcuts so they didn't have to type so much.

Smiley	Meaning
:-)	Happy
:-(	Sad
:-]	Happy sarcasm or smirk
%-)	Happy but confused
%-(	Sad and confused
:-ll	Angry
:-<	Really upset
:-(o)	Yelling
8-0	Shocked
;-)	Winking
:'-(	Crying
:-*	Kiss
X-(	Brain dead
:-&	Tongue-tied
:-#	My lips are sealed
:-D	Laughter
:-}	Grinning
8-)	Wide-eyed
:-\	Undecided

Acronym	Meaning
BRB	Be right back
BTW	By the way
CUL	See you later
F2F	Face to face
FWIW	For what it's worth
FYA	For your amusement
FYI	For your information
GMTA	Great minds think alike
HHOK	Ha ha only kidding
IMHO	In my humble opinion
IOW	In other words
LOL	Laughing out loud
TIA	Thanks in advance
TNX	Thanks
WRT	With respect to
WTG	Way to go

Once your message is sent, there is no way to retrieve it.

Protect Yourself Against E-Mail Break-Ins

If you leave your computer unattended, make sure that no one else can use your e-mail program while you're away. You certainly don't want someone else writing a letter to your boss describing what you think of him or her. And never give your e-mail user name and password to anyone else.

If you travel with a laptop or palmtop computer, password protect your e-mail software.

There's no substitute for personal interaction. Every once in a while, rather than ask a question of a coworker via e-mail, get up from your chair and stroll down to that person's office. You'll stretch your legs and get the break you probably needed but wouldn't otherwise have taken.

Save Important Information

When you send or receive an e-mail message that contains important information, save the file on your hard drive or print out a copy of it and put it in the appropriate file so that you can find it when you need it.

If there's work to do, note it as a to-do item on your Master List.

Using Your E-Mail Software

There are a number of features that come with most e-mail software programs, and I would like to share my thoughts with you on how you can use them to save time and become more productive.

Use your e-mail address book

Your e-mail address book makes it easy for you to keep track of other people's e-mail addresses. You can also use it to store the person's name, mailing address, e-mail address, phone and fax numbers, Web sites, and much more.

So when you receive an e-mail message, add the person to your e-mail address book.

Address book entries can be exported for use in other programs.

Attaching documents and other files to your e-mail message

When you've a document, spreadsheet, or other file you want to send to someone, just attach it to your e-mail message. It's no longer necessary to copy the file onto a floppy disk and mail it. That's just wasted time.

All you've got to do is create your e-mail message, select the attachment command, locate the file on your hard drive, click OK, and the file's attached to your e-mail message. Then click the Send button and it's done.

You can also use Windows 95/98's drag and drop features. Locate the file in Windows Explorer, and drag and drop it onto the e-mail message.

Zipping up files

When you've a very large file, or you want to send a person several files, zipping it up is the easiest way to do it. Here are two very popular zipping programs:

- ✔ **E-mailZIP Deluxe:** E-mailZIP Deluxe makes it easy to zip your files. Just browse your directories and select the files you want to send. (You can also drag and drop.) Type in the person's e-mail address, write your e-mail message, and click Send. Your files are automatically compressed and immediately sent out as an e-mail attachment. For more information, contact JE Software, a division of Janesway Electronics Corp., 404 North Terrace Ave, Mount Vernon, NY 10552-3111; phone 800-431-1348 or 914-699-6710; Web site www.jesoftware.com.

- ✔ **WinZip:** WinZip brings the convenience of Windows to the use of ZIP files and other archive and compression formats. The optional wizard interface makes unzipping easier than ever. WinZip features built-in support for popular Internet file formats, including TAR, gzip, UNIX compress, UUencode, BinHex, and MIME. ARJ, LZH, and ARC files are supported via external programs. WinZip interfaces to most virus scanners. To download a free trial version, visit Nico Mak Computing's Web site at www.winzip.com. For more information, contact Nico Mak Computing, Inc., P.O. Box 540, Mansfield, CT 06268-0540.

Sending Web pages via e-mail

Since we're on the subject of attachments, I'm going to throw this Web tip in, because sending Web pages is sort of like attaching files to e-mail messages.

Many times you'll visit a Web site and find a Web page you would like to send to someone else, or even to yourself. Here's how you do it.

Microsoft Internet Explorer

In Internet Explorer you select File⇨Send, and then select Page by Mail, Link by Mail, or Shortcut to Desktop.

- ✔ **Page by Mail.** When you select Page by Mail, Internet Explorer opens your e-mail software and makes the Web page the e-mail message. Select the recipient(s), press the Send button, and the Web page is sent to the selected recipient(s).

- ✔ **Link by Mail.** When you select Link by Mail, Internet Explorer opens your e-mail software and inserts the Web page's address in the e-mail message. Select the recipient(s), press the Send button, and the link is sent to the selected recipient(s).

- ✔ **Shortcut to Desktop.** The Shortcut to Desktop option places an icon on your Windows desktop. Click the icon, and Windows opens your browser and brings up the selected page.

Netscape Navigator

In Navigator you select File⇨Send. Navigator opens your e-mail software and inserts the Web page's address in the e-mail message. Select the recipient(s), press the Send button, and the link is sent to the selected recipient(s).

Create a signature file

Do you find yourself repeatedly typing your name, company name, address, e-mail address, and/or other information at the end of each e-mail message? If so, here is an easy way to save yourself some typing: Create a signature file.

Most e-mail programs offer a feature that enables you to automatically add some text at the bottom of your e-mail messages. (Think of a signature file as the footer on a word processing document.)

Filtering your e-mail

Most e-mail software programs enable you to filter your e-mail messages. With the filtering option, you can automatically route incoming messages — messages that meet certain criteria — to selected folders at the moment the e-mail message is received. You can set these criteria based upon:

- ✔ **The specific e-mail address of the recipient.** You may have separate mail boxes for sales, `sales@yourcompany.com`; marketing, `marketing@yourcompany.com`; or customer service, `customerservice@yourcompany.com`, for example.

- ✔ **The person who sent the e-mail message.** You may want to flag specific e-mail messages from your boss or key customers or accounts and have them placed in a folder named IMPORTANT, for example.

- ✔ **Key words that are placed in the subject line.** Any message that has the word "FREE" in the subject line is immediately deleted.

- ✔ **And other criteria that you feel are appropriate.**

Once an e-mail message is received that matches the selected criteria, you can have your e-mail system do any of the following:

- ✔ **Move:** Move the message from your inbox to a selected folder.

- ✔ **Copy:** Copy the message from your inbox to a selected folder.

- ✔ **Forward:** Forward the message to a specific person.

- ✔ **Send:** Send an automatic reply.

- ✔ **Leave:** Leave the message on the server. (It is never placed in your inbox.)

- ✔ **Delete:** Delete the message from your server. (You never see the message.)

In Microsoft's Outlook Express, the filtering option is named Inbox Assistant. You open it by selecting Tools⇨Inbox Assistant. In Netscape Communicator's Netscape Mailbox, you access the filters option by selecting Edit⇨Mail Filters. In Qualcomm's Eudora Pro, you access the filters option by selecting Tools⇨Filters.

Receiving Your E-Mail When You're away from Your Computer

There are a number of tools you can use to receive your e-mail when you're away from your computer. Here are a few.

Receive your e-mail on your pager

If you want to make sure you never miss an e-mail message, Software Labs' PageAbility Mail-Link enables you to receive all of your e-mail messages on your alphanumeric pager. PageAbility monitors your e-mail address, and when you get a message, it sends both the subject line and the entire message to your pager. For more information, contact The Software Labs, Inc., 18378 Redmond Way, Redmond, WA 98052; phone 425-869-6802; Web site `www.pageability.com`.

Use your PalmPilot

With your PalmPilot, and Smartcode Software's HandMAIL software, it's easy to receive your e-mail. (You do of course need a PalmPilot modem.) Just download the HandMAIL software from Smartcode's Web site (a free demo version is available) and install it on your PalmPilot. Within minutes you'll be sending and receiving e-mail from your PalmPilot. For more information, contact Smartcode Software, Inc., 5355 Mira Sorrento Place, Suite 100, San Diego, CA 92121; phone 619-597-7544; Web site `www.smartcodesoft.com`. For more information about the PalmPilot, contact 3Com Company, 1565 Charleston Road, Mountainview, CA 94043. Or visit their Web site `www.palmpilot.com`. PalmPilot's Customer Service number is 888-619-7488.

Use the Mobilon Windows CE Handheld PC from Sharp Electronics

The Mobilon, from Sharp Electronics, is a Microsoft Windows CE handheld PC. It comes with a number of software applications including Microsoft's Pocket Outlook. One Pocket Outlook feature — the Inbox — enables you to send and receive Internet e-mail. (With Microsoft's Pocket Internet Explorer, which also comes with the Mobilon, you can surf the Internet.) For more information, contact Sharp Electronics, Sharp Plaza, Mahwah, NJ 07430; phone 800-BE-SHARP; Web site `www.sharp-usa.com`.

Get your e-mail from your telephone

Mail Call enables you to retrieve your e-mail from any telephone. Once you've signed up for the service, just dial into their toll-free number, enter your Personal Identification Number, and their computer retrieves your messages and reads the headers to you. You can then select which messages you wish to listen to. Messages can also be sent to a fax machine. For more information contact Mail Call, Inc., 8910 Miramar Pkwy., Suite 208, Miramar, FL 33025; phone 954-437-4199; Web site `www.mailcall.net`.

Getting Free E-Mail

Many of the more popular Web sites are offering free e-mail as an enticement to getting you to visit their Web site on a regular basis. (The more visitors a Web site has, the more it can charge its advertisers.)

The following sites currently offer free e-mail:

Web Site	Name	Address
Yahoo!	Yahoo Mail	www.yahoo.com
Excite	MailExcite	www.mailexcite.com
Hotmail	Hotmail	www.hotmail.com
Lycos	Lycosmail	www.lycos.com
Net@ddress	Net@ddress	www.netaddress.com
WhoWhere	WhoWhere	www.whowhere.com

Sending E-Mail Messages to Many People

E-mail is a great way to promote your business — of course, I mean sending messages to people who *want* to be on your e-mail mailing list. I'm not encouraging you to send unwanted messages, which is *spamming*.

Most Internet Service Providers (ISPs) limit the number of outgoing e-mail messages to 50 messages at a time. This is done to discourage spamming. There are, however, a number of ISP's that will send your e-mail messages at a cost of several hundred, or several thousand, dollars per session. As an alternative, you can set up your own e-mail server on your own computer and do it yourself. I discuss this in Chapter 15.

Dealing with Spam

Spam is the e-mail equivalent of the junk mail that the U.S. Postal Service delivers to your home and office every day. And what do you do with your junk mail? You throw it away! You should do the same with your junk e-mail, a.k.a. spam.

The best way to avoid junk e-mail is to stay off the spammers' lists.

Finding people on the Internet

While we're on the subject of using e-mail, there are several Web sites you can visit that enable you to search the Internet for e-mail addresses. They are Bigfoot Directory at `www.big-foot.com` and WhoWhere Directory at `www.whowhere.com`.

Unfortunately, that's easier said than done. Sneaky marketers use automated robot programs that infiltrate online chat rooms and electronic bulletin boards to harvest e-mail addresses. The programs then send you take your address and offers to buy no-name stocks that are sure to skyrocket, guaranteed plans to make millions working from home, and lots of links to naughty pictures.

Well, there are some ways to toss the junk e-mail — to can the spam, if you'll pardon the overused pun. And I don't mean merely reading the subject line on new e-mail and then deleting those with "get rich quick" or "sex here now" topics. Here are some tips:

✔ Don't reply to spammers! Never reply by placing "Remove" in the subject line. This tells the spammer that they do in fact have a *live* one, making you a more valuable target.

✔ Be selective when requested to give your e-mail address on a Web page.

  You don't have to give your real e-mail address. You can always make one up.

✔ Be selective when you're asked to complete online forms, especially those with personal details such as hobbies and interests. Doing so makes you a spam target.

✔ Be selective about giving your e-mail address when completing online hardware or software registration cards.

✔ There is a difference between getting e-mail from a legitimate business that is trying to promote its goods and services, and getting spam from a fly-by-night operator that is promoting a get-rich-quick scheme.

✔ Don't list yourself in the member directory of your online service.

✔ Ask your friends to refrain from giving your e-mail address to others.

✔ If you post to news or discussion groups — and you *don't* want a response to your posting — use a different online identity. Don't use your e-mail address.

✔ You're more likely to get spammed if you post messages in Internet newsgroups.

✔ If you post to news or discussion groups — and you *do* want a response to your posting — enter an e-mail address that another reader will understand, but a robot won't. For example, `Shirley@aol.com` could become `ShirleyNOSPAM@NOSPAM.aol.com`.

Unisyn Software has developed a spam-blocking program, Spam Exterminator. SpamEx automatically scans your mailbox at set intervals and checks new messages against the Spam List. When a spam message is found, it is automatically removed. SpamEx has a list of 17,500 known spammers, and you can make your own rules. It works with any POP3 Internet e-mail program. You can download a free trial version from Unisyn's Web site, `www.unisyn.com`. For more information, call Unisyn Software, 213-738-1700.

Places you can go to complain

Here are a few places you can go to complain about spam:

✔ **The Network Abuse Clearinghouse** — `www.abuse.net` — is a free Internet service. It was created by John Levine, one of the authors of *The Internet For Dummies,* 5th Edition (IDG Books Worldwide, Inc.). It is intended to help the Internet community report and control network abuse and abusive users.

Before you can send any messages through abuse.net, you have to register. (This is to prevent spamming and abuse through abuse.net itself.) When you send a message to `domain@abuse.net`, the system automatically re-mails your message to the best reporting address(es) they know for that domain, which is usually `postmaster@domain` or `abuse@domain`.

The Network Abuse Clearinghouse also has some automated abuse reporting tools that you can download.

✔ Another very good anti-spam site is **Fight Spam on the Internet!** — `www.spam.abuse.net/spam`. It provides one of the best collections of anti-spam links and resources to be found anywhere on the Internet. If you know of a page or site or story that would be of interest to the anti-spam community, don't hesitate to bring it to their attention.

Visit any search engine, such as AltaVista — `altavista.digital.com` — and type in "anti-spam" (in quotation marks), and you'll find a long list of sites that offer anti-spamming tips.

✔ **The Federal Trade Commission** — `www.ftc.gov` — has set up a special e-mail address — `uce@ftc.gov` — to receive complaints about fraudulent or deceptive e-mail. The FTC's Web site is `www.ftc.gov`.

Junk e-mail can be managed but not eliminated. Simply read the subject line of any message and if you don't understand it, trash it.

Part IV
Looking Out for #1

The 5th Wave   By Rich Tennant

YOU CAN ALWAYS TRUST
A FOWLER DITCH

LOOK FOR MY
OTHER DITCHES
ALONG RTE 682

ANOTHER
BEAUTIFUL
DITCH
DUG BY
BILL
FOWLER

In this part . . .

*W*ith continued downsizing, the people working in corporate America, people like you and me, have to look out for themselves. The days of lifetime employment are gone. There's no longer a benevolent employer that's going to take care of us throughout our career. If we don't look out for our own best interests, who will?

In Chapter 14, I show you how to improve your ability to communicate your ideas to a group of people. I know that most of us, myself included, are scared to death to stand in front of an audience and make a presentation, but when you can overcome that fear, you can do a very good job of convincing people to your way of thinking, and this skill will help you to promote your ideas, your company's products and services, and yourself.

In Chapter 15, I help you promote yourself. You start by collecting testimonial letters from satisfied customers, clients, and coworkers. To become the recognized expert in your field, get yourself quoted in the local newspapers, start writing articles for newspapers, magazines, and trade journals, and then write the definitive book. Public speaking is another way that you can promote yourself. Finally, I give you some tips on how to get more mileage out of your business cards.

And then, I also discuss two new ways you can promote yourself. The first is with a Web site and the second is by sending out e-mail. With a Web site, you can promote yourself 24 hours a day, seven days a week. And by setting up your own e-mail server on your computer, you've an easy — and inexpensive — way to communicate with your customers, clients, and prospects.

In Chapter 16, I show you how you can get the right results by doing the right things. Goal setting is an enjoyable and challenging experience. You can set reasonable goals for yourself, accomplish them, and then push yourself toward accomplishing another set of goals.

In Chapter 17, I talk about being a success in the business of life. The keys to success come from having a winning attitude and maintaining good work habits. You need to challenge yourself, take responsibility for the things you do, surround yourself with successful people, make the most of your time, and spend more time with your family and friends.

Chapter 14

Make Winning Presentations

● ●

In This Chapter

▶ Overcoming stage fright

▶ Warming up your audience

▶ Relating to your audience

▶ Making your voice sound better

▶ Enhancing your presentation

▶ Making the meeting room speaker-friendly

▶ Setting up the tables and chairs

● ●

*M*ost of us never think about it, but the art of standing in front of a group of people and really dazzling them with a presentation is extremely important.

Now, I know that you probably don't consider yourself to be a public speaker, but whenever you've got to stand up in front of a group of people, it's public speaking. When you're giving a report to your boss, colleagues, or coworkers, you've become a public speaker (even if you're sitting down).

When you're sitting in a meeting and you're asked your opinions about something, you become a public speaker. And when you're participating in a brainstorming session, whenever you start talking, you transform yourself from being an observer to being an active participant — and a public speaker.

A Presentation Is a Show

When you start speaking, you become the center of attention; everybody's eyes are on you as they lean forward to hear what it is that you're going to say. I know it's scary. And you're probably feeling terrified because the spotlight's on you. But this is your opportunity to go out and sell your thoughts, your ideas, and yourself. So you should look at this opportunity to speak and to present this information as a performance, as a show.

And whether you like it or not, when you're making a presentation to one person or to several hundred people, for that brief time when you're standing in front of your audience, you become an actor. You're standing in the center of the stage, and you're the star. The same principles that make for a successful stage or screen performance will also make your presentation a success. You'll be exciting and entertaining, provide useful information, and persuade your audience to say "Yes."

People don't care how much you know unless they know how much you care.

Get rid of those butterflies

It's perfectly natural for you to feel butterflies in your stomach when you've got to stand up and speak before a group of people, or when you're participating in a discussion with your colleagues and coworkers while you're sitting in the conference room. Many professional athletes, actors, singers, and musicians feel a sense of terror just before they're about to perform, so why shouldn't you? But after they get started, that feeling of terror subsides. If you didn't feel nervous, tense, or apprehensive, you wouldn't be human.

With a little bit of practice, you can get rid of those butterflies in your stomach and use that nervous energy to improve the quality of your presentation. Here are some tips:

- ✔ While you are waiting for your turn to speak, you should use these few moments to "warm up." Think about your opening statements or remarks, and go over your material or notes one more time.

- ✔ If you will be addressing a group of people and are waiting to be introduced, read the first page or two of your presentation to yourself.

- ✔ Remind yourself to display lots of energy and enthusiasm and to smile. Remember that these people are your friends.

- ✔ Use your breathing to calm yourself down. Controlled breathing is a great way to get yourself to relax. Start by inhaling deeply through your nose and then, with pursed lips, slowly blow the air out of your mouth as if you were trying to blow out a dozen candles on a birthday cake in one breath. As you exhale, you'll feel your *diaphragm* — the muscle that brings air into and pushes air out of your lungs — contract and become tighter. The more nervous you feel, the harder you should blow and the tighter you should squeeze your diaphragm. This technique will help you to dissipate a lot of nervous energy.

- ✔ Leave a nickel or a quarter in one of your pockets; if you're feeling stress or tension, you can squeeze the coin.

How do you want to be introduced?

When you will be speaking in front of a group of people, someone will usually take a moment to introduce you to your audience. A well-written introduction can build instant rapport between you and your audience and can win them over, even before you begin speaking. Here are some ideas that will help to guarantee that the person who introduces you will say the right things:

✔ Write out the introduction — in full — so that the person who introduces you won't start rambling when introducing you.

✔ The introduction should be double-spaced, using at least an 18-point font (this makes it easy to read), and take no more than 90 seconds to read.

✔ Any words or phrases you want the person to emphasize should be noted by italics or "quotation" marks.

✔ Ask the person who will be introducing you to read your introduction aloud at least two times before introducing you.

✔ Make sure you both know how to pronounce each other's names.

✔ Test the microphone — long before you're about to speak — to make sure it works properly.

Warm up your audience

When you are speaking in front of a group of people, try to loosen up your audience, and yourself, before you begin. This gives them a few moments to get settled, and it gives you a chance to burn up some of your nervous energy.

Open with a bang

Plan the opening of your presentation in the same methodical way that you plan the presentation itself. Say thank you to the person who just gave you such a *wonderful and heart-warming* introduction. And if possible, say something that is funny or humorous. This gives the audience a chance to get settled and relax.

Then think about how you can use your opening line to grab your audience's attention and establish rapport with them.

If you've got some special talents, use them. Can you sing? Dance? Draw? Can you tell stories? Can you tell funny stories? The use of humor can be an important part of making an effective presentation. Funny stories that are based on a personal experience or a real-life example can help you to illustrate a key point and make it easier for your audience to remember those key points.

When you're in front of a group of people, just be yourself. Don't try to be something you're not.

Pay close attention to the length of your opening remarks. If your few moments of small talk are too short, then your audience won't be ready for you; and if it's too long, they'll begin to feel you're wasting their time.

The goal of your speech is to try and make them think. Speak intelligently, persuasively, and logically. Remember, the most moving thing in a speech is always the logic.

Speeches are a tool of leadership. Say *big* things — *great* things — and say them with sincerity.

Talk with your body

No matter how well prepared you are when you give your presentation, it is your nonverbal delivery — your physical presence in front of your audience — that ultimately establishes your credibility.

The first thing you should pay attention to is how you look in front of your audience. Here are some tips:

- ✔ Stand up straight, squeeze your shoulder blades together to open your chest, square your shoulders, and pick up your head.

- ✔ For more balance and stability — and a feeling of power — plant your feet firmly on the floor. To do this, spread your feet about an inch wider than your normal stance, bend your knees slightly, and gently rock forward and backward, for just a moment, so that you can feel your heels, feet, and toes come in contact with the floor. This will keep your weight evenly distributed on both feet.

- ✔ When you move, take long, purposeful strides in the direction you want to go, and then plant your feet on the floor again.

Fifty-five percent of your message is communicated through body language, 38 percent through your vocal cords, and only 7 percent through your words.

You've got two hands — use them

Because more than half of your message is conveyed by your body language, be animated and use your hands and facial expressions to help express yourself. Let your audience use their eyes and their ears to experience what you're saying.

Here are some tips:

- ✔ Keep your hands in view. Don't put them in your pockets or behind your back.

- ✔ Let your gestures flow naturally. Speak with your hands and your arms. Practice being more animated with your gestures in front of a mirror so that you can see how other people see you.

- ✔ When you're making points, spread your hand out and count on your fingers so that your audience will know that you're counting for them.

- ✔ To keep from making jingling sounds when you're walking around, remove keys, change, and any other objects from your pockets.

Keep smiling. The warmth of your smile will help to win your audience over.

Keep your body moving

To keep your audience's attention, don't stand in one place or stay behind the lectern or podium for too long. Keep moving. Let your movement coincide with your words. When you become excited and begin to speak more rapidly, move quickly and it'll stir up the audience. When you calm down and begin to speak at a slower rate of speed, lower the tone of your voice and slow down your body movements. It'll keep your audience sitting on the edges of their seats.

- ✔ When you're giving a list of items, say the item, take one step, and stop, and then say the next item and repeat this movement as you're stating your list.

- ✔ When you're making specific points, turn and face a different part of the room — left and right, front and back.

- ✔ When you want to speak intimately, move forward and lower your voice.

- ✔ When you want to speak with more authority, take a step backward and speak more loudly.

- ✔ Talk to all the people in your audience: the people in the front of the room, the people in the back of the room, the people in the middle, and the people who are sitting on the far left and far right.

- ✔ When someone asks a question, walk toward that person.

When answering a question, listen to the question and then repeat it to the audience before you begin to answer it.

Look at your audience

When you're talking to someone, look at him or her. Eye contact is a very important part of defining, developing, and establishing relationships between people. And by looking into another person's eyes, you can often determine how well the two of you are connecting.

When you're speaking in front of a group of people, you want to establish a relationship with each person in the audience. You want them to feel connected to you, befriended by you, and you want them to give you some of their energy, which in turn gives you more confidence.

Try to win everyone over. Let them feel the warmth of your presence and the warmth of your smile.

✔ When you're standing in front of a small group of people, scan the room and try to make eye contact with as many individuals as you can, especially those who aren't smiling and nodding their heads in agreement. Select a row and then scan from left to right (not front to back), and when you've looked at everyone in that row, scan the row behind it, from right to left, until you've worked your way through the entire audience. Then you should look at the people sitting in the front of the room and start over. Make all members of your audience feel that you're speaking directly to them.

✔ If you're speaking to a large audience, it may not be possible for you to look at each person, so you should make and hold eye contact with various sections of the room following the same pattern of movement. Start at the front of the audience and look from left to right, and then look at the next section of people from right to left, until you've worked your way through the entire audience, and then start over again.

✔ For a little variety, you can play some games with yourself as you're making eye contact with your audience. For example, you can look for everyone with big hair, everyone with short hair, or everyone with no hair. Then look for everyone wearing green, or red, or black, and then look at each person who is sitting in the middle of each section. (And if you see people with yellow hair, green hair, orange hair, or purple hair, don't stare at them because you may forget where you are in your presentation.)

✔ If you're losing some members of your audience — they're dozing off, appear to be daydreaming, or are talking with their neighbors — you've got to work at bringing them back. Walk towards them, give them more eye contact, and pay more attention to them.

To bring attention to your eyes, use a very light powder around them. To bring attention to your mouth, use Vaseline or a light lip gloss.

Now where was I?

Most people find that it can be quite a challenge to hold their speaker's notes, look at the audience, and keep their place all at the same time. So here are a few thoughts:

✔ When you create your outline, only include the key words or phrases. Don't write out your sentences.

✔ Make your speaker's notes easy to read. Print them on a sheet of paper or on index cards, using a very large, easy-to-read font, such as Times Roman, 18 point. (You can use presentation software to create your speaker's notes. I discuss presentation software in the section "Use Pictures, Graphics, and Charts to Enhance Your Presentation." For myself, I just create my speaker's notes in WordPerfect.)

✔ Hold your notes with your left hand and, as you speak, slide your thumb downward so that it's always on the next line of your presentation. When you take your eyes away from your notes to look at your audience, just look for your thumb and you'll know exactly where you are in your presentation.

When you're looking into a person's eyes, don't try to look at both eyes at the same time. This causes you to shift your focus from one eye to the other, and the other person can see your eyes darting back and forth. Instead, you should focus on only one of the person's eyes at a time. This will keep your eyes in a fixed position.

Make your voice sound interesting

Most people make decisions based not on what a person says, but on how that person says it. And when you're speaking in front of a group of people, if your delivery is exciting, the presentation becomes exciting and your audience continues to listen. So when you can make the sound of your voice more interesting — by varying the volume, pitch, modulation, and intonation — it's much easier to keep your audience's attention. The next few sections offer some tips on using your voice effectively.

Pay attention to the speed at which you talk

Don't talk too slowly or you'll bore your audience to death; but don't speak too quickly either, or they may not catch everything you're saying. Just try to speak at the same rate of speed that you use when you're talking to a friend on the phone, about 150 to 200 words per minute.

For added emphasis, add silence

When you're giving a presentation, it's very easy to overwhelm your audience with information. You're giving them so many different things to think about that it's almost impossible for them to process it all. One of the ways you can help your audience grasp all the things you're saying is to use silence as a presentation technique.

✔ When you want to emphasize a specific point, pause for one beat before and after the word you want to make stand out. (A beat would be about a second in length, like your heartbeat when you're lying down and resting, not your heartbeat while you're standing in front of your audience.)

✔ When you want to emphasize the transition from one thought to another, pause for about two beats.

✔ To give your audience a few moments to reflect on the unusual, complex, important, provocative, or evocative statement you just made, pause for about four beats.

✔ When you want to emphasize something dramatically, make your statement and then stop talking. After a few moments the tension will start to build, and when it finally reaches a breaking point, you should commence speaking again.

And to keep your presentation from appearing canned — because you've given it so many times — you should occasionally pause, look toward the ceiling, and rub your chin with your hand, as if you're trying to remember something or you're trying to find just the right word, for three or four beats. This is particularly effective when someone's asking a question that you've answered a thousand times before.

Change your pace frequently

Vary your pace to fit the content or mood of what you're saying. When you're talking about something that's exciting, sound excited and speak a little more quickly. And when you're talking about something that's serious, sound serious and slow things down.

Raise and lower your voice

To keep your audience interested in what you're saying, you should change the volume at which you're speaking. When you get excited, it's okay to speak loudly and more quickly; and when you want to make a very important point, speak softly, or even whisper, and everyone will lean forward as they strain to hear what it is you're saying. When you whisper, everyone listens!

Pronounce all your words clearly and distinctly

Try to pronounce your words — beginning, middle, and end — cleanly and clearly, and keep enough air in your lungs so that you'll be able to end your sentences with power as you put em-PHA-sis on the last syl-LAB-le of the last word. Always try to speak with power and conviction.

Always take a deep breath before you begin to speak. When a person begins speaking in front of a group of people, he or she often gets a rush of adrenaline and then starts talking faster and faster and faster. And like a hundred-car freight train, once you start talking too quickly, it's very difficult to slow yourself down. So always take a breath before you begin a new sentence and a deep breath before you begin a new paragraph. This technique will give you an extra moment to collect your thoughts, in addition to keeping you from talking too quickly. And remember: When your lungs are full of air, your voice sounds deeper and has more power.

Add depth and power to your voice

Here are a few easy and simple exercises that will help you add depth and power to your voice:

- **Humming down.** To lower the normal pitch of your voice, hum down the scale to the lowest note you can reach and hold it for as long as you can. Do this three or four times a day as you're getting dressed in the morning. Within just a few weeks, you'll find that you're speaking with a deeper voice.

- **Make your voice more interesting.** To make your voice sound more interesting, practice counting aloud. Start by counting from 1 to 10 and do this over and over again (and then from 1 to 20, and from 1 to 30). As you say the numbers, begin to make each one sound different from the previous number. Say some louder, others softer, some with a higher voice, and others with a lower voice. Try to make each one sound interesting. Do this for a few weeks, and you'll be able to keep your audience members sitting on the edges of their seats while you're reading the telephone directory.

- **Increase your lung capacity.** When your lungs are empty, they hold about two pints of air; when they're fully inflated, they hold about ten pints — a one-gallon differential — and when you're just sitting around watching television, your lungs contain about five pints of air. The greater the amount of air you have in your lungs, the richer the tone of your voice, the deeper the pitch of your voice, and the more powerful the volume.

Enthusiasm creates energy

Like laughter, enthusiasm is contagious. So let your enthusiasm about your job, career, product, service, or business show in your voice, your gestures, and in your energy level when you're standing in front of an audience. When it's apparent that you enjoy and are excited about the subject of your presentation, you'll keep your audience interested in the things you're saying.

Use your computer to create your slides, overheads, charts, and speaker's notes

Today, you can use presentation software that makes it easy to create professional-looking slides, overhead transparencies, and charts without leaving your office. You can design and create charts, graphs, drawings, and illustrations that can be used to make professional slide shows, overhead transparencies, handouts for meetings, or any other type of information that you would present on paper. In just a matter of minutes, you can create presentations that have impact and get results.

The following are very good presentation software programs:

✔ **Corel WordPerfect Presentations:** Corel WordPerfect Presentations is a part of Corel's WordPerfect Office Suite. Corel Corporation, 1600 Carling Ave., Ottawa, Ontario, Canada K1Z 8R7. Corel Customer Service (North America only) can be reached by calling 1-800-772-6735. Corel Corporate Customer Service can be reached at 613-728-3733. Web site: www.corel.com.

✔ **Harvard Graphics:** Harvard Graphics is published by Software Publishing Corporation, 3 Oak Road, Fairfield, NJ 07004; phone 800-557-3743 or 973-808-1992; Web site www.spco.com. (If you would like to learn more about the Harvard Graphics program, pick up a copy of *Harvard Graphics 2 For Dummies,* by Roger C. Parker, published by IDG Books Worldwide, Inc., at your local bookstore.)

✔ **Freelance Graphics:** Freelance Graphics is published by Lotus Development Corp., 55 Cambridge Pkwy., Cambridge, MA 02142; phone 800-343-5414; Web site www.lotus.com.

✔ **PowerPoint:** PowerPoint is published by Microsoft Corporation, One Microsoft Way, Redmond, WA 98052. For more information, contact Microsoft's Information Center at 800-426-9400. Web site: www.microsoft.com.

To increase your lung capacity, just take a deep breath and, in a whisper, start counting very slowly. With your first breath, you may be able to count to 6, 7, or 8. Take a second breath, and you should be able to count to 10, 12, or 13. With a third breath, you may get up to 15 or 16. And with your fourth or fifth breath, you'll probably be getting close to 20. Do this for just two minutes a day, and within two weeks, you should be able to count to 30, 35, 40, or even higher on a single breath.

With these simple and easy exercises, you'll increase your lung capacity, add power to your voice, and make it sound deeper and stronger.

Use Pictures, Graphics, and Charts to Enhance Your Presentation

When you're planning your presentation, always ask yourself, "What kinds of visuals will best enhance my presentation?" Do you want to work with slides, overheads, or flip charts in addition to your handouts?

Visuals enhance the image of the presentation itself, and visuals get more of the audience's senses involved because they can see a picture of what you're describing. Visuals also enable you to walk a person through all the step-by-step details of your presentation.

Here are some tips to make visual aids work for you:

✔ Just before you begin your presentation, run through your slides or overheads — for the twentieth time — to make sure that they're in the right order and facing forward.

✔ Talk to your audience. Don't talk to the screen, overhead projector, or flip chart. Just glance at the screen to see that it's showing the proper slide and then look at your audience as you continue speaking.

What Handouts Do You Want to Leave Behind?

Whenever you speak in front of a group of people, you should always prepare a handout that audience members can take with them. It doesn't have to be very detailed or complicated. In most cases, a simple outline, a bulleted list, or even a fill-in-the-blank form will do. You just want to use the handout as a reminder of your main points and as a promotional piece. Here are some tips:

✔ If you have a multipage handout, your name, corporate logo, and the title of your presentation should be prominently displayed on the first page. On the following pages, your name, address, and phone number should be placed in a header or footer. It's okay to continue plugging your company, but be subtle.

✔ Each sheet of paper should be numbered. If they become separated, the person can put the information back together again in the correct sequence.

✔ If you're handing out single pieces of paper, place your name, company name, business address, and phone number at the top or bottom of each sheet in your handout. This makes it easy for people to get in touch with you later.

> ✔ If you're the author of a book, make sure that you mention the title on one of the sheets in your handout. (Even if the book is unrelated to the topic at hand, you should still mention it because it increases your credibility.)

Make the Meeting Room Speaker-Friendly

For most of us, the setup of a meeting room isn't something we need to be concerned with very often. But since *Time Management For Dummies,* 2nd Edition, is a reference book that you're going to keep on the shelf for years to come, this section could become very important to you if you should be asked to speak in front of a group of people. (It can also be helpful if you're the person who is responsible for setting up the room for a speaker.)

Whenever you're conducting a business meeting in a conference room or making a presentation to several hundred people in an auditorium, you should do your best to make sure that the conditions of the meeting room meet with your approval. Don't assume that the room will be set up in a way that will be advantageous to your presentation — because it won't!

The layout of the seating, lighting, and acoustics of the room can have a significant impact on your ability to connect with your audience. If it's done properly, a great presentation will be fabulous, a good presentation will be great, and even a not-so-good presentation will come out okay. But if it's done wrong, even a great presentation can be a flop.

Work with the people who will be setting up your meeting room

Tell the meeting planner or the person who is in charge of setting up the room — several weeks in advance of your presentation — how you want the room set up. Draw diagrams to show the desired layout for the chairs and tables.

Provide an itemized list of what you will need in the way of audio or video equipment. After you've had your initial conversation or meeting, confirm everything that was discussed, including any drawings or diagrams you've made for the layout of the room, in writing.

Here's a checklist of things you probably never thought about before that you should consider whenever you're going to give a presentation:

- ✔ How big is the room? You always want to be close to your audience, so the smaller the room, the better. When you're close to your audience, it's much easier to generate energy, enthusiasm, and excitement.

- ✔ How many chairs should be set up? You never know how many people will actually show up for a presentation, but as a general rule, you should set up 30 percent fewer chairs than the number of people you expect. This helps to guarantee that the front of the room will fill up first and that your audience will be close to you.

Check out the meeting room at least an hour before you are to begin your presentation. If the room is not occupied, take a few minutes to rearrange the seating by moving some chairs to the side. This guarantees that people will sit in the front of the room.

- ✔ Have extra chairs available. Have some extra chairs stacked somewhere in the back of the room so that if it becomes necessary to set up additional chairs, they'll be available. Should you need to set up additional chairs, you'll find that this last-minute craziness adds to the energy and excitement in the room and gives everyone the impression that this is important because the turnout was so overwhelmingly large that you had to set up more chairs at the last minute.

If you find that you're giving your presentation in a room that's got more chairs than people, instruct the people who are in charge of the presentation to ask the people in the audience to sit in the front of the room as they walk into the room, before they've settled comfortably into their chairs.

- ✔ How bright is the room? Make sure that the room is well lit so that you can see the audience clearly and so that they can see you.

- ✔ Does the room have a dimmer? If you will be showing slides or using other audiovisual equipment, make sure that the room has a dimmer so that the people in the audience don't have to take notes in the dark.

Ask someone to dim the lights when it's time to show your slides or overheads. You don't want to interrupt your presentation.

- ✔ If you'll be writing things on a flip chart, ask someone from the audience to come up and write down the information that you dictate. This way, you can continue to focus your attention on your audience. If you'll be doing the writing yourself, write quickly and clearly. And remember to bring your own markers.

- ✔ Make sure that all your visuals are big enough for everyone to see clearly.

- ✔ If you want to hang posters or other things on the wall, bring a roll of your own duct tape. To hang a poster, take four 12-inch strips and make each of them into a loop with the sticky side out. Then put a loop on each of the four corners of each poster and stick it to the wall.

✔ Keep the room cool. The temperature of the room is important. If you're expecting a lot of people, keep the meeting room just a little on the cool side, about 68 to 70 degrees, but not so cold that the audience members must put on their coats, scarves, and mittens. If the room becomes too warm, the people in your audience may lose their ability to concentrate and may even start to doze off. (Temperature becomes even more important if you'll be making your presentation just after your audience has eaten a meal.)

✔ What do you see when you look out the window? If the meeting room has a wonderful view, like the hotel's swimming pool, you've got to do something about it. If you can't shut the drapes, find out whether it's possible to change rooms or change the layout of the chairs and tables.

✔ Check out the equipment. Make sure that your equipment works, and make sure you have spare bulbs for your overhead or slide projector. If you'll be using someone else's slide projector, bring along your own 25-foot extension cord for the remote control switch. (And if you really want to be prepared for the unexpected, bring along a 100-foot electrical extension cord.)

✔ And last but not least, if you'll be using a microphone, double-check the sound quality and room acoustics before you begin your presentation.

✔ If you're using a handheld wireless microphone, ask someone from the hotel to put in a fresh battery.

Arranging the Tables (And Chairs)

The closer you are to your audience, the more energy they can absorb from you, and the more you can absorb from them. Traditionally, the seating for a presentation is laid out in rows, like a classroom. Oftentimes, there's even an aisle placed in the center of the rows of chairs. But think about this arrangement for a moment: It's detrimental to the speaker.

When the seats are in rows, the members of the audience are unable to make eye contact with other members of the audience and see how the other people are responding to the presentation. And with an aisle going down the center of the room, directly in front of the speaker, the speaker's audience has effectively been cut in half. When looking straight ahead, the only thing the speaker sees is the back of the room.

Arrange the chairs in a semicircle

As an alternative for arranging the chairs in straight rows, have them arranged in a semicircle, with the speaker almost in the center. This arrangement allows the audience to see both the speaker and the other people in the

I can't stand still!

Do you prefer standing behind a podium or walking around? If you're comfortable standing behind a podium, then the microphone that's attached to the podium should be sufficient.

But if you like to walk around, you should be wearing a lavaliere microphone around your neck — one that has a long cord attached to it — or a wireless microphone.

If you're wearing a wireless microphone, always have a wired microphone available in the event you start picking up conversations between taxi cabs or landing instructions from a nearby airport.

And don't forget: If you're going to wear a wireless microphone, ask the sound technician to install a fresh battery.

---

audience as well. It also brings the people who are sitting at the ends of the aisles closer to the speaker. This setup creates a much more intimate and more personal setting.

Arrange tables at an angle

If both tables and chairs are to be set up, they shouldn't be arranged in nice straight rows. The tables should be arranged so that they're at an angle to the speaker. This way, the audience can see both the speaker and the other members of the audience while they're taking notes. To avoid having an aisle going up the center of the room, the tables should be placed so that they're touching at the corners.

Variations on a theme

Now, there are many different ways of arranging a room, and I'm not going to try to address all of them. I just want to get you thinking about different ways in which you can improve the interaction between the audience and the speaker.

Some Additional Things to Think About

If I haven't given you enough things to think about already, here are a few more:

- ✔ If there are phones in the room, have them disconnected.
- ✔ If Muzak is playing, have it turned off.

- ✔ If there's a public address system, make sure that no announcements will be made while you're giving your presentation.

- ✔ If you will be speaking after a meal has been served, make sure that the people who are catering the meal instruct the waiters and waitresses not to take away dinner dishes after you begin speaking.

- ✔ Check to be sure that there will be no noise emanating from adjacent rooms, the hallway, or other surroundings.

- ✔ Keep water, food, other refreshments, and display materials in the back of the room.

If a meal, soft drinks, or coffee and rolls will be served, you should anticipate that something will go wrong. You may get the wrong food, at the wrong time, in the wrong room. So the day before the meeting is to take place and again on the day of your meeting, verify everything with the person who is in charge of catering your event. If your meeting is scheduled to start at 8:00 a.m., make sure that the caterer understands that you want the coffee and rolls to be there no later than 7:30 a.m.

I know that I've given you a lot of things to think about, maybe more than you ever wanted to know, but many of the things that can interfere with a successful speech or presentation are easily avoidable. And here's one final thought: Always arrive for your presentation at least an hour before you're scheduled to begin speaking. Doing so will give you an opportunity to see how the room has been laid out and to test all the equipment so that you're sure everything works properly.

How Well Did You Do?

After each presentation, critique yourself so that you can do an even better job the next time. Ask yourself questions like these: How high was my energy level? My enthusiasm? How well did I present my information? Did I relate to the audience? What could I have done even better?

Chapter 15

Promote Yourself

● ●

In This Chapter

▶ Collecting letters of reference

▶ Getting yourself quoted in the newspaper

▶ Writing newspaper and magazine articles and *the* book

▶ Promoting yourself through public speaking

▶ Using your business cards

▶ Mastering the art of networking

▶ Promoting yourself on the Internet and with e-mail

● ●

*I*f you want to get ahead in business, and in life, you've got to sell and promote yourself. You've got to toot your own horn. You've got to tell your colleagues, coworkers, and even your boss when you do something important or noteworthy. And you've got to let your clients, customers, friends, and family know when something good happens to you.

Working hard and doing the right things are the basic building blocks of a successful career. And after you've laid that foundation, you ought to let others know that wonderful things are happening to you.

Collect Testimonial Letters

Every time you do something well, ask the person you did it for to send you a brief note that you can put in your file. When you do something well for a customer or client, ask for a letter. When you do a great job on a project or do something very well for one of your company's customers or clients, ask one of your colleagues, coworkers, or even your boss to write you a letter saying what a great job you did. (And don't forget to ask if it would be okay for you to use the letter as a future reference.)

You just never know when these letters could help you in closing a big sale with a future customer or help you land your dream job. To say it plain and simple, letters of recommendation and testimonials from satisfied clients — written on their letterhead — are a great way to promote yourself.

When I started my time-management consulting practice, I asked my satisfied customers to write me letters that I could show to people who were considering hiring me to get them organized. Some of those letters were so good that I'm still using them even though they're several years old.

Testimonial letters or letters of recommendation can come from many sources, in addition to satisfied customers, clients, colleagues, and coworkers. You can also collect letters from your peers within your industry or from members of the professional organizations you belong to. The greater the status of the person writing the letter — the title on the letterhead — the more it helps to build your credibility.

Though the person you're showing the letter to may not be familiar with the individual who wrote the letter, the person may know of the company and will certainly be impressed by the letter writer's title or position within the company.

Many years ago, a man asked John D. Rockefeller if he could borrow some money. Rockefeller thought about it, and then decided not to extend him a loan. He did, however, offer to do something even better. He said that he would invite the man down to the floor of the New York Stock Exchange and would put his arm on his friend's shoulder as the two of them walked across the trading floor. After the two of them took their stroll, the man was able to borrow the money he needed from someone else. This person felt that anyone who was such a good friend of John D. Rockefeller had to be a good credit risk.

Do you know any celebrities, community leaders, or other famous and important people? If you do, can you get them to write you a letter, send you an autographed photograph, or have your picture taken with them? If so, it'll give the impression to your prospective customers, clients, and anybody else that you yourself are special and important.

Here are some tips about getting and using testimonial letters:

✔ Just ask people to write a testimonial letter, a letter of recommendation, or a thank you letter in appreciation for the good job you did for them, and they probably will. Oftentimes, the people will feel honored that you asked.

✔ After a person has agreed to write a testimonial letter, make a note to yourself to follow up in a week or two. If it hasn't arrived by then, the person has probably forgotten about it and needs a gentle reminder.

✔ If the letter writer is extremely busy, offer to write a sample letter yourself that the person could have typed on his or her own letterhead. This makes writing the letter much easier for the person you've asked, and no one can write as good a testimonial letter about you as you can. (If you feel a bit uncomfortable about tooting your horn, that's perfectly natural. Most of us are, but don't let that stop you from asking someone to write you a nice letter.)

✔ If you've got some great letters but they're a bit old, just mask out the date the next time you have them reproduced.

✔ When you make up a brochure or flyer, use some of the quotes from your letters.

✔ Have you thought about recording a testimonial on tape? Perhaps your satisfied client would allow you to make a tape recording of the testimonial. You can then put together a collection of these interviews on a single cassette that you can give to prospective clients or customers in the future.

✔ The next time you send out a brochure or other promotional literature, personalize it. Use a colored marker to highlight key phrases, write handwritten notes in the margin, or use sticky notes to direct the reader to specific pages.

Testimonial letters should become an on-going part of your marketing and promotional efforts. With time, you'll have a collection of letters that show that you've done a number of different things well and have been able to help your customers and clients solve many different kinds of problems.

Have You Been Quoted in a Newspaper or Magazine?

When you're quoted in the newspaper or are the subject of a magazine article, it adds a great deal to your credibility. If you're quoted or interviewed often enough, you soon become a recognized expert on the subject.

Put each and every article in which you're quoted online. Promoting yourself through your Web site is discussed later in this chapter.

Here are some tips on how to get the most mileage out of your newspaper and magazine articles:

✔ To make a professional-looking reprint of a newspaper or magazine article, cut out the name of the newspaper or magazine from the front page and center it at the top of a piece of white paper. Then cut out the article, center it underneath the publication's name, and photocopy the reprint. (If, after a while, you feel that the article's become dated, just mask out the date the next time you reproduce it.)

You can also scan the article into your computer, then lay it out, and print it.

✔ For greater impact, have your article professionally typeset and then have your publicity reprints printed on a glossy paper. (If you would like to go one step further, have the newspaper or magazine's masthead reproduced in a second color.)

Self-promotion really works!

In 1988, I decided that I wanted to write a time-management book, but after thinking about it, I realized that I would need some publicity about myself and my time-management consulting business before a major publisher would take me seriously. It took me several months of trying, but I finally persuaded Bill Gruber, a business columnist for the *Chicago Tribune*, to write a brief, three-inch piece about me. Several weeks later, I got a phone call from Jim Warren, also of the *Tribune,* who wanted to do a more in-depth interview.

All of a sudden, I found that I liked seeing my name in print — it also helped my business — and decided that I would try to get a national newspaper, like *The Wall Street Journal, The New York Times,* or *USA Today* to do a story about me. So I started making calls to editors, and I finally spoke to a senior editor at *USA Today,* who asked me, "Are you the guy in Chicago who cleans off desks for $1,000 a person?" When I said, "Yes," she said, "I'll have a reporter call you later this afternoon."

And on January 18, 1989, I was featured, pictures and all, in *USA Today* as "Mr. Neat, the Clutterbuster." Over the next few weeks, I was interviewed by *Newsweek* and some other national magazines. Within three months, I had my book contract with Simon & Schuster for my first best-seller, *If You Haven't Got the Time to Do It Right, When Will You Find the Time to Do It Over?*

I've now been interviewed by almost every major magazine and newspaper in the country, and have done more than a thousand radio and television interviews. This publicity, coupled with my having written several best-selling books — the newest of which is *Success is a Journey* — has helped me become one of the country's leading authorities on time management.

✔ To turn a radio or television interview into a publicity piece, bring along a camera and ask someone to take a photograph of you and the host during the interview. And don't forget to ask the host to send you a thank-you letter for having been a guest on the program. (Always ask for an audiotape of your radio interviews and a videotape of your television appearances. These could come in handy if you later decide to create a promotional tape. You can also use their quotes on your printed materials.)

Writing, Anyone?

You can develop a great deal of credibility and establish yourself as one of the leading authorities in your chosen field when you write articles for newspapers, magazines, or trade journals. (The money's not very good — you may even do it for free — but the exposure is phenomenal!) Then you can take your printed articles and use them as additional promotional and marketing pieces.

Self-publish your book

Many authors have chosen to self-publish their books instead of working with a commercial publishing house. The big advantage in doing this is that you can make a whole lot more money. You must, however, have a vehicle for selling them.

Many self-published authors are also professional speakers. Whenever they make a speech, they use the speaking opportunity to sell their books, audiotapes, videotapes, workbooks, and other materials to those in attendance.

Many self-published authors have found the Internet to be a very cost-effective way for them to sell their books.

Here are a couple more reasons why you should consider self publishing:

- ✔ You have complete and total editorial control.

- ✔ You can probably turn your manuscript into a book in a fraction of the time it would take a commercial publishing house to do so.

Writing newspaper, magazine, or trade journal articles is one thing, but you can set yourself apart from everybody else when you write "the book." Once you write a book, you're on your way to establishing yourself as the leading authority within your area of expertise. As a published author, you'll receive a great deal of respect from your peers, and there will be a huge increase in your level of credibility. If you were to write several books, you may be able to position yourself as the ultimate authority.

Start Your Own Newsletter

In addition to writing newspaper or magazine articles and/or writing a book, think about publishing your own newsletter.

As a newsletter publisher, you've a great vehicle for promoting yourself and making money.

Because you've got important things to say, a newsletter offers you a cost-effective way to get your message out.

Sell advertising to defray some of your production costs. There may be some companies that have products or services that they would like to sell to the people who are receiving your newsletter.

I create my newsletter — ACT! in ACTion — with Adobe's PageMaker

In 1995 I wrote my first ACT! book, *ACT! For Windows For Dummies*. While working on the book, I learned that there were more than a million ACT! users and came to the conclusion that many of them would want access to the most current ACT! information — information that couldn't be easily supplied in a book. So I started thinking about how I could provide them with timely information, and I came up with an idea: Start an ACT! newsletter.

At that time, I didn't know a thing about newsletters, so I bought some books on the subject and started asking questions of friends who self-published their own newsletters. One of the things that I found out was that with Adobe's PageMaker — PageMaker is the leading desktop publishing program — it's *easy* to create a newsletter. (PageMaker is a high-end desktop publishing program; you can also create a newsletter using word processors such as Corel WordPerfect and Microsoft Word.)

So I got myself a copy of PageMaker and started discovering PageMaker's ins and outs. (I also picked up a copy of IDG's *PageMaker For Dummies* book, by Galen Gruman, which made learning PageMaker even easier.)

In no time at all I had created my newsletter's format. Four months later, I published my first issue.

Today I use PageMaker for every promotional and marketing piece that I create. It's quick, easy to use, and extremely powerful.

Anything you want to do with the printed word, or a graphic image, can be done with PageMaker.

You can use PageMaker to create any type of publication, be it an advertisement, a two-page newsletter, a five-hundred page book, or a four-color magazine.

You can create your Web pages with PageMaker, and your own PDF documents. (PDF is an abbreviation for Adobe's Portable Documents Format. PDF documents are fully-formatted documents that can be read in Adobe's Acrobat Reader, which is available as a free download from Adobe's Web site, www.adobe.com.)

For more information about PageMaker and Adobe's other desktop publishing products, including Adobe Illustrator and Adobe Photoshop, contact Adobe Systems Incorporated, 345 Park Ave., San Jose, CA 95110-2704; phone 408-536-6000. Adobe's Web site is www.adobe.com.

If you would like a *free* sample copy of my self-published ACT! newsletter, *ACT! in ACTion,* fill out the card at the back of this book, or visit my Web site at www.ACTnews.com and complete the online free trial subscription form.

Promote Yourself through Public Speaking

Public speaking is an excellent way to promote and market yourself. It gets you in front of potential customers and clients. It gives you credibility and exposure, and after you've done it a few times, you may discover that people are willing to pay you to make a presentation.

Here are some tips on public speaking:

✔ **Practice, practice, practice!** If you haven't done a lot of speaking in front of groups of people, look for opportunities where you can go out and practice. The more you speak in front of an audience, the easier it gets.

✔ **Try a friendly audience.** Make your first few speeches in front of groups of people where no one in the audience is a client or prospective client. This gives you the opportunity to practice in front of a live audience and work most of the bugs out of your presentation. And if you make some mistakes, it doesn't matter because no one in the audience is doing business with you.

✔ **Watch how you speak.** As you prepare for your presentations, rehearse in front of a mirror and try to imagine that you're standing in front of your audience. This way, you can see your facial expressions and watch your body movements.

✔ **Listen to how you speak.** Record your practice sessions so you can hear what you're saying and how you're saying it.

✔ **Listen to how your audience hears you.** Bring a cassette recorder or a camcorder to your presentation and record your session. Listening to yourself on audio or watching yourself on video is a wonderful way to improve your presentation skills because you can hear, or see, what you said and how you said it.

✔ **Take an acting class.** If you would like a bit more practice performing in front of an audience, enroll in an acting or drama class at your local community college. You might consider trying out for a small part in a community play.

✔ **Watch how other professional speakers perform.** You can learn a lot by watching a pro give a speech. When possible, attend a seminar or borrow, rent, or buy some videotapes. Watch how the pros — like Brian Tracy, Les Brown, and Zig Ziglar — move on stage, use their voices, and make eye contact with the audience.

✔ **Hire a coach.** If you're really serious about your speaking, think about hiring a voice and acting coach to help you improve your presentation style. A good coach can see what you're doing and help you with your diction, body movements, volume, pitch, and timing. You'll find these techniques to be very useful whenever you're making a presentation, whether it's in a client's office or to the company's board of directors. To find a voice coach, give a call to the drama department of your local high school, college, or university, or one of your local theater companies.

To be, or not to be . . . a speaker

One day, when I was in the process of writing my first book, *If You Haven't Got the Time to Do It Right, When Will You Find the Time to Do It Over?*, my editor at Simon & Schuster called to tell me that they were going to send me on a national author's tour. We talked for a few minutes, and afterwards it dawned on me that I didn't have the slightest idea how to conduct myself during a radio, television, or newspaper interview. So I went out and hired a voice and acting coach.

I studied with Leslie Holland, a local actress, once a week for almost a year, and it was one of the best things I ever did. I learned how to speak properly, how to enunciate my words clearly, and, most importantly, how to present myself in front of a television camera. The wonderful thing about this training is that it helped me in many other areas of my business and personal life.

If you're interested in becoming a professional speaker — yes, people will actually pay you to speak — you may want to contact the National Speakers Association, 1500 South Priest Dr., Tempe, AZ 85281; phone 602-968-2552.

If you want to improve your ability to speak in front of a group of people but don't plan to make a career out of it, give Toastmasters International or Dale Carnegie a call. They can be reached at Toastmasters International, P.O. Box 9052, Mission Viejo, CA 92690; phone 949-858-8255, or Dale Carnegie & Associates, 1475 Franklin Ave., Garden City, NY 11530; phone 516-248-5100.

Learn from a great speaking coach

If you want to find out how to make a career as a professional speaker, you *must* give Dottie Walters a call. Dottie's company, Walters Speaker Services, is one of the leading resources for people who want to:

✔ Improve their public speaking skills.

✔ Make a career as a public speaker.

✔ Hire a speaker for a business meeting or conference.

Dottie and her daughter Lilly have written several very good books on how to become a professional speaker. These include *Speak and Grow Rich* and *Secrets of Successful Speakers.* They have also published booklets and audio and videocassettes that will help you enhance your presentations and motivate your audiences.

Their *Sharing Ideas* is the best newsmagazine in the world for professional speakers.

For more information, contact Dottie and Lilly at Walters Speaker Services, PO Box 1120, Glendora, CA 91740-1120; phone 626-335-8069; Web site www.walters-intl.com.

Don't Forget to Pass Out Your Business Cards

To get ahead in business, you've got to promote yourself, and one of the best ways you can do it is by passing out business cards.

A business card offers you several opportunities to promote yourself. When you give someone a card, it gives you the opportunity to talk about yourself, tell the person what you do for a living, and to talk about the goods, products, or services that your company sells.

Don't be shy about giving out your business cards: Give them out liberally. Every time you sit beside someone at a dinner party or a business luncheon, give the person who is sitting next to you a card and tell them what you do for a living. Pass out cards whenever you're standing in line. You could be waiting to cash a check at the bank.

Or maybe you're waiting to pay for your groceries at the supermarket, buying a ticket for the movies, waiting for the gates to open at the ball game, or standing at the ticket counter at the airport. You never know who the people standing next to you are unless you use the opportunity to start talking with them, introduce yourself, hand them a business card, and promote yourself and your business.

Here are some additional tips on using business cards:

✔ When you give potential clients a business card, don't just give them one card: Give out two or three so that they can keep one for themselves and give the others to friends or associates. Business cards are cheap, so give them away every chance you get.

✔ Whenever you buy something from someone, don't pass up the opportunity to give that person a card and say what you do for a living. This kind of opportunity would include your dry cleaner, your banker, the person who cuts your hair, the person who sells you your clothing, as well as the butcher, the baker, and the candlestick maker.

Make it easy for a person to reach you. Include your cell phone, your car phone, your home phone, your e-mail address, and your Web site on your business card.

Take Other People's Business Cards

As important as it is to give away business cards, it's even more important that you take other people's cards. From my own experience, I've found that many times people wanted to have me help them get organized, but they never got around to calling because my business card was lost and buried somewhere in a pile on the desk. But because I had *their* cards, I was able to follow up with them.

If there's money to be made from something, it's your responsibility to stay on top of things. You can't sit around waiting for other people to call you because they won't! So when you meet people, give them one of your business cards, and always take one of theirs. Then follow up with them!

Always carry a pen or pencil and a handful of business cards with you so that you can jot down the name and number of the people you meet, in case they don't happen to have business cards with them. When you get back to the office, add their names to your list of people to call. (If you put the piece of paper with the name and number on it in a pile, it could be weeks before you see it again.)

This is another way that ACT! can help improve your daily productivity. Instead of having another small piece of paper or business on your desktop, just add the person's name to your ACT! database and throw the piece of paper away. Then you can open ACT!'s notepad and write down who this person is, what he or she does for a living, where you met, and why you're going to be calling in two weeks. Then you add that person to your list of people to call. With this system, you'll never lose track of anyone.

What do you do with your business cards?

How many business cards do you have in the lap drawer of your desk? Fifty? A hundred? Two hundred? More? If you're like most people, you've gone to a great deal of effort to meet people and collect their business cards because you thought these people could be of help to you in the future. But what good are these cards if you can't remember who these people are, what they do, where you met them, or why you've bothered to keep their cards in the first place?

This is another way that ACT! can help you become more productive. ACT! is a great place to store the information on your business cards because it gives you an easy way to find the person's name and number when you need it.

If you're really into collecting business cards and don't feel like typing the names, addresses, and phone numbers of hundreds, if not thousands, of business cards into ACT!, you've another alternative. You can scan your business cards directly into your computer with Seiko's Smart Business Card Reader. Seiko Instruments, Inc., 1130 Ringwood Court, San Jose, CA 95131; phone 800-688-0817; Web site `www.seikosmart.com`.

One day, I was having lunch with a client at a local restaurant when a man came over to our table and asked if I was Jeff Mayer. I said that I was, and he asked whether I was still in the business of helping people get organized. I said, "Yes," and then he asked me to call him. He didn't have a business card in his wallet, so I wrote his name and number on the back of one of mine. As soon as I got back to my office, I added his name to my ACT! database and included his name on my list of people to call. It took me almost three weeks before I was able to get him on the telephone so that we could schedule an appointment. But because of ACT!, this business opportunity didn't slip through my fingers.

The Art of Networking

As you go through life, you're going to meet people — lots of people. You're going to meet people at business meetings, at conventions and seminars, and in other business settings. And you're going to meet people in non-business settings as well. You may have a conversation with a person on an airplane, while you're exercising at your local health club, or while you're waiting for a table at your favorite restaurant on a Saturday night.

And every once in a while, you'll meet someone who could be a potential business contact or someone who could help you with your future career moves. These are the people you should keep in touch with and get to know better. With time, you'll find that you have lots of things in common, and the two of you will become friends.

You should work hard to nurture and cultivate these relationships. Take the time to discover what's important and meaningful to these other people, and you'll eventually know more about them than they know about themselves. That's the secret of developing a close relationship and friendship. Business is built around relationships.

ACT! is designed to enhance your relationships

ACT! will help you further your relationships with the important people in your life. As you get to know other people better, you become friends. And one of the ways you can get to know people better is by asking questions. With the passage of time, you should know everything about them.

You'll be able to answer questions such as the following: What do they do for a living? How did they get into this line of work? What are their long-range goals, dreams, and desires? Where do they live? Are they single, married, or divorced? If they're married, what is their spouse's name? What does he or she do for a living? Where or how did they meet? Do they have children? How old? When are their birthdays? Wedding anniversary? What do they like to do on the weekends? What are their hobbies? What are their kids' hobbies? Where did they go to school? How do they spend their vacations?

Every time you meet with a person or talk on the phone and learn a little bit more about the things that are going on in that person's life, you just make a notation in ACT!'s Notepad (ACT!'s Notes/History Tab is shown in Figure 15-1). The Notepad makes life easy because it gives you a convenient place to store lots of miscellaneous information.

One day, I had a business meeting with a potential consulting client, and during the conversation, I asked her how her husband was feeling. She said that he was doing much better, and thanked me for asking about him. Then she asked me how I knew her husband had been ill. I told her that her secretary had mentioned that he was in the hospital during a previous phone conversation. What I didn't mention was that I had recorded that information in ACT! and reviewed it just before the meeting. That's how I knew to ask her how he was doing.

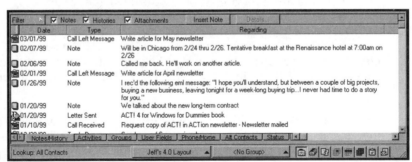

Figure 15-1:
ACT!'s
Notes/
History Tab.

Spend your time with the people who are most important to you

There's an old sales and marketing adage called the 80/20 rule, which states "You get 80 percent of your business from 20 percent of your clients." Said another way: In most businesses, a small number of clients typically generates the majority of the business's sales and profits.

I've heard people talk about this 80/20 rule for many years, and I'm sure that you have too, but there has always been something about it that bothered me. If, in fact, 80 percent of a company's business is coming from just 20 percent of its customers, then wouldn't it make a lot of sense to get to know these people better and minimize the time spent with everyone else? And as you get to know them better, they may be in a position to introduce you to some other people who may be potential clients or customers.

Get to know your friends better

We've all got good friends, people that are important to us, but because life and work are so hectic, we just don't get to spend enough time with them. In today's fast-paced, high-pressure world, you need to spend more time with the people who make you feel better, the people who build you up, the people who stimulate your creative energies.

Therefore, I'm going to suggest that you sit down right now and make a list of the ten business people whose companionship you like and enjoy the most. Figure 15-2 shows an example of such a list.

Now that you've made this list, call each of these people and set up a date to have either lunch or dinner together. In the future, you should plan to break bread with at least one of these people every week. As you meet more people, expand your list of "Business People I Like the Most" and have lunch with them regularly.

Once again, this is another way ACT! can keep you organized. When you schedule an activity such as "Call Jim Smith for lunch" — you may remember him from Chapter 3 — you can designate it as a recurring activity. With the click of a button, you can schedule a reminder to call Jim, say, once every other month for the next two years. This way, you won't lose touch with the important people in your life.

I was working with a client one day, and he began telling me about how he had forgotten to call his closest friend, who just happened to be his biggest customer, to wish him a happy 50th birthday. I suggested that we use ACT! to keep this from ever happening again. With ACT!'s recurring activity feature, we were able to enter the person's birthday for the next several years, and then we selected a lead time of 14 days so that the reminder would appear well in advance of the big day.

The Ten Business People I Like the Most

1. _____

2. _____

3. _____

4. _____

5. _____

6. _____

7. _____

8. _____

9. _____

10. _____

Figure 15-2:
Make a list
of the ten
business
people you
like the
most.

Promoting Yourself on a Web Site

With a Web site, you have the ability to promote yourself and your business 24 hours a day, 7 days a week. You can also reach a much wider audience, and faster, than you ever could offline.

This enables you to save travel time and expenses, and it spares you from preparing and making the same presentation over and over again, because people are coming directly to you.

(If you need to brush up on the World Wide Web and the Internet, pick up a copy of *The Internet For Dummies,* by John R. Levine, Carol Baroudi, and Margaret Levine Young.)

Read on for some tips on using a Web site to your best advantage.

Promote your business

You can put a listing of the products and services you sell — with complete descriptions — up on your Web site. You can use all sorts of media, including video and sound, to promote your products. You can update your online catalog whenever you want to! And think, you can create wonderfully detailed and visually interesting presentations for your products for a fraction of what it would cost to do so offline.

You can also set up your Web site so that when Web visitors express interest in a specific product, they can

✒ Purchase the item online with a credit card.

✒ Request additional information by filling out an online Web form. Once the form has been completed, it can be sent directly to you as e-mail or posted in a database on your Web site.

 Would you like your Web visitors to be able to call you up with questions or to place an order while they're on your site? With Voice Button, a prospect who is visiting your Web site can click an icon and make a call directly to your office while he remains connected to your Web site! Voice Button eliminates the need for the customer to write down the telephone number and dial the call separately. For more information, contact Nortel (Northern Telecom), One Brunswick Square, Atrium Suite 100, St. John, New Brunswick, Canada E2L 4V1; phone 1-800-4-NORTEL; Web site `www.nortel.com/voice-button`.

Collect the names of prospects

When someone visits your Web site, you can use it as a vehicle for capturing their name, address, and other additional information you feel would be useful or important.

You can, for example, ask visitors if they would like to get on your mailing list. If so, they can then fill out an online Web form that stores their information in a Web site database. You can then download the list of names into a spreadsheet or your own database program.

 Create an e-mail mailing list. Invite everybody who visits your site to get on your e-mail mailing list. This is a wonderful, and inexpensive, way to keep your name in front of them. (This is discussed later in this chapter.)

Promote yourself

Every piece of promotional literature you use in your business should be available on your Web site. This should include such things as:

- ✔ **Testimonial letters:** Testimonial letters from satisfied customers (with their permission, of course). You can even include the sender's mailing address, phone number, and/or e-mail address and Web site.

  You can place a link to the author's Web site or e-mail address on your page; if a visitor clicks this link, he or she will go directly to the Web site or e-mail address of the author of your testimonial letter.

- ✔ **Complimentary e-mail messages:** Whenever you receive a complimentary e-mail message from a satisfied customer, copy the message onto a Web page titled "E-mail Messages from Satisfied Customers."

- ✔ **Articles about you:** When you've been quoted in the newspaper or in a magazine, put the article(s) on your Web site.

  If the newspaper or magazine has an online edition, just copy the article onto your site. Remember to place the appropriate copyright information on the page. You should also contact the organization to see whether it's necessary to get permission to place a copy of the article on your Web site.

- ✔ **Articles you've written:** Put articles you've written on your Web site.

- ✔ **Promote your books:** If you've written a book, use your Web site as a place to publicize, promote, and sell your books. You can put sample chapters online with direct links to online bookstores, such as amazon.com and barnesandnoble.com, or you can arrange to accept credit cards on your Web site and sell the books yourself.

Creating your Web site

After you decide that you want to promote yourself and your business on a Web site, you need to decide what sort of a Web site you'd like to have, and whether or not you want to develop the site yourself or hire someone to do it for you.

Think about your Web site's appearance

The design of a good Web site is influenced by many issues:

- ✔ Do you want a lot of flashy graphics?
- ✔ Do you want a lot of text on each page?
- ✔ Do you want fancy fonts, or plain, easy-to-read fonts?
- ✔ What kind of background do you want?

 ✔ How do you want your Web visitors to move from one page to another within your site? Do you prefer graphics buttons, pictures or other graphics, or text links?

 ✔ Do you want to put audio or video clips or multimedia presentations on your site?

Keep your pages functional and make it easy for your visitors to navigate from one page to the next.

Pay attention to every Web site you visit. Keep a pad of paper on your desk and note the things you like, and don't like, about each site. Incorporate these ideas into your Web site.

Make your page accessible for your audience

Think about who will be visiting your Web site. What type of online connection do you think your guests will have? Would you expect them to be using 56K modems? (Many Web surfers are still using slower 28.8 modems.) Or do you think they're using very fast ISDN lines or corporate T-1 connections?

A fancy Web page, with several graphics and a bunch of fancy buttons, takes a lot longer to download than a text-based page. And for someone using a 28.8 modem, it can take a L-O-N-G time to open. And when a page takes a long time to open, the visitor may get tired of waiting and decide to go elsewhere.

Check out the competition

Visit each of your major and minor competitors' Web sites. See what they are doing and how they're doing it. Keep a list of the things that you like about each site and an even more detailed list of things that should be done to *improve* their site.

Then implement the things that you like, and the improvements you think should be made, into your own Web site design.

Bookmark any sites that *really* grab your attention so you can find them later. You can also print out the Web page and put it in a file folder for future reference.

Nail down the content

In addition to product and promotional information, what other information would be meaningful and beneficial to your Web visitors? Here are the kinds of information you could put on your Web site:

 ✔ Links to other sites

 ✔ Informative articles about your business or industry

- ✔ Competitive studies or surveys that show how your products are head and shoulders above the competition

- ✔ Technical information that would be difficult for your customers to find elsewhere

Consider the following tips as you prepare information for your Web site:

- ✔ Brainstorm with your colleagues and coworkers to get their thoughts and ideas as to what should be on your site.

- ✔ Ask your customers what types of information they would like to find on your Web site. Then provide links from that information to online order forms so it's easy for them to make a purchase.

- ✔ Make it easy for your Web guests to contact you. Place your mailing address and phone number at the bottom of each page and include an e-mail link so it's easy for them to send you a quick message.

All Things Web — www.pantos.org/atw — is a site that helps Web designers and authors create usable Web pages. Sections on the site include these topics: The Usable Web, Design Fundamentals, The Need for Speed, and more. Stop by. It's worth a visit.

A Web site is a work-in-process. Once you've published your site, you'll discover that you want to make changes to its design, layout, and content. That's the beauty of having a Web site. You make your changes and publish them, and it's done! (Until you come up with another *great* idea to make your site even better.)

Do you want to design the site yourself?

Today's Web authoring programs are very easy to use. If you can create and format a word processing document, you can create a Web page.

Well, to tell you the truth, designing a Web page and the accompanying Web site isn't quite that easy. But if you're up to the challenge, you can create an attractive and functional site without *too* much effort. (I know because I've done it myself.)

Here are some of the advantages of creating the site yourself:

- ✔ You have complete and total control of the site.

- ✔ When you want to make changes to the site, you can do it immediately.

- ✔ You don't have to *try* to explain to a Web designer what it is you want and then wait for two weeks before it's done wrong.

- ✔ You'll save yourself some money. (It could even be a lot of money.)

When I first put up my site — www.actnews.com — I got frequent messages from visitors who let me know that links didn't work properly, that I had made spelling, punctuation, or grammatical errors, and that they noticed lots of other problems. (Web surfers are a picky lot!) Whenever I received one of these messages, I just opened FrontPage, my Web publishing software, made the changes, published them, and went back to work. I often wondered how long it would have taken to get these *minor* chances made if it had been necessary for me to contact a *professional* Web designer.

Here are some of the disadvantages of creating the site yourself:

- ✔ You're responsible for the design of the site.
- ✔ You're responsible for keeping the site up-to-date.
- ✔ You have to correct anything that doesn't work on the site, like bad links and spelling, punctuation, or grammatical errors.

Visit AltaVista — altavista.digital.com — and enter "web site design tips" (keep the quotation marks) as the search string. Spend some time on each of the sites that appear on the list, and you'll become a Web site design expert in no time at all.

Design your Web site with the major search engines in mind. This helps guarantee that the *right* people will find your site. Search engines are covered later in this chapter.

If you decide to undertake this project on your own, a number of easy-to-use Web-page tool kits are available, including the following popular programs:

- ✔ **Microsoft FrontPage:** Microsoft FrontPage makes it easy to create great-looking Web sites. Its easy-to-use features let you create professional Web sites without programming. For more information, contact Microsoft, One Microsoft Way, Redmond, WA 98052-6399; phone 800-426-9400, extension 552; Web site www.microsoft.com/frontpage.

- ✔ **Corel WebMaster Suite:** Corel WebMaster Suite delivers the tools you need to create and manage your Web site. It offers a state-of-the-art Web authoring tool, professional site management functionality, sophisticated graphics and animation, and more. For more information, contact Corel Corporation, 1600 Carling Ave., Ottawa, Ontario, Canada K1Z 8R7. Corel Customer Service (North America only) can be reached by calling 800-772-6735. Corel Corporate Customer Service can be reached at 613-728-3733. Corel's Web site is www.corel.com.

- ✔ **Adobe PageMill:** Adobe PageMill is as easy to use as your favorite word processor. With Adobe PageMill, you can build a well-designed, content-rich Web site without knowing anything about HTML or other complex applications. For more information, contact Adobe Systems Incorporated, 345 Park Ave., San Jose, CA 95110-2704; phone 800-833-6687 or 408-536-6000; Web site www.adobe.com.

✔ **Symantec Visual Page:** Visual Page makes it easy for you to create pro-fessional-looking Web sites. It has a full WYSIWYG (what-you-see-is-what-you-get) design mode, drag-and-drop placement, a spell checker, and a clean interface. For more information, contact Symantec Corporation, 10201 Torre Ave., Cupertino, CA 95014; phone 800-441-7234; Web site www.symantec.com/vpage.

Web authoring tools are also included in Netscape Communicator 4 and Microsoft Internet Explorer 4. Because both Web browsers can be down-loaded for free, the Netscape Composer and Microsoft FrontPage Express editors are free as well.

Visit your local bookstore and ask for the Internet section. You'll find hun-dreds of books on Web site development.

Hire a professional Web designer

As an alternative to designing the Web site yourself, you can hire someone to do it for you.

These are some of the things a professional Web designer can do:

✔ Design your Web site.

✔ Create custom graphics.

✔ Scan in your corporate logo for use within the site.

✔ Scan in photographs of key personnel (like you, of course).

✔ Scan in photographs of your products.

✔ Use *cool* graphics and buttons.

✔ Create Web forms and write Java scripts.

✔ Utilize multimedia, including animation, audio, and video clips.

✔ Integrate your Web site with a database.

✔ Register your domain name.

✔ Enable you to process credit card transactions.

✔ Create an online catalog.

✔ Create an online marketing and promotion campaign.

✔ Get your site listed with many search engines.

If you're so inclined, the designer can even help you sell advertising on your Web site by developing a banner ad campaign. (Banner ads are those graph-ics you see on a Web page that are advertising some company's product or service.)

Thousands of people design Web sites. And you can be sure that some are better than others. So what should you do?

I suggest that you start by speaking with your friends who have put up their own Web sites. Ask them about their Web experiences. Study their sites, and, if you like the way they have been designed, ask for the name of their designer.

Wander around the Web — visiting one site after another. When you find a site whose design you like, send the designer an e-mail message and ask him to contact you. (Almost every site lists the Web site designer at the bottom of the home page.)

Visit each Web designer's site and look for links to sites that he or she has designed. Make sure you like the designer's style and the way in which the Web pages are laid out. Call several of the businesses whose sites the designer has created and ask to speak with the person who works with the designer to learn more about the quality, timeliness, and cost of the designer's work.

When you contact a professional Web designer regarding the possibility of putting together your site, ask the following important questions:

- How much is designing a site going to cost?
- How long will it take to design the site?
- How much do you charge to maintain the site? (How frequently will you want to update the site? Daily? Weekly? Monthly?)
- How long will it take you to make the changes once I've told you what I want?

Find a host for your site

There are two parts to having a Web site. The first part is the creation of the site itself, which is usually done on someone's desktop computer (yours or the Web site designer's). Once the Web site's been designed it needs to be published to a Web server, which is a computer that *hosts* your site.

If you've hired a Web designer, he or she will probably take care of this step for you.

If, on the other hand, you've designed your site yourself, you'll have to look for a company that hosts Web sites. Once again, speak with your friends and ask for their recommendations. Here are a few questions to ask:

- Is someone always on staff and available to handle daily emergencies?
- How do you handle emergency situations over the weekend or during a holiday? If my site goes down or develops problems over a holiday weekend, is there an emergency number I can call to notify an engineer of the problem?

Depending upon your needs, you may want a Web host that offers you some or all of the services that a Web designer offers. (See the list earlier in the chapter.)

I've been using AIS Network Corporation to host my Web site for several years. Its service has been just G-R-E-A-T. Once I had a problem on a Saturday night on a holiday weekend and got a return phone call — and a solution to the problem — within an hour. For more information, contact AIS Network Corporation, 1171 Tower Road, Schaumburg, IL 60173; phone 847-882-0493; e-mail ais@aisnetwork.net, Web site www.aisnetwork.com.

Cost will certainly be a factor when selecting a host for your site. Most hosts charge a one-time setup fee and a monthly fee thereafter. However, a number of sites offer free Web hosting, including the following:

- ✔ **Geocities:** www.geocities.com
- ✔ **Tripod:** www.tripod.com/build
- ✔ **Angelfire:** www.angelfire.com
- ✔ **InfoSeek:** www.infoseek.com

For a more up-to-date listing of sites that offer free Web hosting, visit AltaVista, www.altavista.digital.com, or your favorite search engine and type in "Free Web Hosting." (Include the quotation marks in your search string.)

Registering your domain name

After you've decided to set up a Web site, something else needs to be done: You need to get yourself a domain name.

What's a domain name? Just think of a *domain name* as your customized *registered* Internet license plate. Like the vanity plate on your car, once you've registered the domain name, no one else can use that name. It's yours! For example, the domain name for my ACT! Web site is www.ACTnews.com.

To find out whether a domain name is available, visit the Network Solutions InterNIC Registration Services Web site at www.internic.net. Here you can enter a name to see if it's taken or available. Just type in the domain name (don't include an http://www. or www. in front of the name), and the InterNIC search engine will tell you the name and address of the owner. If there is no owner, the domain name is yours!

The cost for processing the initial domain name registration and maintaining the domain name record for two years is $70 (U.S.). The cost for the renewal of the domain name is $35 and is assessed each year on the anniversary of the original registration.

If someone will be registering your domain name, ask what the charge is for this service. (The guy who registered my domain name charged me $100 for the privilege. Some favor!)

Getting your Web site listed

After you've created your Web site, you *must* get your site listed with the major search engines and directories. Otherwise people will never find you.

What is a search engine? Simply put, a *search engine* is an Internet program that enables you to find information. You enter some key words in a search form and click the Search button. Through the miracle of modern technology, the search engine gives you a page of links where you can go to find this information. Neat, huh? A directory provides basically the same service — finding Web sites that match some search criteria.

Many search engines and directories are available on the Internet. The following list discusses the most popular ones and offers directions to their add-a-Web-site page:

- **AltaVista** (www.altavista.digital.com): At the very bottom of the page is a link that reads "Add a Page." Click that link, and a page opens that describes how Scooter, its Web crawler, will visit your site and add your page(s) to AltaVista's Web site database. Scroll down to the bottom of the page and enter your Web site's address.

- **Excite** (www.excite.com): On this site, the Add URL link is hidden, so you've got to click the MORE link and then click the Add URL link.

- **HotBot** (www.hotbot.com): Click the Add URL link at the bottom of the page.

- **Infoseek** (www.infoseek.com): Click the Add URL link at the bottom of the page.

- **Lycos** (www.lycos.com): Click the Add Your Site To Lycos link at the bottom of the page.

- **Yahoo!** (www.yahoo.com): Click the Suggest a Site link at the bottom of the page.

Improving your Web site's ranking

There are a number of factors that affect a page's ranking — where it appears within the list when a search is performed — including the following:

- The words in the Web page's title.
- Keywords (META tags).

- ✔ Word frequency. The number of times specific words appear within the Web page.

- ✔ Web page length. The number of words within the Web page itself.

The title of a page is the name you give it when you create and save the page. This is how you find a Web page's title:

- ✔ **Microsoft Internet Explorer:** In Microsoft Internet Explorer, you view a page's title by selecting File⇨Page Properties. You can also view the Web page's title by selecting View⇨Source. The page's HTML text appears in your computer's text editor. Look for the line located near the top of the page that starts with ⟨title⟩.

- ✔ **Netscape Navigator:** In Netscape Navigator, you view a page's title by selecting View⇨Page Information. The page's title appears in Netscape's Document Info window. You can also view the Web page's HTML code by selecting View⇨Page Source. Look for the ⟨title⟩ line near the top of the page.

Because many search engines use the title in their index, be very descriptive in your page title. You should also include any additional key words that you think people would use to search for your site in the page's title. Use descriptive titles and include key words in every Web page that you publish on your Web site.

A META tag gives a search engine specific information, such as keywords or site summaries, about a site. In Web lingo, META tags are defined as "information about information."

These tags are part of the HTML code. They stay behind the scenes — the Web site visitor never sees them. A Web author may include long sentences or several paragraphs, within a META tag. Certain search engines then read the information in the tags as a way to help them index the site.

Some search engines, like AltaVista, utilize META tags in their index. Others, like Excite, do not. In AltaVista, for example, the META tag controls how your Web page is indexed. In the absence of any other information, AltaVista indexes every word in your document (except for comments) and uses the first few words of the document as a short abstract.

You can, however, control how your Web page is indexed by using the META tag to specify both additional keywords to index and a short description. I'll use me as an example.

```
<META  name="description" content="Jeffrey J. Mayer is a lead-
          ing time management and Symantec ACT! expert.">
<META  name="keywords" content="Jeffrey J. Mayer, ACT!,
          Symantec ACT!, time management, contact management,
          Chicago">
```

AltaVista will index the description and keywords up to a limit of 1,024 characters.

This is how you view a Web page's META tags:

> ✔ **Microsoft Internet Explorer:** In Microsoft Internet Explorer, you view a page's META tags by selecting View⇨Source. The page's HTML text appears in your computer's text editor. Look for the line located near the top of the page that starts with:
>
> ```
> <meta name="description" content=
> <meta name="keywords" content=
> ```
>
> ✔ **Netscape Navigator:** In Netscape Navigator, you view a page's META tags by selecting View⇨Page Source. The page's HTML text appears in Netscape's Document Info window.

Danny Sullivan is an Internet consultant and journalist who created Search Engine Watch, www.searchenginewatch.com. He's been covering search engines since late 1995, when he undertook a study of how Web pages were indexed. That study, along with tips and information, was published online in "A WebMaster's Guide To Search Engines." The guide has been incorporated into Search Engine Watch. Visit Danny's site, and you'll become a search engine expert in no time at all.

Most search engines use a ranking algorithm to determine the order in which matching documents are returned on the results page. Each document gets a grade based on how many of the search terms it contains, where the words are in the document, and how close to each other they are.

Visit your competitor's Web site and check out its META tags and page properties. Use the same words and phrases that they use.

Finding yourself on the Web

After you've listed your Web site, you need to go back to each of the search engines and see where you are positioned in each keyword search.

The Web sites that show up at the top of the search list receive the most visitors.

Enter the key words, or specific queries, that you think someone would use to search for your company, product, or service and see how close you come to being ranked at the top of the list.

If you didn't appear on the first two or three pages, you have more work to do, because nobody will ever find you. Here are some thoughts on improving your ranking:

- ✔ Visit the Web sites that came up at the top of the list and study them for ideas that you can use to improve your rating. Check out their page titles, META tags, and the words that are used within the page. Make a note of everything they have done that you *think* contributes to their being positioned at the top of the list.

- ✔ Edit your page titles and META tags to reflect these new ideas for moving up in the listing.

- ✔ Resubmit your Web site to the search engine.

- ✔ Come back in a few weeks to see whether your ranking improved.

Cross-link your site. If the Web sites that are coming up at the top of the list are not in direct competition with you, contact them and see if they would put a link from their site to yours, and you would do the same for them.

The more links you have, the more important your site becomes.

Most search engines schedule re-crawls of Web sites based upon the degree of change they encounter. If you update your Web site regularly, it will get more frequent visits and will rank higher in the search engines' search results.

Promoting Yourself with E-Mail

In days gone by, we used to promote our businesses by sending out mass mailings to our customers, prospects, and anyone else we wanted to include on our mailing lists.

When the PC came along, we all went wild when we saw the power of WordPerfect's and DOS's mail merge features. Now we had the power to take a list of names in a database or word processing merge file and merge them with a form letter. All we had to do was fold the letters, stuff them, put on a postage stamp or run them through the postal meter, and we were done. It sure beat sending the list and a form letter to a mailing house.

Then faxing caught on. With WinFax PRO, you could take a form letter, merge it with a list of names, and send a customized — and personalized — fax to everybody on the list. You no longer had to fold and stuff letters, put on postage stamps, and mail the letters. This process was cost-effective and time-effective.

Now, with easy-to-use e-mail programs, you can merge a form letter with a list of e-mail addresses and send it out to hundreds or thousands of people at a time with almost no expense.

I do want to mention that you must take great care to send your e-mail messages only to people who want to receive them. People hate to have what they think is "junk e-mail" (called *spam* in the Internet world) gumming up their computer's inbox.

Here are some ways in which you can promote your e-mail newsletter:

✔ Include an online form on your Web site for visitors to complete if they want to subscribe to your newsletter.

✔ Mention your e-mail mailing list on your business card.

✔ Ask everybody you speak with if they would like to be added to your mailing list.

You must also watch how many newsletters you send out at a time. Companies (Internet Service Providers) that provide e-mail services have rules about the volume of e-mail you can send at one time. So contact your e-mail company and ask if they have any restrictions before you start sending out your newsletter. Or, if you are technically inclined, you can set up an *e-mail server* on your own computer and become your own e-mail company, which I just happen to discuss in the sidebar "My thoughts on setting up your own e-mail server."

My thoughts on setting up your own e-mail server

Many Internet Service Providers (ISPs) limit how many e-mail messages can be transmitted at any one time. The limitation is thought of as a way to reduce spamming. And I don't disagree with the ISPs' practices for an instant.

But what do you do when you've got a long list of people who want to be on your e-mail list? The answer is: Set up your own e-mail server. With an e-mail server, you send and receive all of your e-mail directly from your computer. You are no longer using your ISP's e-mail system.

I started doing this a while ago. One day I tried to send out several hundred e-mail messages, and my ISP sent me a *nasty* note accusing me of spamming. It didn't care that these people had asked me to include them on my e-mail mailing list. My ISP said that I could send only 50 messages at a time. I could, on the other hand, use its bulk e-mail service to send the messages at a cost of several hundred dollars for each transmission. I thought that was nuts.

I happened to tell this story to a friend one day, and he suggested that I install an e-mail server on my computer. This feature would enable me to send as many e-mail messages as I wanted. No questions asked.

I logged onto AltaVista, my favorite search engine, typed "e-mail servers" as my search string, and started visiting the sites that appeared on the list. Eventually I found an e-mail server called MDaemon — www.mdaemon.com — that is published by Deerfield.com. MDaemon enables an organization to implement an inexpensive but powerful e-mail mail system. With MDaemon, users can send e-mail to one another on their own intranet, and to anyone on the internet. There is no need for expensive gateways, routers, or dedicated lines.

So I downloaded a free 30-day trial version of an e-mail server and started playing with it. I must volunteer that I had a bit of difficulty setting it up because the program made reference to many Internet and e-mail terms that I wasn't familiar with. However, with a phone call to the company's tech support department, I was able to quickly configure the program to work with Eudora PRO, my e-mail program. The more I used it, the more I was amazed at what I was able to do.

With MDaemon, I'm now able to transmit timely information via e-mail — about 3,000 messages an hour — to the people who want to be on my e-mail mailing list, with little or no effort, directly from my desktop computer. All I've got to do is write the e-mail message and merge the message with my list of e-mail addresses. And because I pay a flat monthly fee for my Internet connection, there's no expense. (I want to mention that I am using an ISDN line, so my transmission speed is rather fast, about 128 Kbps (kilobits per second). If you're using a 56K modem, you could send about 1,000+ messages an hour. (Transmission speed does, however, depend upon the length of your message.)

Using this server has improved my efficiency, made my life a bit easier, and helped me to make more money. It can do the same for you.

For more information about MDaemon, visit www.mdaemon.com or contact Deerfield.com, 4241 Old U.S. 27 South, P.O. Box 851, Gaylord, MI 49735; phone 517-732-8856; Web site www.deerfield.com.

Chapter 16

Do the Right Things and You'll Get the Right Results

Day after day, I hear people tell me about all the wonderful things they will be doing in the future. They talk, and they talk, and they talk, but when I ask them *how* they plan to do these wonderful things, they give me one of those "I can't believe that you're asking me this question" looks. I'm sure the same thing has happened to you at least once in the last month.

Now, there's a big difference between talking and doing, and there's an even bigger difference between daily activities and overall results. When you focus your energies on your *activities,* you can accomplish the majority of the things you set out to do because it's easy to manage *activities.*

On the other hand, you can't manage *results.* Results are the end product; they're the pot of gold at the end of the rainbow. Results come after a lot of hard work and effort. And for many of us, favorable results don't come easy; we've got to work at it.

So instead of focusing on results, it's much more important to sit down and identify which activities need to be done and then go out and do them. And before you know it, you've achieved more than you ever dreamed.

Sweat the Details

Most people hate details. They don't like getting down to the nitty-gritty. They don't like getting down on their hands and knees and getting dirt under their fingernails. They don't want to be *bothered.* Details just get in the way.

But by focusing on the details, you can achieve not only the results you want, but you can usually do it in less time and with less effort. In today's unforgiving business environment, if you don't take the time to work out the details — before you get started on a project — you'll end up working much harder than you have to. The project's going to take longer to complete, and it will cost more than was originally budgeted.

Be Smarter Than the Next Guy or Gal

To succeed in today's fast-paced world, simply working hard doesn't cut it. You've got to be smarter and more creative than the next person, and it's almost impossible to be creative when you're spending all of your time working or putting out fires and very little of your time thinking and planning. When you're able to separate your "thinking and planning" from your "doing," the "doing" becomes much easier.

In American business, "thinking" isn't considered "working." Only when a person's "doing" something is he or she considered to be working. It doesn't matter that the task that is being done is busy work, not productive work. At least the person's working!

Do the Things That Are Important

To be successful in today's extremely competitive business environment, you must spend as much time as you can doing the things that are important, the things that will make your company money, and as little time as possible doing the things that keep you busy but hardly productive.

A journey of a thousand miles begins with a single step . . . forward

If you want to be able to spend more time thinking, you've got to start looking at your daily activities, not your hoped-for results. You may remember the old Chinese proverb: "A journey of a thousand miles begins with a single step."

Over the years, I've often thought about this saying because there was something about it that I was uncomfortable with, and finally I realized what it was. The proverb should be: "A journey of a thousand miles begins with a single step — forward."

Tack a small sign on the wall of your office that reads: "How much money am I making from my present task?" This subtle reminder will help you to keep focused. It's just too easy to get sidetracked. When you find yourself doing something that isn't making you any money, stop doing it! Start working on something that will put some money in your pocket.

That's why the Master List and ACT! are such enormous productivity-improving tools. By looking at your Master List or the ACT! Task List throughout the day, it's easy to identify which tasks are important. Then you set aside some time and do them.

Live in the Here and Now

It's very easy to look way into the future and dream about all of the things you're going to do and achieve. But to do them successfully, you've got to be focused on the here and now.

When you arrive at work in the morning, you should know what you're going to do before you sit down at your desk. If you come into the office and have to ask yourself, "What am I going to do today?" you're already in trouble. Manage your daily activities, and the results will take care of themselves.

Let's play Twenty Questions

A few years ago, I was having a conversation with several people who were career salesmen. (In case you're wondering, all of the people who were participating in this conversation were men. If there had been a woman in the group, I would have used the word *salespeople* in place of the word *salesmen*. And if all of them had been women, I would have used the word *saleswomen* in place of *salesmen*.)

I found their conversation to be very interesting because they were always focusing on the end result. Here it was the beginning of January, and they were telling me how many widgets they planned to sell during the coming year.

But when I began to ask them some pointed and direct questions about *how* they planned to go about selling all these widgets, they became very uncomfortable. They began to squirm when I asked questions like: "How many appointments do you have scheduled with prospective widget buyers this month? This week? Today?" "How many people do you plan to call on the phone for the purpose of scheduling an appointment this week? Today? This morning? This afternoon?" "What do you plan to be doing at 9:00 a.m. tomorrow morning?"

And finally I would ask, "Why are you wasting your valuable time talking to me when you should be making a presentation to a prospective widget buyer?" To say the least, they didn't care for the questions I was asking and the conversation ended shortly thereafter.

Set Activity Goals

I don't know about you, but I'm not a long-term goal setter. I'm just a short-term goal setter. When you break things down into their smallest parts, everything becomes easier. Just spend your time and energy doing the right things every day. Set *activity* goals for yourself, not results goals, and the results will take care of themselves.

Set goals that are reasonable

Set goals for yourself that are reasonable and well within reach. When you're trying to achieve something that's way beyond your immediate grasp, you're likely to give up long before you have a chance at achieving your goal.

Yes, you should certainly have big dreams, goals, and desires, but if you want to make those dreams come true, you'll have to successfully complete a lot of little dreams along the way. So start by setting modest goals for yourself, ones that are within your grasp, ones that are easy to achieve. Then when you reach that first goal, set another, slightly more difficult goal for yourself.

Look at the goals you set for yourself in the same way that a high jumper approaches the challenge of a jump over the bar. He doesn't get up one morning and decide to jump 7 feet when the best he has ever done is 5 feet 9 inches.

This high jumper may dream of clearing 7 feet, but for the time being, the immediate challenge is successfully clearing 5 feet 10 inches. After clearing this height, he can raise the bar another inch, or a fraction thereof, and try again. With each success, the high jumper challenges himself a little bit more and raises the bar higher and higher.

You should approach your goals in the same manner. You should be setting goals — achievable goals — for yourself, accomplishing them, and then setting another goal, one that's slightly more difficult. You shouldn't expect to make quantum leaps in your achievements overnight. That's not being realistic.

But you should be able to move forward a little bit at a time, day in and day out. And after a while, if you take the time to look at where you are today and compare that with where you were when you started, you'll see that you accomplished more than you ever dreamed.

The winning time in the 1948 Olympic marathon would just be good enough to qualify for this year's Boston Marathon. Over the past 50 years, runners have gotten stronger, faster, and better, but it didn't happen at once; it happened a little bit at a time, over a long period of time.

I could lose a few pounds

Here's an example of goal setting that we all can relate to: losing weight. I don't know about you, but I could stand to lose a few pounds, and I know that I would like to lose it immediately. So what would happen if I starved myself for a week? Yes, I would lose my ten pounds, and would probably gain it back within a month, maybe even sooner.

But look at how the dynamics of goal setting change when I break my big goal into a lot of little ones. Instead of trying to lose ten pounds as quickly as I can, what would happen if I changed my goal to lose a pound a week?

If I lost a pound a week for ten weeks, I will have lost my ten pounds. To make this goal even easier, what do you think would happen if I tried to lose a quarter of a pound every two days? Is that reasonable? You bet! And after I lost the weight, do you think I would regain it? I don't!

Give yourself enough time

An important part of goal setting — the one that many people often overlook — is the part that pertains to time. Most people don't give themselves enough time to accomplish their goals. They always think that they can accomplish their goals in a shorter period of time than is reasonable. Then they feel that they failed because they didn't make their self-imposed deadline.

In the end, they aren't being fair to themselves, and it's unfortunate. Had they given themselves more time, they could have accomplished their goals with flying colors. But because they're in such a hurry, they shorten their time frames and place an unnecessary burden on themselves. Somehow, they believe that a goal that would normally take a week to accomplish should be completed in a day, and a goal that would take a month to accomplish should be completed in a week.

Set many short-term goals

The shorter the time frame of your goal, the more real it becomes. It's okay to set long-term or annual goals, but if you want to achieve them, you have to create a plan that breaks them down into smaller and smaller goals. Annual goals should become quarterly goals; quarterly goals should become monthly goals; monthly goals should become weekly goals.

Now don't stop at weekly goals. Break them down even further. Have some fun and play some games with yourself.

- ✔ What is your goal for today?
- ✔ What is your goal for this morning?
- ✔ What is your goal for this afternoon?
- ✔ What is your goal for the next 30 minutes?

After you've broken your larger goals down into very small goals, they should appear to be within your grasp. If they aren't, then maybe you've got to rethink your entire plan and start over again.

And when you've accomplished your short-term goal, take a moment to pat yourself on the back and congratulate yourself for a job well done, and then keep going.

Write your goals on paper

The most important part of the planning process is to write your goals down on paper so that you can see them. Identifying your goals and then putting them down on paper will take some time, thought, and consideration on your part, but as I've said before, the more time you can spend thinking and planning your course of action, the easier it will be.

When you write down your goals, always remember to date that piece of paper.

Writing your goals on paper serves several purposes. First, it shows that you are committed to accomplishing these goals, and by putting them down on paper, it gives you a point of reference from which you can compare your progress at any given point in time with your original plan of action.

After you've stated your overall goals, keep a copy of them on display, where you and your family, friends, and colleagues can see them. Tape a copy of your long and short-term goals on your bathroom mirror so that you can see them every morning and evening. And post a copy of your goals on the wall in your office.

Review your goals regularly

At the end of each week, spend a few minutes reviewing and analyzing your progress during the past week. This information can be very helpful as you plan your activities for the coming week.

Review and analyze your progress every Friday afternoon. This will enable you to prepare yourself mentally for the challenges that lie ahead in the coming week. When you arrive on Monday morning, you'll know exactly what you need to do. Just sit down and do it!

Sharing your dreams with your friends

Share your goals and dreams with your friends, colleagues, and coworkers, and discuss your plans to achieve them. Many of your friends will have thoughts or ideas that can help you accomplish your goals, and they would certainly like to be kept abreast of your progress.

Maintain a daily record of your activities, and keep a daily list of the things you accomplished. These sheets of paper should be placed in a file folder labeled "Things I Accomplished." When you want to see how far you've actually come, just pull out the file and look at your list of accomplishments.

Chapter 17

A Winning Attitude and Good Work Habits Are the Keys to Success

· ·

In This Chapter

▶ Understanding the importance of good work habits

▶ Challenging yourself

▶ Expanding your horizons

▶ Being the best you that you can be

▶ Making the most of your time

· ·

1 know that a lot of people are looking very hard for the secret of success, but they won't find it in a book, lecture, or seminar. You find success inside yourself. It's your attitude, your perspective on life, your willingness to learn, and your willingness to try new things that will determine your ability to achieve the things you desire. Only *you* can motivate yourself. Other people can show you how to do something, but you've got to do it *yourself.*

You Need Good Work Habits

Many of our work habits were acquired early in our careers, but just because you've done something one way for a long time doesn't mean that you've got to continue doing it the same way in the future.

Look at everything you do, and ask yourself, "Why do I do these things this way?" "What would happen if I did them a bit differently?" "Is it possible to streamline my activities and still achieve the same results in less time and with less effort?"

The proof is in the pudding

Early in my business career, Pauline Novak, a very close friend, sat me down and asked me a pointed question. She said, "Jeff, which do you prefer: pleasing habits or pleasing results?"

As I pondered her question, I became uncomfortable and started squirming in my chair like a worm on the end of a hook. After what seemed like an eternity, I sheepishly said that I preferred pleasing results.

From that point on, I started to take a harder look at the things I did, why I did them, and how I did them.

To be successful in today's highly competitive world, it's important that we ask these types of questions more often. And when you become more efficient and effective at work, there's another added benefit: You get to leave the office at a reasonable hour and go home!

Challenge Yourself

Look for new mountains to climb and new rivers to cross. Just because you've never done something before doesn't mean that you shouldn't try to do it. Or even if you tried to do something and weren't successful, it doesn't mean that you shouldn't try a second or third time. Don't be afraid of failure.

People who are successful have failed before. (I know that I learn much more from my failures than from my successes. How about you?) Learn from your mistakes so that you won't repeat them a second time. Cherish your failures. They make your successes sweeter and much more rewarding and fulfilling.

When I was younger, I had a wonderful tennis instructor who had a very interesting outlook on the game and on life. He said to me, "Jeff, if you're getting beat, change your game. And if you're still losing, change your game again. In the end, you may still get beat, but lose as many different ways as you can!"

If you haven't experienced failure, you haven't been trying hard enough. When you succeed, relish the fruits of your hard work. When you fail, see failure not as an end in and of itself, but as an opportunity for learning. It gives you the opportunity to look back and to analyze what happened. Ask yourself these questions:

> ✔ What did I do right?
>
> ✔ What did I do wrong?
>
> ✔ What worked?
>
> ✔ What didn't?
>
> ✔ Why did this happen?

Then go back out and try again.

The only time you must not fail is the last time you try.

Expand Your Horizons

Do things you never did before.

> ✔ Look for new responsibilities and challenge yourself.
>
> ✔ Look for new opportunities and don't be afraid to take chances.
>
> ✔ Look into the future and expand your horizons.
>
> ✔ Learn about other things that go beyond your present area of expertise.
>
> ✔ Challenge your mind and imagination.
>
> ✔ Make decisions. People who hesitate go nowhere.

Take Responsibility for the Things You Do

Once you begin setting goals for yourself, you start to accept personal responsibility, and you become accountable for the things you do. When you take responsibility for your actions, you quickly discover who you are, learn what you're made of, and determine what it is that you stand for.

> ✔ When you make a promise, keep it!
>
> ✔ When you say you're going to do something, do it!
>
> ✔ When you promise something by a certain date or at a certain time, deliver it!

Surround Yourself with Successful People

If you want to be successful, you've got to think and act like you are successful. Success in business, and in life, is an all-consuming attitude. Successful people set high standards for themselves and have made a commitment to personal excellence in everything that they do.

There are plenty of successful people out there. Go out and meet them. Make them your friends. Surround yourself with successful people. Catch their enthusiasm and let them catch yours. Give yourself the opportunity to share each other's successes.

Work hard and strive to do your best. Try to excel at everything you do.

Be the Best You That You Can Be

Your greatest asset is the fact that you are unique. You are blessed with wonderful skills, talents, and abilities, and no one else has those same skills, talents, and abilities. Therefore, it's important that you work hard to be the best *you* that *you* can be.

Get a hit when it means something

How many times have you watched a baseball player get a hit that didn't mean anything? At the moment he hit the ball, the outcome of the game had already been decided.

But what happens when there's pressure, when it's the bottom of the ninth, the winning run's on third base, and the game is on the line? How often does the batter come through with that game-winning hit? Not very often. Instead, he usually strikes out, oftentimes without even taking a swing at the ball. (I'm a Cubs fan, so I've been watching this happen for decades.)

So who do you think is the more valuable player: the one who gets three hits in a game but strikes out when the winning run is on third, or the player who strikes out three times but hits the game-winning single in the bottom of the ninth?

As you go through life, there will always be some defining moments and wonderful opportunities that come your way. When one of these moments comes along, take a big swing, hit the ball, and make the most of it.

Make the Most of Your Time

Now that you've read or skimmed *Time Management For Dummies,* 2nd Edition, it's time to put some of these wonderful time-management tips, ideas, techniques, and strategies to work. Because this is a reference book, keep it handy so that you can refer to it frequently. There is so much useful information in it that you should look through it every few weeks to see whether you can pick up some additional tip(s) that will help you be a little more productive and efficient in your work.

Your overall objective in learning how to use your time more effectively is to get your work done on time and to do it well. When you've done that, it's time to go home.

With the time you've saved at work, you have more time for yourself. You can spend more time doing the things that you love and enjoy. You can spend more time with your family, friends, and the other people who are important to you. You can see a movie or a play, or watch a ball game. You can read a book, magazine, or newspaper. You can take a vacation. You've earned it!

Part V
Time Management on the Go

The 5th Wave — By Rich Tennant

"I know my modem's in the microwave. It seems to increase transmission speed. Can you punch in 'Defrost'? I have a lot of e-mails going out."

In this part . . .

Turn to this part when you need to take your time management show on the road — whether you're headed home to set up an office or traveling out of town.

Chapter 18

Setting Up Your Home Office

. . . .

In This Chapter

▶ Putting together a home office

▶ Understanding your filing and storage space needs

▶ Creating good lighting

▶ Figuring out your telephone needs

▶ Answering your telephone

▶ Getting the right Internet connection

▶ Discovering additional equipment for your home office

. . . .

*W*hen you're working from home, the demands on your time — and the opportunity to become distracted — are even greater than when you work in an office. So here are two things to remember:

✔ **You need to be organized.** If you're going to work out of your home, you've got to be organized. And that's the subject that I address in Chapter 2 of this book. If you haven't read Chapter 2, I would suggest that you go back and do so now.

✔ **You need a good follow-up system.** You also need a good follow-up system so that you can stay on top of all of your unfinished work, tasks, and projects. If you don't have a good follow-up system, important things often slip through the cracks, leaving you with a time-consuming problem that could easily have been avoided. The subject of how to set up a good follow-up system is discussed in Chapter 3 of this book.

In this chapter, I tell you how to set up an efficient and productive home office so that you can maximize the benefits of working from home.

Where Should I Put My Home Office?

Depending upon your usage requirements and your available space, you can put a home office almost anywhere. You can work out of the kitchen, dining room, bedroom, a second or unused bedroom, the attic, or the basement.

But wherever you put your home office, you must think of it as a real office. If possible, you should stay away from high-traffic, high-noise, areas. And the people with whom you live — your family, significant other, or roommate — should accept the fact that when you're in your office, you're working. They should respect the fact that when you're in your office, you need privacy and shouldn't be disturbed.

Setting up your home office

After you've decided where your office will be located, you've got to set it up. That means you need a desk or table, chair, telephone, fax machine, filing space, a computer, and a lot of other things. The manner in which you set up your home office depends upon what type of work you'll be doing and how many hours a day you'll be doing it. So here are some questions to ask yourself:

- Will you be sitting at your computer for a good portion of the day?
- Will you be writing things by hand, as opposed to typing them into the computer?
- How many hours per day will you be on the telephone?
- Will you be meeting with customers or clients in your home office?

You need a desk and file drawers

Because you're going to have a home office, you need to have a desk.

When you select a desk, you should first determine how large you want it to be. And then you should address the question of drawer space.

You can have a desk with several small drawers, a lap drawer, a file drawer, or a combination thereof. You may even decide that you would just like to have a flat work surface without any drawers and use something else to hold your files, papers, and other miscellaneous things.

Steelcase's Turnstone division specializes in small office/home office furnishings. They offer a complete line of office furnishings, including desks, chairs, filing cabinets, and more. Steelcase — the world's largest manufacturer and designer of office systems — offers a complete line of home office desks and furnishings. To locate your nearest Steelcase dealer, call 800-333-9939. You can reach Steelcase's Turnstone division at 800-887-6786. Steelcase's Web site is at www.steelcase.com. Steelcase Inc. is located in Grand Rapids, MI 49501.

You need a comfortable chair

After you've selected your work surface, you've got to find the right chair because you'll be sitting in it every day for hours at a time. Sitting for long periods of time in an uncomfortable chair, like sleeping on an uncomfortable mattress, can result in health problems, especially backaches. Backaches and other illnesses translate into lost productivity. In fact, if you're suffering from backaches and/or your legs are going to sleep, you may be the victim of a poorly designed chair.

Sit in a chair that fits your body

A well-designed chair is one that adjusts to the shape of your body and allows you to find comfortable positions while you're working. Once it is properly adjusted, it not only supports your back, but it also reduces the strain on your shoulders, neck, arms, and hands. These are some of the features you should look for in a chair:

- **Adjustable seat height:** The seat height should be easily adjustable. When sitting at your computer, your elbows should be at the same height as the keyboard. If the keyboard is sitting on the desktop, the height of your seat will probably need to be raised to a height that is higher than you're normally accustomed to. As a result, your feet will no longer be resting comfortably on the floor. To compensate, you'll need a footrest to support your feet. If the keyboard height is adjustable, then you can lower the height of your seat so that your feet will comfortably reach the floor.

- **Adjustable backrest:** The backrest should be adjustable up and down and should fit the curve of your lower back. You want your back to be fully supported so that you can sit up straight, with your head positioned directly over your shoulders. Your arms should be resting comfortably at your sides. If you need additional back support, use cushions or foam padding.

- **Adjustable seat cushion:** The seat cushion should have a slight forward slope and shouldn't dig into the back of your legs. This takes the pressure off your spine and transfers it to your thighs and feet. With an adjustable seat cushion you can select the degree of slope that is most comfortable.

- **Adjustable seat depth:** The seat depth adjustment enables you to move the seat cushion forward or backward, depending upon the length of your legs.

- **Adjustable arms:** The arms should be adjustable so that you can change the height and angle of each arm. This allows the chair to conform to the shape of your body.

The most comfortable office chair I ever sat in

Every feature that I have just described has been incorporated into the Criterion chair from Steelcase. It is by far the most comfortable office chair I have ever used.

Fitting the chair to both the job and the body of the person who is using it can be quite a challenge. Steelcase not only includes every possible adjustment in its Criterion chair, but it has made the adjustments very easy to use.

The feature that I like the most is the individually adjustable arm rests that are designed to support the hands and forearms. When you're typing, your hands aren't resting on the keyboard; they're floating over the keyboard.

I can honestly say that my Criterion chair has gotten a lot of use. I've been sitting in a Criterion chair for six, eight, or ten hours each day for almost six years. I can assure you that it would have been impossible for me to spend so many hours at the computer in a chair that wasn't as well designed as the Criterion. Criterion chairs come with either a high- or a mid-back. The armrests are optional. For a catalog and a current price list, call 800-333-9939. Steelcase's Web site is www.steelcase.com. Steelcase Inc. is located in Grand Rapids, MI 49501.

✔ **Swivel, tilt, and roll:** The chair should swivel left and right, tilt forward and backward, and roll on casters. These features give you more mobility and ease of motion, making that task of trying to reach something that is slightly out of reach much easier.

You Need Filing and Storage Space

After you've made the decision about the type of desk and chair you want, you next have to give consideration to how you want to store your papers, documents, and office supplies. If you don't want to purchase a traditional multidrawer filing cabinet, you have some alternatives.

For example, you could purchase a small filing cabinet — with one file drawer and one small drawer — that rolls on a caster and is small enough to fit under a table. Or maybe you would like to put all of your files and papers in a dresser so the room doesn't look so much like an office.

Use expandable filing pockets. In Chapter 2, I talked about how you can use expandable file pockets to make your filing system work better. You can use the expandable file pockets in other ways in addition to putting them inside filing cabinets.

For example, you can put your papers inside an expandable file pocket and then put it on a shelf inside one of your closets. With a black marker, you can write a name or title that describes the contents of the expandable file pocket on the side of the file pocket that faces out.

To conserve space and save yourself the cost of purchasing a filing cabinet, install adjustable shelves in a closet and put your expandable file pockets on the shelves. (That's what I've done.)

✔ **Buy a dresser.** As an alternative to purchasing a filing cabinet, you can also use a dresser — with adjustable shelves — as a place to store all of your files, papers, and all of the other things you need to run your business from your home. You can then use the top of the dresser as a place to put your printer and fax machine.

✔ **Install shelves on your walls.** One of the best ways to get papers, files, books, software manuals, and lots of other miscellaneous things off your desk is to hang shelves on the wall and put all of this stuff on the shelves.

Don't leave everything in piles. Whatever you end up doing, don't leave everything in piles; it's just impossible to get your work done, do it well, and get it done on time. If you still have piles all over the place, it's time to read (or reread) Chapter 2 of this book.

Good Lighting Makes You More Productive

Many people don't give enough consideration to the lighting in their home office. You'll find that you're much more productive when you've got the right type of lighting for each task you need to perform. You should design your home office with the understanding that the lighting you need to read a letter, for example, is different than the lighting you need to work at your computer.

Your objective is to create a work environment where

✔ The light is bright enough for you to read your papers and documents easily without any eye strain.

✔ You have enough indirect light so that you can work at your computer without seeing glare or reflections on your screen.

To control the amount of daylight that's coming into your home office, consider installing adjustable blinds. Adjustable blinds enable you to block, filter, or redirect bright sunlight away from your workspace.

What Are Your Telephone Needs?

If you're going to be running a business out of your home, you've got to treat it like a business, and that means you need to have a proper telephone system. Whatever your needs, you have a lot of options. So here are some thoughts about phone systems.

You need at least two lines

To run a business properly, you need to have at least two telephone lines; otherwise, your customers, clients, and anyone else who calls will get a busy signal. And you certainly don't want to miss a call from one of your important customers or clients.

Do you need a dedicated line for your fax machine?

Fax machines have become a major part of all of our business lives. It's almost impossible to imagine conducting business without one today. If you send and receive a lot of faxes, it may be worth the expense of installing a dedicated line solely for your fax machine. You do, however, have some other choices. Here are a few of them.

Running two businesses from the home

My wife, Mitzi, and I both run our respective businesses out of our home. She's an interior designer, and I'm a time management consultant and author. (But you already knew that.)

When we installed our phone system, we put in two lines and ordered the call-waiting service for the second line. Here's how it works: If someone calls on line one and it's in use, the call is automatically transferred to line two. If both lines are busy, the call-waiting feature is activated on the second line.

This system worked well for us for almost ten years. Then I started accepting telephone credit card transactions, so I had to install a third telephone line.

And finally, I got tired of waiting for Web pages to appear in my browser, so I bit the bullet and installed an ISDN line for a faster Internet connection. (I'm looking forward to the day when I'll be able to use a Digital Subscriber Line (DSL) or utilize a cable modem. I discuss this a bit later in this chapter.) Subscribe to Caller ID; it's a great service. With Caller ID you know who is calling before you answer the phone. This enables you to choose the calls you want to answer, sending the other calls to the answering machine.

Share your fax and voice lines

Many local telephone companies offer a service for single line users that distinguishes between a voice call and a fax call. When you get a fax, the call is routed to your fax machine, and when you get a voice call, your telephone rings.

Buy a switching box

You can purchase a small switching box that automatically routes your calls. When you receive a fax, the call goes to the fax machine; otherwise, your telephone rings. One of the neat features of the switching box is that you can answer the phone from anywhere in the house; by pressing 0, you can send the call to the answering machine; and by pressing another number, 22 for example, you can send the call to your fax machine.

Command Communications makes a complete line of automatic switching products. Calls can be routed to an answering machine, a fax machine, or your computer's modem. (You can even convert your fax machine into a scanner. With just the touch of a button your fax machine sends images directly into your PC's fax/modem.) For more information, contact Command Communications, 10800 East Bethany Drive, Aurora, CO 80014; phone 303-751-7000; Web site www.command-comm.com.

Many of the new fax machines already have switching boxes installed. Some of the more advanced fax machines also have built-in voice mail systems.

Do you send and receive your faxes directly from your computer?

If you're one of the many people who use faxing software, such as Symantec's WinFax PRO, you send and receive your faxes directly from your computer and may not even have an old-fashioned fax machine. (I discuss fax machines and WinFax PRO later in this chapter.)

If this is the case, you should consider installing a separate telephone line for your computer.

Sign your faxes with a digitized signature. A digitized signature is your handwritten signature reproduced in its identical form. It can be used within WinFax PRO, Word, WordPerfect, and many more computer software programs. For more information, contact Orbit Enterprises at 800-767-6724 or 630-469-3405, or visit their Web site at www.digitize.com.

How can I have a single-line fax or answering machine pick up a call when I've got two phone lines?

You can solve this problem by purchasing a routing box from Radio Shack for about $15.

Whenever the phone rings — it doesn't matter if the call is coming in on line one or line two — the routing box sends the call to the switching box.

The switching box then determines if the call is a voice call or fax transmission. If it's a voice

call, it is sent to the answering machine. If it's a fax transmission, it's sent to the fax machine.

The routing box will save you the expense of purchasing a two-line answering machine and a two-line fax machine (which may not even exist).

Do you want to share your voice line with your computer?

When your computer and telephone share the same line, you can use the computer to dial the phone for you. The autodialing feature is one of the very powerful features of ACT! and many other contact managers.

With a TAPI (Telephony Application Programming Interface) compliant computer telephone, you can control your incoming and outgoing telephone calls from your computer.

Do you need a separate telephone line for your Internet connection?

If you spend a lot of time online, you should consider installing a separate line for your computer. With a dedicated line for your Internet connections, you can surf the Web and still use your telephone. (I discuss getting an Internet connection in just a few moments.)

You do need a telephone!

We all seem to take the telephone for granted. We're accustomed to having fancy phone systems at our offices but don't think about giving ourselves the same conveniences in our home offices.

So when purchasing a telephone, you should have these features:

- ✔ Buttons for two or more lines
- ✔ Conference calling
- ✔ Speed dialing
- ✔ Speaker phone
- ✔ Caller ID display

Nortel's Venture phone system will make you more productive

Nortel's Venture three-line telephone offers the ideal communications solution for small offices or home offices. The Venture system offers the same timesaving, productivity-improving telephone features that you would find in large corporate offices. You start with a single three-line telephone, and as your communication needs grow, you can expand the system to eight networked telephones.

The Venture's features include:

✔ **Voice mail system:** A built-in digital voice mail system that has 14 mailboxes that are available for general and private use. Each mailbox can have its own customized greeting.

✔ **Speakerphone:** A full-duplex speakerphone that makes your voice sound like you're speaking in the handset instead of into the speakerphone.

✔ **Caller ID and Call Waiting Display:** With the integrated Caller ID and Call Waiting Display, you can see who's calling, even when you're on another call. (Of course, you must subscribe to the Caller ID and Call Waiting services.)

✔ **Voice Announced Caller ID:** With the Voice Announced Caller ID integration, the Venture announces over the speakerphone the names and numbers of callers who are listed in the directory whenever they call.

✔ **Call Log:** The Call Log stores the names and numbers of 200 callers.

✔ **Phone Directories:** One Private and three Personal Directories for 200 names and numbers to access and dial important numbers.

With the Venture Enhanced Feature Adapter, you can add more functions to your Venture phone system. These include Music On Hold, Fax Machine Connection, Call Detail Recording and Printing, and Loudspeaker Paging. With the Venture's Doorphone feature, you can answer the front door from any phone in your Venture system and open the door by activating the door's electronic door latch.

For more information about the Venture phone system, contact Nortel (Northern Telecom), One Brunswick Square, Atrium Suite 100, St. John, New Brunswick, Canada E2L 4V1; phone 1-800-4-NORTEL; Web site www.nortel.com.

Who's Going to Answer Your Telephone?

If you're going to be running a business out of your home, someone's got to answer your phone when you're not there. Depending upon your needs and your budget, you have a number of choices.

Get an answering machine

The easiest thing you can do is purchase an answering machine. Today you have lots of choices. You can purchase just a simple, no frills machine, a machine that can answer two or three lines, or something in between.

Panasonic's newest answering machines feature digital sound for both the incoming and outgoing messages. Because the answering machine is digital, you have the capability of creating individual mailboxes so that you can organize your messages. And with digital recording, the sound is crystal clear. Panasonic Company, One Panasonic Way, Secaucus, NJ 07094. For the name of your nearest Panasonic dealer, call 201-348-9090.

Install a voice mail system on your computer and improve your productivity

Symantec's Talkworks PRO brings professional voice and fax messaging to home offices and small businesses. Talkworks has integrated voice mail, message-notification, call tracking, and fax-on-demand capabilities into one software package that will keep you in touch with your customers 24 hours a day, 7 days a week.

Talkworks' features include:

- An answering machine with multiple mailboxes and customizable and pre-recorded greetings
- New message delivery and paging
- Mailbox paging
- Call and fax tracking
- Voice/fax discrimination

- Fax on demand
- Dual modem support

Talkworks PRO saves details of every call using the Caller ID service available through your local phone company. Whether someone leaves a message, sends a fax, or hangs up, Talkworks PRO automatically saves a caller's name, telephone number, and time of call. (Talkworks PRO integrates call logging with ACT!. This includes incoming calls, outgoing calls, and voice messages.)

For more information, contact Symantec Corporation, 10201 Torre Avenue, Cupertino, CA 95014; phone 800-441-7234. Their Web site is www.symantec.com/talkworks.

Hire an answering service

If you want a real person to answer your phone instead of a machine with a recorded message, you should look into hiring an answering service.

Get a voice mail system from your local telephone company

Your local telephone company may offer a full-service voice mail system that enables you to record your own messages, with separate voice mail boxes, and call at any time of the day or night to hear the messages that you've received. These messages can be saved or archived for future reference.

Getting the Right Internet Connection Saves You Time

Surfing the Internet can be a huge time-waster when you're using a regular modem. It just takes too long for Web pages to come up on your browser. However, with a different type of Internet connection, you can save yourself hours of time and dramatically increase your productivity.

There are several different kinds of Internet connections available, and depending upon your Internet usage, and your budget, you may want to consider installing an ISDN (Integrated Services Digital Network) or DSL (Digital Subscriber Line) telephone line. Your local cable company may also be offering high-speed Internet connections with a cable modem.

(I do want to mention that ISDN, DSL, and cable connections may not be available in your town or community at this time. You'll have to contact your local phone or cable company for more information. Hopefully these Internet options will become available, at a reasonable price, in the future.)

What is bandwidth?

Before I describe the different types of Internet connections that are available, a brief discussion on bandwidth is appropriate.

What is bandwidth? Bandwidth is the term that is used to describe the rate of speed that data travels across your Internet connection. Think of bandwidth as the rate of flow of water through a hose. You get more water from a fire hose than from a garden hose because it flows faster; in other words, it has more bandwidth.

So if you're using a 56K modem and connecting with the Internet over a local telephone line (also referred to as an analog line), information is traveling at 56,600 bits per second (bps). You're getting information twice as fast as the person who is using a 28.8K modem, but only half as fast as the person who is using an ISDN line at 128 kilobits per second (Kbps).

The fastest analog modems (56K modems) transfer information at the rate of 56,600 bits per second. If you're still using a 28.8K, or slower, modem you should give serious consideration to upgrading. You're wasting too much time waiting for Web pages to appear within your browser.

ISDN (Integrated Services Digital Network)

An ISDN line is a special telephone line that enables you to send and receive both voice and data (digital) transmissions over ordinary copper telephone lines. When you use an ISDN line to connect to the Internet, Web pages open up very quickly in your browser. The top transmission speed is 128 Kbps.

To utilize an ISDN line, you have to have a special ISDN modem and have your local phone company install an ISDN line in your home or office. ISDN lines are not available in all parts of the country.

DSL (Digital Subscriber Line)

A DSL connection enables you to transmit digital information at very high speeds over the telephone company's copper phone lines. DSL was designed to exploit the one-way nature of most Internet communication, in which large amounts of information flow to the user and only a small amount of information flows from the user.

DSL can transmit data at speeds ranging from 1.544 megabits per second (Mbps) to 8 Mbps. This makes it about 50 to 100 times faster than a connection over a typical telephone line.

One of the other advantages of a DSL line is that there is no dial-up connection. You are always connected to the Internet.

Cable modems

Several years ago, the cable television companies realized that their shielded wires, which are protected against electromagnetic interference, could carry much more information than the largely unshielded wires used by the telephone company. So they began to offer Internet connections in addition to their basic cable service.

At the present time, cable modems are available in only a handful of cities, but its attraction is huge because of the huge bandwidth — the speed of a cable modem is between 1 Mbps to 10 Mbps — that is available. Over the next few years, most of the cable companies will be offering Internet access.

Additional Equipment for Your Home Office That Will Make You More Productive

When you're working from your home, you need more than just a computer and telephone for your home office. A fax machine, or faxing software, and a good printer will save you time and make you more productive. You may also find that a label printer, a business card scanner, and a desktop scanner can help you get more things done in less time and with less effort.

Today's fax machines do a lot more than just send and receive faxes

Yes, you can purchase a thermal paper or plain paper fax machine today. But if you really want to improve your productivity, you should look into a multi-function fax machine. A multi-function machine is really 5 machines built into one:

- ✔ It's a Fax.
- ✔ It's a Printer.
- ✔ It's a Copier.
- ✔ It's a PC Fax.
- ✔ It's a Scanner.

I've been using Brother fax machines for years, and I recently upgraded to their MFC 4650 multi-function machine. These are some of the features that I find very powerful:

- ✔ The fax output is high quality, 600 dpi (dots per inch) laser printing.
- ✔ There is a high-speed, 14.4 fax modem.
- ✔ The document feeder holds 20 pages.
- ✔ The Dual Access function enables you to scan and send a document at the same time that a fax is being received.

The biggest timesaving feature is that you don't need to stand by the machine and wait for the transmission to end before you can go back to your desk, with your original document. When you send a fax, the document is immediately scanned into memory. Then the fax machine dials the phone and sends the transmission.

Here's a brief description of the MCF 4650's features:

- ✔ **Printer features:** The MCF 4650 prints up to 6 page per minute laser output at 600 x 600 dpi resolution. It prints 3 x 5 inch cards, envelopes, and heavy paper stocks.

- ✔ **Copier features:** You can make up to 99 copies at a 400 dpi resolution that are automatically sorted. Copies can be reduced by 50 percent or enlarged to 200 percent.

- ✔ **Scanner features:** The 4650 comes with Visioneer's PaperPort document management software, and has Xerox's TextBridge OCR software. It scans at up to seven pages per minute with 600 x 600 dpi resolution.

- ✔ **PC Fax features:** With the Smith Micro's PC Fax software, you can send faxes directly from your PC and receive faxes into your PC to view before printing. You can also use the 4650 to send out fax broadcasts and create detailed fax logs. (With a NetCentric Internet fax provider and NetCentric's FaxStorm software, which is included, you can send low cost faxes via the Internet.)

Brother International makes a complete line of fax machines for small office and home offices, as well as the corporate office. For more information, call Brother International Corporation, 100 Somerset Corporate Boulevard, Bridgewater, NJ 08807-0911. For the name of your nearest Brother dealer, call 800-284-4357 or visit their Web site at www.brother.com.

You need a good printer

One of the reasons you're able to work out of the home and be so extremely productive at the same time is the personal computer. With today's super-fast machines and powerful software, you can produce the kinds of letters, documents, presentations, and proposals in hours that used to take a group of people the better part of a day.

But the creation of the work inside the computer is only the first part of the process. The second part is getting it to look good on paper. And if you want it to look as good on paper as it does on your computer screen, you need to have a good printer.

Brother International makes a complete line of printers for the home and the office. Their newest line of laser printers — the HL-1040 and HL-1050 — offers high-quality printing at affordable prices.

- ✔ **HL-1040:** The HL-1040 has 2MB of standard memory and has a print speed of up to 10 pages per minute at 600 x 600 dpi (dots per inch).

- ✔ **HL-1050:** The HL-1050 has 4MB, (expandable to 36MB), of standard memory and has a print speed of up to 10 pages per minute at 600 x 600 dpi and 1200 x 600 dpi printing for graphics. With the Universal Serial Bus (USB), you can connect multiple peripheral devices to your computer.

With Brother's Straight Paper Path design you can print on a wide variety of paper stocks and sizes — from 3 x 5-inch index cards, to letter envelopes, to legal-sized paper.

Send and receive your faxes directly from your computer

One of the biggest timesaving and productivity-improving inventions in the last decade has been the fax machine. And although fax machines have made it possible to send and receive information in an instant, most of us still follow a cumbersome procedure: We print hard copies of that letter or document that we just created in the computer. Then we walk to the fax machine, insert the document into the paper feeder, and send the fax. This assumes that the machine isn't already in use. If it is, we wait.

And what happens when someone sends you a fax? Unless the machine is nearby, you have no way of knowing whether a fax has been received, so it may sit there for hours before you get it.

With Symantec's WinFax PRO, you can send and receive all your faxes directly from your computer without ever touching a piece of paper. There's no more walking back and forth to the fax machine; no more standing in line waiting for the machine to become available; and no more greasy, curly paper to deal with. And best of all, when you receive a fax, you're notified instantly and can review it onscreen or print it.

WinFax PRO will even send a message to your pager or cell phone announcing the arrival of a fax. You can also have your incoming faxes automatically forwarded to another fax number.

If you send a lot of faxes, WinFax PRO can save you a lot of time and money. For more information, contact Symantec Corporation, 10201 Torre Avenue, Cupertino, CA 95014; phone 800-441-7234. Their Web site is www.symantec.com/winfax.

If you need a high-end laser printer, the HL-1660e is a phenomenal machine! (It's the one that I now use.) It's designed for the person who needs high-quality text and graphics output and network connectivity. It handles complex printing tasks easily and effortlessly. The HL-1660e is fast. It prints at the rate of 17 pages per minute at a resolution of 600 x 600 dpi for text and 1200 x 600 dpi for graphics. Printed text and graphics look so good that you would think the printed document was created by a professional printer.

The HL-1660e comes with 8MB of RAM that can be easily upgraded to 72MB. It even comes with a 500-sheet, multipurpose paper tray.

If you need even more speed, Brother's newest printer, the HL-2060, prints at the rate of 21 pages per minute at a resolution of 600 x 600 dpi for text and 1200 x 600 dpi for graphics.

If you need a color printer, Brother's HS-5000 series color laser printer has a lot of printing power. It prints crisp 600 x 600 dpi color resolution at up to 4 pages per minute.

I've been using Brother printers for more than ten years (not the HL-1660e; it's brand new) — and have written nine books with them. Day after day, these printers have done what they are designed to do. They print, and print, and print. The only time the printer stops is when it runs out of paper or the toner cartridge needs to be replaced. They are dependable.

Brother International makes a complete line of printers for the small office and home offices, as well as the corporate office. For more information, call Brother International Corporation, 100 Somerset Corporate Boulevard, Bridgewater, NJ 08807-0911. For the name of your nearest Brother dealer, call 800-284-4357 or visit their Web site at www.brother.com.

Print your mailing labels with a label printer

How do you print a single label? Good question, isn't it? Somehow, I don't think that laser printers were designed to print a single label. Typing a label on one of those old fashioned things — an electric typewriter — was always a time-consuming task. (I hope you're not still using one of them!)

But printing a label with the Seiko Smart Label Printer Pro is easy. The SLP Printer Pro attaches to the serial port of your computer and prints labels from a roll, one at a time, instead of from a sheet. Seiko has even developed software that searches for the address in your letter and then automatically prints the label, with bar codes, for you. What could be easier? I use mine every day and find that it's a great productivity-improvement tool.

You can even use the Seiko Smart Label Printer Pro to print labels for file folders, packages, diskettes, name badges, videotapes, and more.

For more information about the Smart Label Printer Pro, contact Seiko Instruments USA Inc., 1130 Ringwood Court, San Jose, CA 95131; phone 800-888-0817. Seiko's Web site is www.seikosmart.com.

Scan your business cards into your computer

How many business cards do you have in the lap drawer of your desk? What good are they to you? Why don't you put the information inside your computer and put it to use?

Yes, I know. Typing them into your computer is a time-consuming task. That said, you should look into purchasing a Seiko Smart Business Card Reader. You'll get the names of the important people in your life into your computer in no time at all and have much more time to build your relationships.

The Seiko Smart Business Card Reader automates the task of typing business card information into your computer. This is what it does: It scans a business card, recognizes the text, and then intelligently determines where the name, address, and other important information is positioned on the card. Then the Smart Business Card Reader places the data into the appropriate fields in your contact management program. The Smart Business Card Reader works with ACT!, GoldMine, Maximizer, Organizer, Sidekick, the PalmPilot, and more.

For more information about the Smart Business Card Reader, contact Seiko Instruments USA Inc., 1130 Ringwood Court, San Jose, CA 95131; phone 800-888-0817. Seiko's Web site is www.seikosmart.com.

Scan your documents into your computer

When you've important documents you want to retain, why not scan them into your computer instead of putting them in a file folder? Visioneer's PaperPort Strobe scanner — it's small, (just 11 inches wide x 2 inches high x 2.5 inches deep), sleek, and fits easily between your keyboard and monitor and weighs just 1.5 pounds — makes it easy for you to scan your documents.

You can scan typical office documents at up to 15 pages per minute (depending upon the scan mode you've selected and the speed of your computer's processor). And, you can also scan in business cards and color photos.

Here are some more things you can do with a PaperPort scanner:

- ✔ Annotate or edit images and text with PaperPort's editing tools.
- ✔ Call out the important items in a document simply by highlighting them in yellow and labeling them with sticky notes.
- ✔ Drag-and-drop a scanned document onto your favorite word processor and Visioneer's software automatically begins the OCR process. A few moments later, the document is ready for editing. (PaperPort Strobe has direct PaperPort Links to over 185 of the most popular software applications. Just drag-and-drop your scanned image or document to any of the link bar icons to immediately launch applications without any other steps.)
- ✔ Drag-and-drop documents and forms to the printer to produce multiple copies of the original.
- ✔ When you want to send a scanned document via e-mail, just select the document you want to e-mail. Drag it onto the e-mail icon, and PaperPort automatically launches an e-mail window and attaches your file in PaperPort format.

If you want a flatbed scanner, Visioneer's PaperPort family of flatbed scanners offer scanners with 300 x 600 dpi to 600 x 1200 dpi. The scanners all include the awarding-winning PaperPort software. And, you don't have to even open up your computer case to install a SCSI card. Just plug your scanner into an existing parallel port, install the software, and you are ready to start scanning!

For more information about PaperPort scanners, contact Visioneer, 34800 Campus Drive, Fremont, CA 94555; phone 800-787-7007 or 510-608-6300. Their Web site is www.visioneer.com.

Chapter 19

Creating a Healthy Work Environment

Are you an office couch potato? Do you come into work, sit down at your desk, and stay there for the rest of the day? Do you take a break for lunch, or do you eat it at your desk? Well, if you do, it's time that you put some movement back into your life.

The human body was designed to move, and we spend too much time sitting at our desks and not enough time moving around. So here are some stretching exercises that will warm up, relax, and stretch the muscles in your hands, fingers, and the rest of your body. And because most of us would like to find ways to make our lives easier, I've included some information about how to automate your keystrokes with macros. If your hands hurt from spending too much time at the computer keyboard, I've got some good news for you: I'm going to tell you about the Kinesis Ergonomic Keyboard and the Kensington Expert Mouse. And if your back hurts, maybe you need a new chair. Steelcase's Criterion chair is a great one.

Be Nice to Your Hands

You probably don't give your hands and fingers much thought, but look at the extensive workout they're getting at your computer's keyboard. For example, if a person spends five hours per day typing at the rate of 60 words (360 keystrokes) per minute, that's 100,000 keystrokes per day, 500,000 keystrokes per week, and 25,000,000 keystrokes per year. Cut it down to 40 words per minute for only three hours per day, and you've still got more than

43,000 keystrokes per day and 215,000 keystrokes per week. In addition, your body isn't moving because you're sitting in the same chair for hours at a time.

To compound the problem, much of this work is done by the little fingers. We use our pinkies to press and hold down the Shift, Ctrl, Alt, Return/Enter, Backspace, and Tab keys. When you type for hours at a time, day after day, the muscles and tendons in the fingers, hands, and arms become susceptible to injury.

So here are a few simple exercises that will help your hands, arms, and fingers stay healthy. Take a few moments to do them several times per day.

- **Massage your hands.** Gently massage the palms of your hands and fingers for 30 to 60 seconds each.

- **Stretch your lower forearm.** To stretch the underside of your forearm, turn your palm facing up, and, with your other hand, gently press your fingers away from your body until you feel your muscles begin to stretch. Hold for 5 seconds and then relax. Repeat 3 to 5 times.

- **Stretch your upper forearm.** To stretch the topside of your forearm, make a fist, and with your other hand, press it toward your body until you feel your muscles begin to stretch. Hold for 5 seconds and then relax. Repeat 3 to 5 times.

- **Rotate your wrists.** Hold your arms away from your sides and slowly rotate both wrists ten times in each direction as if you were drawing circles with your fingertips.

- **Stretch your fingers.** Spread the fingers of both hands far apart and hold for 2 seconds and then make your hands into fists and hold the fists for 2 seconds. Repeat 3 to 5 times.

Give your hands a break from typing at least once every 30 minutes. Shake them for a few moments to get the blood circulating and then switch to another activity that uses the hands differently before you resume typing.

Energize Your Body

The human body was designed to move, so you shouldn't stay seated in that nice comfortable office chair, in the same position at your desk, for hours on end. When you stay seated for too long, your muscles get stiff, you become fatigued, and your productivity goes south. Here are a few exercises that will get your blood flowing again and stretch your tired muscles; within a few minutes, you'll feel refreshed and invigorated.

Do these at least once in the morning and again in the afternoon. And while you're at it, don't forget to take a break. Get up from your desk and stretch your legs at least once every hour.

- ✔ **Stretch your whole body.** Stand up, raise your hands above your head, and try to touch the ceiling. For variation, try to touch the ceiling with one hand at a time. Hold the stretch for 5 to 10 seconds. Repeat several times.

- ✔ **Stretch your back.** Hold your arms straight out from your sides, and with your palms forward, take a deep breath and push your hands gently backward. Hold the stretch 3 to 5 seconds and exhale. Repeat the stretch 3 to 5 times. This exercise will help you stand up straight and get rid of your rounded shoulders.

- ✔ **Roll your shoulders.** To loosen up your shoulders, stand up and pretend you're swimming the backstroke. First bring one arm backward, and then the other. Repeat 3 to 5 times.

- ✔ **Shrug your shoulders.** Slowly lift your shoulders toward your ears, and then roll them backward and down again, making a complete circle. Repeat 3 to 5 times.

- ✔ **Squeeze your shoulder blades.** Stand up straight, clasp your hands behind your head, and squeeze your shoulder blades together. Take a deep breath, and, as you exhale, allow your muscles to relax.

- ✔ **Stretch your neck.** Straighten and arch your back, sit up straight, and hold your head high. Relax your neck by lifting your head and try to gently touch your right ear to your right shoulder, stretching the muscles on the left side of your neck. Let your head roll down to the center, rest a moment, and pick up your head again. Now try to touch your left ear to your left shoulder and let your head roll down to the center; then pick it up. Repeat this 2 or 3 times.

Automate Your Keystrokes with Macros

Because many of the things you do at the keyboard are repetitive, you can use the computer to automate those keystrokes. Keyboard macros — they're like the redial feature on your phone — will make you much more productive because the computer can play back a series of recorded keystrokes much faster than you can type them. And they'll also reduce the wear and tear on your hands and fingers, thereby reducing the possibility of sustaining a hand, finger, or arm injury. See the user's manual of your favorite software applications to learn more about how macros work.

Position Your Hands Properly on the Keyboard

We all come in different shapes and sizes — some of us are tall; others are short; one person may have large hands; another person's hands may be petite. Because of this, you need to be able to adjust your work area to fit your own physical needs. To create a working environment that is right for you, you must take a number of different factors into consideration: the height of your desk, chair, and keyboard; the position of your monitor; and the intensity of the interior lighting under which you're working. If your office equipment forces you to sit in an unnatural position — especially if your wrists are cocked — your risk of injury is greatly increased.

Up until now, you've probably never given any thought regarding how you should position yourself at the keyboard. Most people position the height of their chair so that their feet rest comfortably on the floor, without any regard to the position of their hands in relation to the keyboard. A better way is to make sure your hands are properly positioned at the keyboard — then make any other necessary adjustments.

When sitting at the keyboard, you want to type with a flat wrist, positioned at or just below elbow level, so that your forearms are at a 90-degree angle to your upper arms. Your arms should rest comfortably at your sides; your wrists should be relaxed; and your fingers should be gently curved. Typing with a cocked wrist, either upward or downward, places extra stress on the tendons and nerves as they pass through the wrist. When a person sits in a chair that is either too high or too low in relation to the keyboard, it often causes a person to type with their wrists cocked.

If the height of the keyboard is adjustable, it's easy to achieve this 90-degree position. If the keyboard is sitting on a desk or table whose height cannot be changed, you can compensate for this by raising your chair to the proper height and using a footrest to support your feet.

Here are some keyboard tips:

- If the keyboard is too large for your hands or fingers, try to reach the outlying keys by lifting your hand and arm from the shoulder rather than twisting your wrists or straining to reach those keys with your fingers.

- When typing, avoid resting your wrists on the edge of the work surface. Doing so can put additional pressure on those same tendons and nerves that you're trying to treat so gingerly.

✔ To reduce the strain on your wrists, muscles, and tendons, consider using a padded wrist or palm rest that you can place in front of the keyboard. A wrist rest can be especially helpful during brief typing breaks.

✔ When typing, keep your hands relaxed, type gently, and don't pound the keys.

Do Your Hands Hurt? Then Try a Different Keyboard

I spend a lot of time at my computer keyboard — about six to eight hours each day, and I've been doing it for the better part of the past ten years. Several years ago my hands, fingers, and forearms begin to ache. Somehow I don't think that the human body was designed to spend hours on end typing away.

So after a few visits to my favorite massage therapist, I decided to try one of those fancy ergonomic keyboards. A few days later, my Kinesis Ergonomic Keyboard arrived in the mail, and after using it for a few days, my hands stopped hurting. I've now written two books with it, and I just love it.

Kinesis's designers have given a lot of thought and consideration as to how the human hand and body relate to the keyboard, and they've done some neat things in their design of the keyboard.

(The keyboard looks more like the control panel from the Starship Enterprise than a computer keyboard.) Here are some of the things that they did:

✔ The keyboard is divided into two concave wells that are placed six inches apart. This feature separates the hands, allowing the elbows and arms to rest at shoulder width.

✔ The keys are positioned in a slight arc, instead of in a straight line, which takes into consideration that your fingers are of different lengths — thus conforming the keyboard to the shape of the hand.

✔ They repositioned some of the keys that were formerly pressed with the little finger — the Backspace, Delete, Ctrl, Alt, Home, End, PgUp, PgDn, Return/Enter, and Spacebar keys — and grouped them together in two sets of thumb pads.

✔ They added a foot pedal you can use in place of the Shift key, and they include a little bit of memory in the keyboard so that you can record keyboard macros and save yourself the time and effort of retyping the same words or program commands over and over and over.

If you've been experiencing finger, hand, or arm discomfort, the Kinesis Ergonomic Keyboard (shown in Figure 19-1) is certainly worth trying. Kinesis Ergonomic Keyboard, Kinesis Corporation, 915 118th Avenue Southeast, Bellevue, WA 98005; phone 800-454-6374; Web site www.kinesis.ergo.com.

Figure 19-1:
The Kinesis
Ergonomic
Keyboard.

Position Your Monitor so That You Don't Have to Lean Forward

After you've discovered the proper position for your body in relation to the keyboard, you need to address the position of your monitor. Here are some tips:

- ✔ The top of the monitor should be positioned so that it's even with or slightly below your forehead. You should be able to look straight at the screen without being forced to tilt your head forward and downward.

- ✔ A monitor support arm can be used to raise your monitor to the desired height. These arms allow the monitor to float above the desktop and offer tremendous flexibility because you can position them at any height and distance from your eyes that you want. (I've raised my monitor almost six inches by placing it on a monitor stand.)

✔ To make the task of typing easier and at the same time reduce the strain on your neck, attach a copy holder to the side of your monitor. The copy holder holds the papers right next to the screen, minimizing eye and neck movement.

A Footrest Improves Your Circulation

A footrest is an important — and often overlooked — piece of office furniture. It can reduce the pressure on the back of your thighs, minimize lower back strain by raising your feet, and improve the circulation of blood throughout your body. Most importantly, it compensates for the lack of flexibility between your chair and your desk. By supporting your legs and feet, it allows you to sit higher than would normally be comfortable.

Tired of Mousing? Get a Trackball

If you would like an alternative to using a mouse, you should try Kensington's Expert Mouse trackball. Its ergonomic design offers you maximum mousing comfort while at the same time giving you precision control over your cursor's movement. And because a trackball remains stationary — you only move the ball, not the entire device — it doesn't take up much desktop space.

The Expert Mouse's large trackball — almost the size of a billiard ball — is easily controlled by your fingertips and offers very smooth cursor movement. The buttons, which are placed symmetrically on each side of the ball, have a light, easy-to-press feel and accommodate both left- and right-handed users. The real beauty of the Expert Mouse is in the software. It has several user-programmable functions that give you the ability to adjust and modify how the cursor responds to the movement of the trackball.

✔ **Custom Acceleration.** The Custom Acceleration feature enables you to adjust the cursor acceleration, which is the speed at which your cursor moves in relation to how far and how quickly you move the trackball.

✔ **Brilliant Cursor.** With a single click of a trackball button, your cursor will jump to different, predefined points, or hot spots, on your screen.

✔ **Slow Cursor.** The Slow Cursor feature gives you ultra-precise, pixel-by-pixel control over your cursor's movements. This feature is especially useful for placing graphics, drawings, or page layouts in exact locations on your screen.

One evening, my trackball stopped working. I called tech support, told them what happened, and they said that they would send out a replacement (it has a five-year warranty). The next morning it arrived by Federal Express.

I've been using the Expert Mouse for years. It's easy to use; it's easy on my hands, arms, and fingers; and it helps me be more productive. Expert Mouse, Kensington Microware Limited, 2855 Campus Drive, San Mateo, CA 94403; phone 800-280-8318; Web site www.kensington.com.

Does Your Back Hurt? Then Get a New Chair

If you're spending a lot of time sitting at your desk and your back hurts, you should be sitting in a chair that gives your back, neck, shoulders, and arms proper support. (I talked about Steelcase's Criterion chair in Chapter 18, "Setting Up Your Home Office.")

Chapter 20

Planning Your Business Trip

• •

In This Chapter

▶ Making plane and hotel reservations

▶ Packing your luggage efficiently

▶ Getting to the airport

▶ Spending as little time at the baggage pick-up as possible

▶ Creating an itinerary

▶ Corresponding with people at home

▶ Taking your computer along on the trip

▶ Keeping yourself safe

▶ Traveling across the border

• •

*R*ead on to find out what you need to know before you take your show on the road.

Writing an Itinerary

When you're planning your trip, write out an itinerary. In your itinerary you should include the names, addresses, and phone and fax numbers of everybody with whom you'll be meeting and the hotels at which you'll be staying. It should also include the beginning and ending times for your meetings.

Send a copy of your itinerary to each one of the people with whom you'll be meeting.

Before you leave for the airport, always call to confirm your meeting plans. You don't want to fly across the country to learn that the person you're supposed to be meeting is out of the country.

TIP

E-tickets and buying tickets online

Beware of e-tickets — especially during the busy holiday season — if you *think* you may need to change carriers. When a flight on one carrier is canceled, travelers with paper tickets can usually walk over to another carrier and have their tickets honored. Travelers with electronic tickets (tickets that are recorded in the airline's computer but aren't printed on paper) don't have such luck. They have to stand in line to get a paper ticket from their original carrier before they can get on another airline's flight.

There are a number of Web sites that offer discount airplane tickets.

Priceline — www.priceline.com — is a buying service that lets you name your price for airline tickets, and the airlines pick the flights where they have empty seats. Just post your request and guarantee your offer with a major credit card. Priceline then goes about finding a seller who decides whether or not to fill the request.

With Priceline, there is no auction, no bidding, and no back and forth. Simply name your price and let Priceline find a seller.

Other sites to visit for discount travel and hotels are:

✔ **Cheap Tickets, Inc.** — www.cheaptickets.com — is a consolidator based in Honolulu. It sells published and unpublished discount fares for flights on domestic and foreign airlines.

✔ **Best Fares Online** — www.bestfares.com — is the Web-based version of Tom Parson's *Best Fares Discount Travel Magazine.*

Purchasing Your Ticket

When you purchase your ticket, it's best to charge it to a credit card. This payment method may provide you with certain protections under federal credit regulations, which can be meaningful should the airline go on strike or declare bankruptcy.

When you receive your ticket, check to make sure that all of the information on it is correct. Fares change all the time, so check frequently to see if the cost of your ticket has gone down. If it has, you can have your ticket reissued at the lower fare.

Always try to have your tickets and boarding passes in hand before you go to the airport. This speeds your check-in process. And always reconfirm your flight a day or two before your scheduled departure. Flight schedules do change.

Making Your Hotel Reservation

When you make your hotel reservation, be specific about what type of room you want.

- ✔ Do you want a smoking or non-smoking room?
- ✔ What size, type, or kind of bed do you want?
- ✔ Can you request a location (such as a room away from the elevator and ice machine?)

If you've got any specific wants or needs, ask for them. Here are some additional questions to ask:

- ✔ What is included in the price? Breakfast?
- ✔ What are the additional charges for taxes and service?
- ✔ What do they charge for local and long-distance phone service?
- ✔ Does the view change the price? Garden view? Water view?
- ✔ What is their cancellation policy? Do they charge a fee if you don't stay for the number of days in your original reservation?
- ✔ If you're driving, do they have parking? If so, is there a charge?

When you've finished making your reservation, write down the hotel's confirmation number and ask them to fax you a written confirmation.

- ✔ If you're having trouble getting the reservation you want when calling a hotel's toll-free number, try calling the hotel directly. The likelihood that you'll get your special request is greatly increased. The best time to call would be during a *slow* time of day, usually between 10 a.m. and 3 p.m.
- ✔ Always ask for directions from the airport or train station to the hotel. If you'll be taking a taxi, ask what the estimated cost should be.
- ✔ Always confirm your reservations a few days before you're scheduled to arrive.
- ✔ Start a database of the best hotels in each city you visit. Look for hotels with multiple phone lines and jacks in each room, fax machines, late check-in, exercise rooms, and so on. ACT! is great for keeping track of this kind of information.

Book discount hotels over the Internet

Hotel Discounts (www.hoteldiscount.com) highlights some of the best hotels in 16 major cities worldwide. Just click on your destination city, and they display a visual sample of participating hotel locations, rates, and available dates. Browse as much as you like, and then make a reservation at the hotel of your choice. You can reserve a room instantly by filling out the online form or by calling their toll-free number, 800-715-7666. (International customers can contact them by voice at 214-361-7311, ext. 1128.)

Once you place your reservation, you receive an instant booking number. The hotel room and tax charges are prepaid and charged to your credit card. When you check out of your hotel, you only owe the hotel for incidental room charges. Depending on the length of your stay, you may have saved yourself hundreds of dollars.

Hotel Discounts is a *free* service. There are no membership fees or minimum night stays required.

Using the Internet to Plan Your Trip

The Internet has become a great time-saving and information gathering tool. Here is a *brief* overview of how you can use the Internet to save you time with your business and vacation travel needs.

Visit an online travel agency

These are some of the more popular Web sites from which you can plan your business and vacation travel. Think of them as your online travel agent.

- ✔ **Travelocity:** www2.travelocity.com
- ✔ **Preview Travel:** www.previewtravel.com
- ✔ **Expedia:** ww.expedia.com
- ✔ **1travel:** travel.com
- ✔ **International Travel Network:** www.itn.com

Visit your favorite airline's Web site

Would you like to plan your business trip and make your reservation with your favorite airline online? Well, here are the Web sites of the major airlines:

- ✔ **America West:** www.americawest.com
- ✔ **American:** www.americanair.com
- ✔ **Continental:** www.flycontinental.com
- ✔ **Delta:** www.delta-air.com
- ✔ **Northwest:** www.nwa.com
- ✔ **Southwest:** www.southwest.com
- ✔ **Trans World Airlines:** www.twa.com
- ✔ **United:** www.ual.com
- ✔ **US Airways:** www.usair.com

You can also check on gate information and the arrival and departure times of specific flights, as well as check on the number of miles in your frequent flyer account.

Remembering to Bring Money

When you go on a trip, you need to think about your money needs. If you're going to take cash or traveler's checks, or some of each, you *do* need to go to the bank to get some.

When you purchase traveler's checks, record the serial number, denomination, and the date and location of the issuing bank or agency. Keep one copy of this information in a safe and separate place at home and a second copy with you. (But not with your traveler's checks.) If you lose your traveler's checks, you can get replacements quickly.

Almost every major credit card can be used for purchases and cash advances worldwide. Bring along a copy of the credit card numbers, but don't keep the list with the credit cards.

If your credit cards or traveler's checks are lost or stolen, immediately notify the credit card companies and the local police.

Getting money in the event of an emergency

Take along the local telephone number for your bank so you can have money transferred to you, should you need emergency funds.

If you're in a pinch, call Western Union

If in spite of all your precautions you find yourself strapped for cash, Western Union is there to help. Call a relative or friend who can send money through Western Union. A toll-free number is available in most countries. Money will be available within minutes of its being deposited. Western Union's service is generally available seven days a week in more than 140 countries around the world.

You can obtain the local Western Union phone number before you travel by calling 800-325-6000 or checking the local phone directory of the country you're visiting.

Acquiring foreign currency

If you're traveling overseas, you need to think about your foreign currency needs.

Consider prepaying your trip in dollars before leaving the U.S. This spares you the fuss over exchanging money for your major expenses. You can probably prepay everything from your hotels, to fixed-priced meals and concerts, to city tours and museum trips.

Here are some additional thoughts about converting dollars to foreign currency:

✔ Before you depart, purchase a small amount of foreign currency to use for buses, taxis, phones, or tips when you first arrive in a foreign city. Foreign exchange facilities at airports may be closed when your flight arrives.

✔ Foreign currency can be purchased at some U.S. banks, foreign exchange firms, foreign exchange windows, or even vending machines at many international airports in the United States.

✔ Don't convert money at kiosks unless there are several of them grouped together. The lone counter is unlikely to offer competitive exchange rates.

✔ Do convert money at local banks, but ask other tourists and hotel concierges for advice on finding the banks that don't charge *exorbitant* exchange fees — on top of the conversion expenses — to exchange dollars.

✔ Don't convert money that's already been exchanged into other currencies. For example, if your trip is taking you to Great Britain, Italy, France, and elsewhere, don't change U.S. dollars into pounds, and then change pounds into lira, and then change lira into francs. Going from one currency to another can deflate your buying power by 10 percent with each transaction. Try your best to *guess* how much local currency you'll need for your stay within each country.

The Universal Currency Converter (www.xe.net/currency) allows you to perform interactive foreign exchange rate conversions on the Internet. Type the amount of source currency in the input box, then select the source and destination currencies in the output box, and click the Perform Currency Conversion button.

Packing Your Luggage

The three words "I forgot something" strike terror in the hearts of all travelers. On the following pages, you'll learn how to do a more thorough job of planning and preparing for your business and personal trips.

Make a list of everything you need to do in preparation for your trip. This list should include things you need to purchase, people you need to call, and anything else that comes to mind. As you complete each item, check it off the list.

Lay everything you *think* you'll absolutely, positively need to take with you on your bed before you start packing. Then go through each item, one by one, and put the stuff you *really* don't need back in the closet or dresser drawer.

When you're traveling in the U.S., you can probably replace anything you forget to bring with an acceptable substitute. However, when you're traveling outside the U.S., you *must* always bring everything that you'll need. Even the simplest things, the things that we take for granted, are often hard, if not impossible, to get in foreign countries.

Taking the right clothing

When you travel, give thought to the *type* of clothing you should bring along. Here are some clothing tips:

- Bring along enough underwear, socks, and nylons — one pair per day — to last the entire trip.
- Pack clothes that are neutral in color, don't show dirt, and are made of wrinkle-resistant fibers.
- Take clothes that mix and match.
- Bring two pairs of shoes. Wear one; pack one.
- Never travel with *new* shoes.
- Bring comfortable clothing to wear in your hotel room.
- If you're bringing two suits (outfits), wear one and pack one.

Tips for women

- As you're laying your outfits on the bed, try to think of everything that goes with each particular outfit: shoes, belt, stockings, slip, necklace, earrings, and so forth.

- To make your outfits look different, bring along a few extra scarves and/or blouses.

- In addition to packing enough underwear, bring some extra pairs of socks and extra pantyhose.

- For casual wear, leggings are great. They're comfortable, and they don't take up much space. (Don't bring jeans, because they're bulky.)

- Pack a comfortable pair of slippers.

- Wear or pack a pair of business shoes (black works with everything) and plan your wardrobe so that everything works together.

- Bring/wear a second pair of comfortable shoes. Make sure that both pairs have low to medium heels (up to 1 ½ inches). You want your feet to be comfortable.

- Carry a light trench coat on the airplane.

- Never pack your jewelry. Bring only a few pieces that will go with everything.

Tips for men

- Bring, or wear, one pair of dress shoes (black) and a comfortable pair of running shoes.

- Pack casual clothes, like sweats, for lounging in your room.

- Pack one suit and wear the other (if your trip is long enough to require two suits).

- When you arrive in your hotel room, hang your suits up as soon as possible. You can steam out wrinkles by hanging your suits in the bathroom and turning on the shower and running hot water for 10 to 15 minutes.

- If you don't feel like packing several suits, shirts, socks, underwear, T-shirts, and other clothing, have the hotel's dry cleaning or laundry service wash them for you. (Make sure that your company will reimburse you for this expense because it's not cheap.)

- If you're meeting new or different people every day, they won't know that you've only got two ties with you.

Packing small when it comes to toiletries

Here are some thoughts about packing toiletries:

✔ Take the smallest possible size of each of your toiletries — razor, shaving cream (or electric razor), toothbrush, toothpaste, nail clippers, deodorant, lotion, and so on. If small sizes aren't available, buy some small containers and take only as much as you need.

✔ Keep a duplicate set of your toiletries — and for women, cosmetics — packed in a travel bag. Then you'll no longer have to pack them.

✔ Place your bottles in a Ziploc plastic bag. This ensures that if they leak, they won't stain your clothes.

✔ Bring an emergency medical kit that contains your favorite painkiller, a cold remedy, an upset-stomach medicine, and Band-Aids.

✔ Bring extra Ziploc plastic bags. They are great for holding small miscellaneous things as well as wet bathing suits and leaky bottles.

Bringing along a few extras

Here's a list of some additional things you may want to bring with you on your trips:

✔ A battery-powered clock and/or clock radio.

✔ A steamer and/or a travel iron with fold-down handles. (If you don't want to bring a travel iron, you can usually borrow an iron and ironing board from the hotel.)

✔ A folding hair dryer and a curling iron. (Remember to bring along a voltage converter and plugs if you're traveling outside the U.S.)

✔ For men: a travel electric shaver with built-in $^{110}/_{220}$ volt converters.

When traveling overseas, bring a 220-volt power converter and plug adapters.

✔ A Swiss army knife — with lots of neat features — can come in handy while you're traveling.

✔ A portable radio or Walkman.

✔ An umbrella.

✔ If you can't live without coffee in the morning, bring along a small coffee kit — including little packets of instant coffee, sugar, and powdered cream — with an immersion heater.

If the value of your personal belongings is worth more than the airline's liability limit (usually $1,250 per passenger for domestic flights and $640 per bag on international trips), call your insurance agent to make sure that you will be reimbursed in the event that your luggage is lost.

Choosing carry-on items

If you'll be checking your luggage, here's a list of items that you should consider carrying with you on the plane:

- ✔ Your valuables: your cash, credit cards, traveler's checks, and jewelry.
- ✔ Your airline tickets, passport, visas, and tour vouchers.
- ✔ Your prescription medicine, over-the-counter drugs, house and car keys, and eyeglasses.
- ✔ Any important business or personal papers and anything that has sentimental value.
- ✔ Any fragile or breakable items, such as your camera, eyeglasses, contact lenses (with case and solution), hearing aid with extra batteries, and any glass containers.
- ✔ Name, address, and phone number of destination hotel, business contacts, and/or relatives at destination.
- ✔ Clothing for your first day at the destination, should you have something important to do that day.
- ✔ Always bring some toiletries and one change of underwear if you're checking your luggage. (If the airline misplaces your luggage, it may be a few days before they find it and return it to you.)
- ✔ Toothbrush and toothpaste in a Ziploc plastic bag.
- ✔ Breath mints.
- ✔ Comb and brush.
- ✔ Makeup, hair spray, styling mousse, spare earrings.
- ✔ For men, a shaving kit.

Pack your jewelry, prescription medicine, and other valuable things in a small bag and place it at the top of your carry-on bag. If, for some reason, you're required to check your carry-on bag, it's easy for you to remove your valuables and keep them on your person.

Don't pack anything in a carry-on bag that could be considered a weapon (scissors, a knife, and so on). If you're hungry, bring your own food and something to drink. It's always a good idea to bring bottled water because it's very easy to become dehydrated.

Clean out your purse or wallet and leave the stuff you don't need at home. This could include your library card, the local grocery store's check cashing card, and the health club's photo ID. Before you leave the house or your office on your way to the airport, **Check to See That You Have Your Tickets!**

Look in your briefcase, purse, travel bag, or coat pocket several times before you walk out the door and one final time before your car, taxi, or limo drives away to make sure you have the things you need.

Here are some additional travel tips:

- ✔ Get yourself luggage that has built-in wheels. It takes the lug out of luggage. (Or get yourself a wheely.)

- ✔ Instead of carrying a briefcase, bring a large tote that can double as your briefcase.

- ✔ Bring along an inflatable neck pillow. An inflatable neck pillow cushions your neck and holds your head up while you doze off on the plane.

- ✔ If you tend to perspire, you might want to pack a fresh shirt or blouse and some antiperspirant.

- ✔ Purchase carry-on bags that have large outside-zippered compartments. You can use them to store your in-flight reading material. Put your luggage in the overhead bin with the zippered compartment on top. This way, it's easy to retrieve a magazine, book, or some of your business materials.

- ✔ Use a small travel case to store all of the things that you would like to keep with you during your flight. Keep the travel case in the outside-zippered compartment of your carry-on bag. Then once you're aboard the plane, remove the case from your carry-on bag just before you place it in the overhead compartment.

- ✔ If you wear contact lenses, remove them during the flight and wear your glasses instead.

- ✔ Just before landing, take your toiletries bag with you to the washroom and freshen up.

- ✔ When you're flying in casual clothes and have an important business or social meeting planned upon your arrival or for the next day, always carry your more formal clothing with you.

- ✔ You can also store your magazines, books, and business materials in your briefcase or a small carry-on bag that fits under the seat.

- ✔ I know I'm repeating myself, but when you leave your home or office for the airport, always check one final time to see that you've got your airline ticket, your passport if you are leaving the country, and your money.

- ✔ Don't overpack luggage that you will be checking. This puts extra pressure on the latches, making it easier for them to spring open.

✔ A heavy bag that fits in an overhead bin may still cause the bin to exceed its weight limit.

✔ Lock your bags. Locks aren't very effective against determined thieves, but they make it harder for the bags to spring open accidentally.

✔ Put a bright, colorful luggage tag on the outside of your baggage. It should include your name, home address, and home and work phone numbers. Such tags will make it easy for you to spot your bags as they come down the carousel.

✔ Put your name, address, and phone number information inside each bag and add an address and telephone number where you can be reached at your destination city.

✔ Always bring something to keep you occupied: one or two good books (preferably paperback), some magazines, and a Walkman, CD player, or cassette player.

✔ Don't forget to bring all of the papers and other support material you need for your business trips.

✔ Bring expense reports, a letter-sized pad of paper, pens and pencils, a pocket tape recorder, and your detailed itinerary (including names, addresses, phone numbers, and the dates and times of your meetings). Also include a list of hotels, car rental agencies, and important phone numbers for people you may have to contact while you're out of town.

✔ Document all your expenses. Keep a daily journal of your activities and collect receipts.

✔ Leave a copy of your itinerary with your secretary, assistant, or manager; a family member or neighbor; and the people you'll be meeting with while you're out of town.

✔ Tickets, passports, cash, and credit cards are all things you can't afford to misplace.

✔ Take a photograph of your luggage, and carry the photo in your carry-on luggage. This is handy in case your luggage is lost.

Expense reporting made easy

One thing that everybody who travels hates to do is complete their expense reports. It's a dreadful, boring, and time-consuming task.

Today, many businesses are discovering they can dramatically reduce their employees travel and entertainment costs through the use of expense reporting software. Here are several programs that make this task much easier.

Xpense Management Solution from Concur Technologies

✔ Xpense Management Solution from Concur Technologies (formally Portable Software) enables you to

Prepare expense reports more easily.

Automatically populate corporate charge card and travel booking data.

Reimburse travelers more quickly.

For more information, contact Concur Technologies at 6222 185th Avenue, NE, Redmond, WA 98052; phone 800-478-7411 or 425-702-8808; Web site www.concur.com.

Employee Payables from Captura Software, Inc.

✔ Employee Payables is an automated expense management system. It was designed for large global, multidivisional companies that have complex travel policies. Employee Payables makes it easy for employees to record expenses while on the road.

The familiar, easy-to-use interface captures complex expense data at the source. Employees download credit card transactions and categorize them, enter cash expenses, and, with a few quick steps, group the transactions into an expense report and submit them.

For more information, contact Captura Software, Inc., 1629 220th Street SE, Suite 101, Bothell, WA 98021; phone 800 547 2223; Web site www.captura.com.

Extensity Expense Reports by Extensity, Inc.

✔ Extensity Expense Reports can help you immediately improve the accuracy and efficiency of your expense management process with the flexibility to meet your growing needs. Built for the Web using 100 percent pure Java, Extensity Expense Reports automates the entire expense reporting process from creation through approval and payment.

Extensity Expense Reports is easily configured to model any company's unique business processes and policies.

For more information, contact Extensity, Inc., 2200 Powell Street, Suite 400, Emeryville, CA 94608; phone; 510-594-5700 Web site www.extensity.com.

Getting to the Airport

Traffic to the airport is always troublesome, especially when you're running late, so always leave yourself some extra commuting time. If you're driving — as opposed to taking public transportation, a taxi, or limo — and are unfamiliar with the local roads, allow yourself some extra time. You could get lost along the way.

If you're going to leave your car in an airport parking lot, allow extra time to find a parking spot (most airports are short of parking). Public transportation, a taxi, or a limo may be an attractive alternative. If you frequently use the same car rental company, you may be able to leave your car in the rental company's parking lot and take the courtesy van to and from the terminal.

Once you get inside the terminal, anticipate delays at security checkpoints and passenger check-ins. Infrequent fliers always hold up the line.

Checking in at the Airport

Once you arrive at the airport, you've got to check in.

Here are some tips about checking your luggage:

- ✔ Don't check in at the last minute. Even if you make the flight, your bag(s) may not.

- ✔ Watch the agent who is checking your bags to make sure that he or she attaches a destination tag to each one. Then check to see that these tags show the three-letter code for your destination airport.

- ✔ Ask where your bags are being checked to. (They may not be checked to your final destination if you must clear customs before you reach your final destination or if you're taking a connecting flight involving two airlines that don't have an interline baggage agreement.)

- ✔ Always get a claim check for every bag that you check. Don't throw the claim checks away until your bags are returned and you have left the baggage-claim area.

- ✔ Always remove any airline tags that may still be on the bag from your last trip.

Here are some tips for checking in for your flight:

✔ Check in at least 30 minutes before your flight. Airlines can give your reserved seat to someone else even if you already have your boarding pass. (You can lose your entire reservation if you haven't checked in 10 minutes before scheduled departure time on a domestic flight. Many of today's flights are oversold, so the last passengers to check in are the first to be bumped, even if they have met the 10-minute deadline.)

If you don't check in early enough, the airline can bump you and give your seat to someone else without providing any compensation.

✔ Bring a photo ID with your name on it when you fly.

✔ After you check in, examine your ticket to make sure that the agent didn't accidentally remove two coupons.

✔ Be nice, polite, and patient with the airline ticket agent who is checking you in. He or she is the person who can help you if you've got a problem.

✔ If you need any type of assistance — you've got a sore leg or sore back and don't feel like walking to the gate — ask one of the airline employees if it's possible to have someone drive you to your gate in their oversized golf cart.

✔ If you're traveling with your children, keep a color picture of your child's face in your purse or wallet in case he or she gets lost in a crowded airport or shopping area.

✔ If you are bumped because your flight is over booked, read the Over Booking Notice in your ticket and then ask for a copy of the rules mentioned in that notice. (This information applies only to oversold flights.)

✔ If the airline offers you a free ticket, ask about restrictions. Does the ticket have an expiration date? Can it be used at any time, or are certain holiday periods blacked out? Can it be used for international flights? Do you need to follow any specific procedures when using this ticket?

Reducing Stress on the Airplane

Traveling today is a real pain in the butt. I don't care what the airlines say; all we ever do is sit and wait, and wait, and wait. We wait to board the plane. We wait for it to leave the gate. We wait for the plane to take off. We wait for it to land. And if we don't carry everything we own on board, we wait for our luggage.

With this in mind, there are a lot of things you can do to reduce the amount of time you waste in airports. The following travel tips should help to reduce the stress and strain of airplane travel.

✔ Take the earliest flight available. An early departure is less likely to be delayed because of the ripple effects of delays throughout the day.

✔ Fly Tuesdays through Thursdays, or Sunday mornings, when possible.

✔ Try not to go to the airport at the busiest times — the times when everybody else is going to the airport.

✔ Get a good travel agent and train him or her to get you the seat assignments you want.

✔ Always get your seat assignments, with boarding passes, for the entire trip.

✔ Avoid bulkhead seats. There is no seat in front of you under which to place small items you may need in flight, and parents traveling with infants are often seated there. An exit row may be a better option and usually offers more leg room.

✔ Always be one of the first people to board the plane. This will guarantee that you'll be able to store your carry-on luggage in one of the overhead bins. Then you can settle in your seat and start working while the latecomers are trying to find a place to put their bags.

✔ Bring your own food and beverage. Most airlines are cutting back on their in-flight meals (which aren't very good in the first place) and are only offering peanuts and soft drinks. (If you want to have some fun with the flight attendants, stop at a deli on your way to the airport and pick up a nice fat sandwich; it makes them go crazy.)

✔ Always have alternate plans in case of flight delays or cancellations.

Is your flight on time?

How's this for a neat tool: You're on a flight home after a long trip, and you want to find out where you are and how soon you'll be landing. So you fire up your laptop, connect to the Internet through the airplane telephone and log onto FlightTracker at www.thetrip.com. (Once you log on, select FlightTracker under Guides and Tools — the exact address is www.flight.thetrip.com/flightstatus.) In a few moments, you've an answer to your questions.

FlightTracker uses real-time flight data based on FAA radar data that shows up-to-the-minute status of all flights that are flying, have recently flown, or are about to take off between major cities within the United States. FlightTracker reports the current position of any flight, its departure and arrival airports, speed and altitude, aircraft type, current heading, nearest city, and departure and arrival times.

That's putting the power of the Internet at your fingertips!

When you need to confirm the time of an arriving or departing flight, call your airline's automated flight arrival and departure telephone number — they often include gate information — for estimated times instead of waiting for a reservations agent.

When you're traveling, expect to encounter delays in your air travel plans. Planes are always delayed because of mechanical problems, the weather, or lots of other things that the airlines never tell you about. So prepare for those delays by bringing additional work that you can do on the plane and a list of people to call if you're stuck in the airport. And in case you need to take a break, bring along some magazines, a good book, your Walkman with your favorite audiocassette, or your favorite CDs that you can play on your laptop's CD-ROM.

Staying Comfortable on the Flight

During a long — or not so long — flight your body can become quite stiff. In no time at all, you're very uncomfortable because you're confined to the small space of an airplane seat.

The combination of cramped seats that limit movement and the pressure of the seat cushions on the back of your thighs impairs circulation in the legs. This often results in swollen ankles and feet.

So here are some suggestions to help make your trip more comfortable:

- Wear comfortable clothing without a binding waistband.

- Place a small pillow in the small of your back. It gives you additional back support.

- Use an inflatable neck pillow. It gives your head and neck additional support. It also makes it easier for you to doze off or fall asleep.

- Get up from your seat and walk up and down the aisle at least once an hour. (It's easier if you've got an aisle seat.) And when you have time to kill between connecting flights, take a brisk walk through the airport.

- To prevent dehydration, drink lots of water (bring your own bottle) or caffeine-free, non-alcoholic drinks. Eight ounces an hour is a good rule. (Non-carbonated drinks reduce bloating.)

- Use saline eye drops before, during, and after the flight. If you wear contact lenses, you should wear your glasses instead.

✔ If you're tired of listening to annoying and distracting noises while you're flying, try Noise Cancellation Technologies's NoiseBuster. NoiseBuster's "anti-noisewave" technology blocks out the constant drone of the airplane's engines and lots of other unwanted sounds — like screaming children — and allows you to concentrate on your work and hear yourself think. I use NoiseBuster whenever I fly and find that I actually feel relaxed and refreshed after my flight. For more information contact Noise Cancellation Technologies, Inc., 800 Summer Street, Stamford, CT 06901; phone 800-278-3526.

Exercising in your seat

Here are exercises you can do while sitting in your seat. Do them once every hour, and they will keep you from getting stiff.

✔ Stretch your arms up.

✔ Stretch your legs out.

✔ Rotate your head.

✔ Rotate your wrists.

✔ Rotate your ankles.

✔ Flex your hands and feet.

✔ Roll your shoulders.

✔ Stretch your lower back by tucking in your stomach and bending downward.

✔ Contract and relax the muscles in your stomach.

✔ Contract and relax the muscles in your buttocks.

✔ Raise your knees one at a time to the opposite elbow.

Protecting your ears

Earaches are a common source of in-flight health problems. As the plane descends, the Eustachian tube in the middle ear tends to collapse as the outside pressure builds.

The middle ear may even become filled with fluid and become blocked. In the most severe cases, the middle ear can even rupture.

You can reduce this risk by taking a decongestant before the plane takes off and again an hour before the plane begins its descent.

If the flight is more than four hours in length, try using a nasal spray. Apply the spray 30 to 60 minutes before landing and do it a second time as the plane begins its descent.

Use the Valsalva maneuver; if your ears fail to open by themselves, try this:

1. Close your mouth.

2. Pinch your nose.

3. Force air up from your lungs into your ears.

   You should hear the middle ear click open.

This should give you temporary relief. To equalize pressure through the rest of the plane's descent, repeat the maneuver as often as is necessary.

Chewing gum is also helpful.

Getting Your Bags after Your Flight

Once you arrive, you've got to get your bags. Here are some thoughts:

- ✔ Check the baggage tags to make sure they belong to you (since so many bags look alike).

- ✔ If your luggage arrives open, unlocked, or visibly damaged, check immediately to see if any of the contents are missing or damaged. If so, report it to the appropriate airline officials.

- ✔ Report any baggage problems to your airline before leaving the airport.

To avoid long lines for taxis at major airports, hire a Skycap — even if you have only a briefcase or purse for them to carry. They usually have a deal with the taxi dispatcher who will arrange a taxi for you.

Every once in a while you may find that you've arrived at your destination but your luggage didn't. (Well, it may happen more than *once* in a while.)

Here are some tips that will help you deal with the airline if you arrive at your destination, but your luggage doesn't.

- ✔ When you're talking with the baggage clerks or other airline personnel, try to give them an accurate description of your luggage; it may make it easier for them to find it. (In an earlier tip, I suggested that you take a photo of your luggage.)

✔ Insist that the airline fill out a form and give you a copy, even if they say the bags will be arriving on the next flight. Get the agent's name and an appropriate telephone number — not the reservations number — for following up.

✔ If an airline employee or representative takes your baggage claim checks, make sure this is noted on all copies of the claim report. Keep a record of the claim check numbers.

✔ Ask the person who is helping you if arrangements can be made for the airline to deliver the bags to your hotel or home — without charge — when they are found.

✔ Ask if the airline will give you an advance or reimburse you for any items you must buy while your bag is missing.

When your luggage arrives at your hotel, open it immediately. If something is missing or has been damaged, call the airline. Make a note of the name and position or title of the person with whom you spoke, as well as the date and time of the call. Ask the person what you should do next and confirm this conversation with a certified letter.

Getting reimbursed for lost or damaged luggage

If your luggage is lost on a U.S. domestic trip (a trip starting and ending within the U.S. and not a connection to an international flight), you can receive up to $1,250 in reimbursement from the airline.

To be reimbursed, you need to notify the airline of the loss, delay, or damage to your luggage in writing within seven days of the time when you should have received the luggage. You will also need to provide receipts of your expenses. (Send your letter to the head of the airline's local office in the city where the luggage was lost. Send a copy of your letter to the airline's corporate office.)

Write a *nice* letter. When you write your letter to the customer relations office, include your frequent flyer number and go into great detail about how terribly you were inconvenienced by the loss of your luggage as you ask for compensation. You should include an itemized list of the replacement items you needed to purchase.

If your luggage was lost on an international trip, the airline's liability for loss, delay, or damage is approximately $9 per pound. (Since the average bag weighs less than 44 pounds, you may receive almost $400. The maximum liability is 70 pounds, or about $730.)

You may be able to get more money for your lost luggage if you tell the agent that your luggage contains valuables at the time you check in.

Check out your homeowners or renters insurance policy to make sure it covers your possessions when you're traveling. Many items such as jewelry, furs, cameras, and precious metals are excluded from a typical homeowners policy and must be insured specifically.

Renting a Car

Renting a car can be a big time waster, especially when you're in a hurry to leave the airport and go to your next meeting or your hotel. Here are a few tips that will help you speed up the process:

- ✔ If you know you're going to need a rental car, always call and make a reservation in advance.

- ✔ If you're going to be arriving late, call the car rental company, from the airplane if necessary, to let them know that you're still coming.

- ✔ Don't ask questions about your car rental options when you're at the reservations counter. Ask your car rental questions at the time you're making your reservation. And if you'll be using discounts, don't forget to mention it at the time you make your reservation.

- ✔ Once you are at the rental counter, avoid any changes in your reservation.

- ✔ Know your insurance needs before you book your reservation. If you're not sure whether your auto policy covers rentals, call your insurance agent or credit-card company. This is especially important if you're renting a car outside the United States.

- ✔ Reserve a rental car from several companies and pick the shorter line when you arrive at the airport. (Remember to ask if there is a penalty for not honoring your reservation at the time you book the reservation.)

- ✔ Join your favorite car rental company's express program. This enables you to avoid standing in long lines at the counter, and zip straight to your car. (Most car rental companies charge an annual fee for this program, but it may be waived if you're a frequent business traveler.)

Get off the beaten path

If you will be in need of a map or driving directions once you arrive at your destination, visit Mapquest at www.mapquest.com. Here you can find a specific place, get driving directions, print out your map, and more.

If you're looking for offbeat attractions, visit Roadside America (www.roadsideamerica.com.) This Web site is chock-full of odd and hilarious travel destinations, ready for you to explore. Their Welcome Center is designed to help you understand Roadside America and more easily navigate 500+ pages of interstate adventure. The Roadside America Web site was created by Doug Kirby, Ken Smith, and Mike Wilkins, and is loosely based on the Roadside America books written by the same three characters.

Keeping in Touch with the Folks Back Home

When you take a trip, designate one person at home as your contact person. This is the person you'll call for any messages. And tell all your family and friends that if they must get in touch with you, they should leave a message with that one person. The frequency of your calls will depend upon the nature — and length — of your personal or business travel.

Your contact person should have a copy of your schedule and itinerary, complete with hotel names, phone numbers, and fax numbers, if possible. Faxing and e-mail are convenient ways to communicate when you're many time zones away from home.

Make sure that someone knows how to get in touch with you at all times. (This may be even more important when you're traveling for fun rather than business.)

To save a lot of money, don't use the hotel phone! It's the most expensive way to make a call because hotels routinely add stiff surcharges to long-distance phone calls. Use a telephone calling card instead.

If you're traveling abroad, AT&T's USA Direct is a great service. You dial a local access number in your host country and are connected with an AT&T operator, who then connects your call in the U.S. The call is charged to your AT&T Calling Card or as a collect call to your home or business telephone. AT&T has a companion service, AT&T World Connect, which allows you to call a person in country B while you are in country A. For additional information, call your AT&T representative or 800-331-1140 before you leave the country.

You can also use e-mail to stay in touch while you're on the road. Of course, you can take your laptop with you whenever you travel, but you do have some other alternatives — like the PalmPilot or Sharp's Mobilon, which are discussed in Chapter 22 — if you don't feel like lugging it around.

Traveling with Your Computer

Computers are great, and you can do some amazing things with those 2, 3, or 4 pound laptops. But they aren't much good if they run out of juice or you can't connect them to the hotel's telephone. So when you're traveling with a computer, think about your communication needs before you leave for the airport. Here are some tips:

✔ When you make your hotel reservation, request a modem-ready room. (Most of the major hotel chains have installed modem-ready telephones.)

✔ Make sure that your laptop is fully charged when you arrive at the airport. Security personnel might ask you to turn it on to verify that it's a real computer.

✔ Always bring along a fully charged replacement battery so that you can continue working after the first one runs out of energy.

✔ Bring along a collection of extension cords so that you can use your portable computer comfortably in your hotel room. Include an extension power cord, an extension phone line cord, and extra in-line and duplex phone jacks. (When you check out in the morning, don't forget to pack everything up and take it with you.)

✔ Always travel with a screwdriver and a pocket knife so that you can remove wall plates and strip insulation from phone wires, if necessary. If you really want to be prepared, bring along an acoustic coupler to attach to your phone, alligator clips to attach your modem to phone wires, and a line tester to locate live phone wires.

✔ Always bring along some blank disks to back up your information.

✔ Put your ancillary accessories, like external floppy drives, in your luggage. You don't need to carry them with you.

Here are three tips for overseas travel:

✔ When traveling overseas, check your computer's power adapter. Make sure it can accommodate 110/120 and 220/240 voltages and line frequencies of 50/60Hz. If it doesn't, purchase a power converter.

✔ Bring along power adapter plugs that fit the electrical outlets of the countries you'll be visiting. An assortment of electrical wall plugs can be found at most computer stores.

✔ Bring along the appropriate modem-line adapter plugs.

Password protect your information

Always protect your information with a password. You should use your computer's password protection so that someone else can't even turn it on (in addition to putting a password on each of your applications).

When selecting a password, don't choose one that's easy to figure out — like the name of your wife or your daughter. On the other hand, you don't want to select a password that's so hard to remember that you have to write it down.

Protecting your computer while you're traveling

Here are some computer protection tips. They'll help you keep your computer safe and sound:

- ✔ If you're carrying a brand new, super-duper, fancy-schmancy notebook, don't flaunt it. Store it in a plain but sturdy briefcase or traveling bag so that it won't be a tempting target for thieves. Never use a laptop carrying case. It's like a billboard saying "steal this."

- ✔ Keep the computer out of sight while in the airport or on the plane — except when you need to use it.

- ✔ Keep your computer with you at all times, even when you go to the restroom.

- ✔ Password protect your computer so that it won't even boot up.

- ✔ Put a name and address on your computer if it is lost.

- ✔ Never check your computer with your carry-on luggage.

- ✔ If your hotel room has a safe and your laptop fits in it, use it! Otherwise, see if you can check it at the front desk.

- ✔ And finally, call your insurance agent, or contact your corporate insurance department, to make sure that your computer is insured.

Protecting Yourself While You're Traveling

While you're traveling, you should always be alert and aware of everything that's going on around you. You always want to be safe and secure.

Staying alert

Be very suspicious of anyone who comes up to you and remarks about something on your clothes, or who asks you a question with the intention of distracting you. Frequently, this person is part of a team. While he or she has your attention, the teammate has your wallet.

When using public transportation, be especially alert to those around you who might try to jostle you.

Here are some additional safety tips:

- Watch out for motorbikes coming up from behind. Keep your purse, if you have one, away from the street side and hang onto it as the motorbike passes. Don't let it swing loosely from your shoulder.

- Carry your belongings in a secure manner. When you're walking down a crowded street, be very careful. If you're carrying a shoulder bag, you should keep it tucked under your arm and held securely by the strap. Instead of putting your wallet in your pants pocket, wear a money belt.

- Wear an internal money pouch around your neck and under your clothes, if possible.

- Don't keep your wallet in your back hip pocket. You have no idea how easily a deft pickpocket can lift it out!

- Never leave anything, not even an umbrella, visible inside your rental car. You increase your chances of being robbed by 60 percent.

- Never leave your car unattended — or where you can't see it — when it's packed with your belongings.

You are most theft prone while visiting tourist attractions.

You don't want to make yourself an easy target, so always be wary of:

- Small groups of loiterers in parking lots, alleyways, and doorways.

- Individuals who are watching you go into a bank or ATM area.

- People who are sitting in parked cars and appear to be watching you.

- Loiterers in public places.

- People who are following you from place to place.

- People who are near you in confined areas, such as between parked cars, in passageways, subways, or garages.

- Strangers who ask you for the time or other information. They may be trying to distract you.

- People who are jostling you on buses, trains, or subways.

If you travel in places where violent theft is a possibility, carry two wallets: one for you, and one for them.

Avoiding potentially dangerous situations

To avoid a situation that could lead to a personal attack, stay away from:

- ✔ Shrubs, trees, and concealed doorways or other areas where people may hide.
- ✔ Isolated streets, parking lots, elevators, restrooms, and Laundromats, especially at night.
- ✔ Badly lit or isolated ATM machines at night.

You may want to consider carrying a personal safety aid such as a personal attack alarm, mace, or pepper spray.

Car-jacking: a story you don't want to bring home

Here are some tips so you won't become a car-jacking victim:

- ✔ Look all around you before entering your car in a parking lot or garage.
- ✔ Have your car key in hand before entering the lot or garage.
- ✔ Look in your back seat before getting in.
- ✔ Lock your car doors immediately.
- ✔ Leave space between you and the car ahead at traffic lights. This will give you room to get away should someone approach you.
- ✔ If someone does approach your car, be prepared to blare your horn, flash your lights, and step on the gas.

Don't leave anything of value in your car.

Staying safe in your hotel room

Hotels with good security never give out guest room numbers or other guest information. And the reservations clerk never announces a guest's room number or places a guest's room key with the room number side up when other people are in a position to see it.

Here are some tips to keep you safe and sound while you're in your hotel room:

✔ Never open your hotel room door without looking through the peephole first. If you don't know the person, or if the person claims to be with the hotel staff and you know you didn't send for anyone, call the front desk or hotel security to verify whether or not this uninvited visitor is who he or she claims to be.

✔ Never invite a stranger — a person you just met — into your room.

✔ If the room door has a key-type lock, insist that the cylinder be changed before accepting the room. (For additional security, you can purchase a personal alarm that fits inside the doorjamb of your room.)

✔ Always keep a good hold on your room key and make sure that, upon opening your room door, you remember to remove the key. Do not leave it dangling in your lock. If you are afraid that you may lose it while out, leave it with the desk clerk for safekeeping.

✔ Never leave exit/fire doors propped open. The doors are there to keep you safe.

✔ Never remove or disconnect the battery from your smoke detector.

✔ Don't leave your laptop or notebook computer lying around in your hotel room. Lock it in your suitcase. (You can purchase small, programmable motion detector alarms to protect your computer.) Some hotels allow you to check your computer at the front desk.

✔ Small children should always be accompanied by an adult at the hotel swimming pool, even if a hotel lifeguard is present.

✔ Never use your hotel room for business! Always conduct any business meeting in the hotel lobby, the restaurant, or the lounge.

✔ Rooms located near an exit can provide easy access for criminals.

Protecting your home while you're away

When you're away from your house, you want to keep it safe and secure. Here are some suggestions:

✔ Buy and use an alarm system, preferably with an external remote control. This kind of alarm is a small price to pay for peace of mind and the security of your family and your belongings.

✔ Check the locks on your doors and windows; replace any that aren't working properly.

✔ Use deadbolt locks — with keys on both sides on all first-floor doors.

✔ Jimmy-proof your windows. Drill a hole through the top and bottom sashes of all first-floor windows and insert a screw or bolt.

✔ Secure sliding doors. Insert a wooden pole along the inside track between the operating door and the jam.

✓ Lock the interior door to your garage.

✓ Collect all of your keys. Gather all spare keys that are hanging on hooks or nails near breakable windows. Don't hand out keys to cleaning services or other tradespeople and don't leave keys in mailboxes or planters, under doormats, or taped under your car's fender.

✓ Equip all your windows, especially double-hung windows, with locks or braces.

✓ Equip the track of sliding doors with a pin stop.

✓ Use outside lighting around your house to light hidden areas.

✓ Set your home alarm before leaving and hook it to an automatic dialer if you don't have security monitoring.

✓ Install automatic solar-sensitive or motion-detector sensors on exterior lights.

✓ Stop your paper and mail delivery when you're traveling.

✓ Ask a neighbor to remove anything thrown in your yard or in front of your door in your absence.

✓ Attach a timer to a few lights in different parts of your house.

✓ Don't close all your curtains. This usually indicates that no one is home.

✓ If you've a pool, make sure that it is covered, and that all entrance gates are locked while you are away. Use a pool alarm that sounds when anyone enters the water. This will help alert neighbors should someone sneak in for a swim.

✓ Install a ball valve on the main water line where it enters the house. This enables you to turn off the water when you leave and guarantees that your home won't flood if a pipe bursts.

✓ Leave a key and an itinerary with a trusted neighbor. Even though you canceled the mail and daily newspapers, it's a good idea to have someone check for unexpected deliveries, miscellaneous solicitations, and giveaway newspapers that have been thrown in your driveway.

Here are two final thoughts:

✓ Consider hiring a house sitter or pet sitter. Even if you don't have a pet, they can come in every few days and water your plants.

✓ Make an appointment with your local police and fire department to have someone come out and identify your home's most vulnerable safety points.

Traveling to Foreign Countries

If you are going to travel outside the United States, you will need certain travel documents. Though document requirements vary from country to country, when you leave the U.S., you need to have the following documents in order to reenter the country: a passport or other proof of citizenship, plus a visa or a tourist card. (When you enter a foreign country, you may also need evidence that you have enough money for your stay there and/or have an ongoing or return ticket.)

Getting a U.S. passport

A U.S. citizen needs a passport to depart or enter the United States and to enter and depart from most foreign countries. (Your travel agent or airline can tell you if you need a passport for the country you plan to visit.) Even if you are not required to have a passport to visit a country, U.S. Immigration requires you to prove your U.S. citizenship and identity when you reenter the United States.

These documents verify proof of U.S. citizenship:

- ✔ A U.S. passport
- ✔ An expired U.S. passport
- ✔ A certified copy of your birth certificate
- ✔ A Certificate of Naturalization
- ✔ A Certificate of Citizenship
- ✔ A Report of Birth Abroad of a Citizen of the United States

A valid driver's license or a government identification card that includes a photo or a physical description is adequate to prove your identity, but it is not proof of citizenship.

If your passport will expire within six months of your travel dates, you may not be permitted to enter certain countries. (If you return to the United States with an expired passport, you will be subject to a passport waiver fee.)

You can get a passport at one of the 13 U.S. government passport agencies, or from one of the 2,500-plus state and federal courts, or from the 900-plus U.S. post offices.

Apply for your passport several months before your trip and allow at least two additional weeks for each visa that you have requested. (It's a good idea to obtain your visas before you leave the United States because you may not be able to obtain visas for certain countries once you have departed.)

Here are some things you should know about applying for a passport:

- ✔ If you are a first-time passport applicant and are age 13 or older, you must apply in person. (Under age 13, a parent or legal guardian may appear on your behalf.)

- ✔ You can apply by mail if you were issued a passport within the past 12 years and if you were older than 18 years at the time it was issued. To apply by mail, use application form DSP-82.

To apply for a passport you need to bring:

- ✔ A completed, but unsigned, passport application (form DSP-11).

- ✔ Proof of U.S. citizenship. You can use either a previous passport or a certified copy of your birth certificate. (If you were born abroad, a Certificate of Naturalization, a Certificate of Citizenship, Report of Birth Abroad of a U.S. Citizen, or a Certificate of Birth [Form FS-545 or DS-1350] will confirm proof of citizenship.)

Establish proof of identity

You must also establish your identity to the satisfaction of the person accepting your passport application. The following items are generally acceptable documents of identity if they contain your signature and if they readily identify you by physical description or photograph:

- ✔ A previous U.S. passport

- ✔ A Certificate of Naturalization or a Certificate of Citizenship

- ✔ A valid driver's license

- ✔ A government (federal, state, or municipal) identification card

You need two photographs

Present two identical 2 inch x 2 inch black and white or color photographs of yourself taken within the past six months. They must show a front view against a plain, light background.

The fee for a 10-year passport for a first-time applicant who is over the age of 18 is $65. (The $10 execution fee is included.) For persons under the age of 18, a five-year passport costs $40. You can pay with cash, personal check, bank draft, or money order.

Hire someone to apply for your passport

There are a number of companies that will apply for a passport, obtain a visa, or process documents for international business transactions that require approval from the State Department and foreign consular offices for you. This will save you the time, trouble, hassle, and headaches of doing it yourself. They do of course, charge a fee for their services.

For more information you can contact:

✔ **Express Visa Service Inc.** 800-488-0021. They've offices in New York, Chicago, Los Angeles, Miami, and Houston.

✔ **Travisa.** 800-222-2589. They've offices in Washington, D.C.; Chicago; Detroit; San Juan, P.R.; and San Francisco.

✔ **Travel Document Systems Inc.** 800-874-5100. Their office is in Washington, D.C.

You may also apply by mail if:

✔ You have been issued a passport within 12 years prior to your new application.

✔ You are able to submit your most recent U.S. passport with your new application.

✔ Your previous passport was issued on or after your 18th birthday.

✔ You use the same name as that on your most recent passport, or you have had your name changed by marriage or court order.

To apply for a passport by mail, you'll need to obtain an Application for Passport by Mail form (Form DSP-82) from one of the offices accepting applications or from your travel agent and complete the information requested. The cost is $55. (The $10 acceptance fee is not required for applicants eligible to apply by mail.)

When you receive your passport, sign it right away!

To get more information about passports, you can order a brochure entitled "Passports: Applying for Them the Easy Way," from the Federal Consumer Information Center in Pueblo, CO 81009. The cost is 50 cents each.

Protect your passport

Your passport is the most valuable document you will carry abroad. It confirms your U.S. citizenship. Guard it carefully. When you must carry your passport, hide it securely on your person.

Do not leave it in a handbag or an exposed pocket. Whenever possible, leave your passport in the hotel safe, not in an empty hotel room or packed in your luggage. One family member should not carry all the passports for the entire family.

When you return to the U.S. and go through Immigration and Customs, have your passport and other documents — such as an International Certificate of Vaccination, a medical letter, or a Customs certificate of registration for foreign-made personal articles — ready. If you need to support your customs declaration, have your receipts available. And try to pack your luggage in such a way to make the inspection by the Customs agent easier.

Obtaining visas

A visa is an endorsement or stamp placed in your passport by a foreign government that permits you to visit that country for a specified purpose and a limited length of time. To obtain a visa, apply directly to the embassy or nearest consulate of each country you plan to visit, or consult a travel agent.

For more information about visas, write to the Consumer Information Center, Dept. 371B, Pueblo, CO 81009 to request Foreign Entry Requirements, a State Department document that outlines visa and entry requirements for every country and includes foreign embassy phone numbers. Enclose 50 cents with your request to cover copying.

Securing adequate health insurance

If you become seriously ill or are injured while you're traveling overseas, obtaining medical treatment and hospital care can be very costly. Check with your health insurance carrier before you leave the United States to see what benefits, if any, you will be provided.

If your health insurance policy does not cover you abroad, you can purchase a temporary, short-term health and emergency assistance policy. (One of the benefits that is included in a health and emergency assistance policy is coverage for medical evacuation to the United States.) To find out more about short-term health and emergency assistance policies, contact your travel agent or your health insurance company.

Bringing a letter from your doctor

If you have any preexisting medical conditions and will be traveling abroad, bring along a letter from your doctor that describes your condition. The letter should include information about any prescription medicine that you must take. With any luck, this letter will be sufficient for you to bring the medication into the foreign country.

Leave any medication in its original containers, labels and all.

Getting assistance should you become ill

Should you should become ill or be injured while you're overseas, contact the nearest U.S. embassy or consulate and ask them for a list of local doctors, dentists, medical specialists, clinics, and hospitals. If your illness or injury is serious, the consul can help you find medical assistance and can contact your family or friends and notify them of your condition. A consul can also assist in the transfer of funds from the United States.

Getting information about political problems abroad

There is a lot of political unrest in many foreign countries today. Before you leave on your trip, there are several Web sites you should visit to get the latest travel information.

- **Bureau of Consular Affairs of the U.S. Department of State:** The U.S. Department of State has received numerous inquiries from the traveling American public about overseas travel. It frequently provides Worldwide Caution and the Consular Information Sheets and Public Announcements or Travel Warnings for many foreign countries. The Department provides this information in written form so that it is consistent for every traveler and allows the traveler to make his or her own determination based on the available information. This is some of the information you will find on the Bureau of Consular Affairs Web site:

  - Travel Warnings/Consular Information Sheets

  - Services/Information for Americans Abroad

  - Travel Publications

  - Passport Information

  - Visa Services

- Judicial Assistance

- U.S. Embassy and Consulate Web sites Worldwide

So make it a point to visit the Bureau of Consular Affairs Web site at `http://travel.state.gov`.

✔ **Centers for Disease Control and Prevention:** The Centers for Disease Control and Prevention Web site has very timely information on health issues throughout the world. Geographic Health Recommendations are offered for

- Africa

- Asia

- Australia and the South Pacific

- Caribbean

- Eastern and Western Europe

- Indian Region

- Mexico, Central, and South America

- Middle East

If health issues are a concern, visit the CDC's Web site at `www.cdc.gov/travel`.

Subscribe to Kroll Travel Watch

Kroll Associates, the world's leading risk management, security, and investigations firm, has a service, Kroll Travel Watch, that provides business and leisure travelers with the critical, updated information they need for safe and hassle-free travel. Kroll Travel Watch is the world's leading source for constantly updated travel security information. It monitors on a daily basis nearly 300 cities in over 100 countries around the world.

Kroll Travel Watch distributes two-page City Advisories on demand to corporations and individuals by fax and over the Internet, 24 hours a day, 7 days a week. Clients receive only the advisories they request.

Kroll Travel Watch City Advisories provide travelers with the information they need to feel comfortable in familiar and unfamiliar destinations alike. Travel Watch helps travelers avoid threats to their personal safety and to their valuables with specific information about security alerts, health warnings, the latest airport scams, and parts of town to avoid. It also offers a wide variety of practical information about everything from standard taxi fares to the locations of airport currency exchange counters. In every City Advisory, travelers will find the following city advisory information:

- ✔ **Updated Local News Affecting Travel:** Security alerts, weather advisories, transport strikes, and more.

- ✔ **Safety and Security Considerations:** What parts of town to avoid, the best way to get around town, what to wear, and more.

- ✔ **Airport Information:** What to expect from customs and immigration, airport facilities, local scams, things to be aware of, and more.

- ✔ **Transportation to the City:** All the secure options, from taxis to public buses, with fares and trip duration.

- ✔ **Health Considerations:** Required inoculations, water quality, what foods to avoid, health alerts, and more.

- ✔ **Emergency Telephone Numbers:** Police, ambulance, embassies, and consulates.

- ✔ **Upcoming Festivals and Events:** Conventions, national and religious holidays, dignitary visits, and sporting events.

- ✔ **Average Weather, Time Zones, and Exchanges:** Average temperatures and precipitation, time zone information, and exchange rates.

For more information, contact Kroll Associates Inc., 900 Third Avenue, New York, NY 10022; phone 212-593-1000. To order a single full City Advisory via fax, call their 24-hour order line at 800-824-7502. From outside the U.S., you can call 703-319-1112. Kroll's Web site is: `www.krollassociates.com`.

A few final foreign travel thoughts

Here are a few final thoughts on foreign travel:

- ✔ **Leave an itinerary.** Leave a detailed itinerary (with names, addresses, and phone numbers of persons and places to be visited) with relatives, friends, and/or business associates in the United States so that they can reach you in an emergency. Also include a photocopy of your passport information page.

  Make a list of all your important numbers: your passport information, your credit card numbers, your traveler's checks, and airline ticket numbers. Leave a copy at home and carry a copy with you — separate from your valuables.

- ✔ **Leave your valuables at home.** Don't bring anything on your trip that you would hate to lose. Leave your expensive jewelry, family photographs, or objects of sentimental value at home.

- ✔ **Obtain a foreign driver's license and auto insurance.** Many countries do not recognize a U.S. driver's license. If you intend to drive overseas, check with the embassy or consulate of the countries you will be visiting to get information about their driver's license, road permit, and auto insurance requirements.

✔ **Bring proof of prior possession for foreign-made items.** If you're planning to take foreign-made personal articles abroad — such as watches, cameras, or video recorders — bring along proof of ownership (a receipt, bill of sale, an insurance policy, or a jeweler's appraisal). Otherwise, these items could be subject to duty and taxes when you return to the U.S.

✔ **Reconfirm Your Plane Reservations.** When traveling overseas, reconfirm your return reservation at least 72 hours before departure. If your name does not appear on the reservations list, you may not be able to get on your departure flight. When you confirm your reservations in person, ask for a written confirmation. And if you confirm it by phone, ask for the person's name and position and write down the date and time of the call.

Part VI
Technology and Time Management

The 5th Wave   By Rich Tennant

"Room service? Please send someone up to refresh the mini bar, make up the room, and defrag the harddrive."

In this part . . .

Your time management techniques need to stay in sync with changing technology. Turn to this part to get the most out of today's time management tools.

Chapter 21

Getting More Out of Your Computer

● ●

In This Chapter

▶ Dealing with disk space problems

▶ Increasing speed

▶ Adding memory

▶ Upgrading your software

▶ Bumping your modem speed

▶ Discovering what your next computer has to offer

● ●

Do you get up every morning, look at the newspaper, see that the prices for new computers keep on dropping, and kick yourself for what you paid for your present machine? I sure do. But I've gotten over it, and you should, too.

Today, you should think of your computer as a disposable item. If you can get two, or maybe three, good years of use out of it, you certainly got your money's worth. The couple of thousand dollars you spent on the machine has paid for itself in increased productivity many times over.

And when you purchase your next computer, you'll once again see that the increased speed and performance are saving you time and helping you to get more things done in less time with less effort and making you money.

When I bought my first word processor in 1988 — a dedicated word processor, not a computer — it cost me almost $2,000, plus another $500 for a sheet feeder. (Yes, that's right.) In 1990 I bought my first computer, a 386, 16Mhz machine with a 14-inch monitor and a 300 dpi printer. The whole system cost almost $4,000. What can you purchase today for $4,000?

Now don't get nervous. I'm not writing this chapter because I think you should go out and purchase a new computer this very minute. (You can, however, purchase a super-fast Pentium computer for under $1,000.)

Get the latest computer prices on the Internet

Every computer company has a Web site where you can go to get information on their newest, fanciest, and most powerful machines. Here are the Web sites of some of the most popular computer manufacturers.

- Dell: www.dell.com
- Compaq: www.compaq.com
- Gateway: www.gateway.com
- Hewlett Packard: www.hp.com
- IBM: www.ibm.com
- NEC: www.nec.com

I know this is obvious, or at least it should be, but please notice that every computer manufacturer's Web site uses its name. So you can probably guess the name of the Web site for other computer manufacturers.

Also, every computer magazine has its own Web site where you can go to read about the newest hardware and software products. Here are some of the more popular sites:

- CNET: www.cnet.com
- ZIFF-DAVIS: www.zdnet.com
- PC Magazine: www.zdnet.com/pcmag
- Windows Magazine: www.winmag.com

I'm writing this chapter because there are a lot of things you can do with your present machine to improve its performance without replacing it. At some point, you will have to replace it, but you may be able to put off the new purchase for a year; by then, computers will be even cheaper.

(Later in this chapter I tell you what bells and whistles I think you should consider adding to your next computer.)

If you're wondering why I'm including information on computers in a time management book, the answer is easy: When you're sitting at your computer and waiting for the machine to complete a task, like sorting a database, performing a mail merge, or redrawing the screen when you're using your graphics program or surfing the Internet, you're wasting time. And since time is money, you should get the most out of your computer.

Some of the things I mention in the next few pages are a bit technical. If you're not familiar with the insides and inner workings of a computer, don't try to do any of these things yourself. Just invite your favorite computer guru over for dinner, and then casually ask him or her to help you with a little project.

If You're Still Using a 486 or An Early Pentium, It's Time to Replace It!

OK, I lied. You should get nervous. If you're still using an old 486, or a not-quite-so-old Pentium computer — and you're not running Windows 95/98 — you don't have to read any further. Your machine is too old to be saved. It just doesn't have the horsepower to take you into the 21st century. It's like driving an old car. It may take you where you want to go, but you'll get there very S-L-O-W-L-Y, and it might break down along the way.

If time is money, why waste it waiting for computer screens or Web pages to appear on your computer monitor? I suggest you immediately turn to the section "Bells and Whistles for Your Next Computer," later in this chapter.

If You Need More Disk Space, Get a New Hard Drive

If you don't have enough disk space on your hard drive — today's new computer programs have so many bells and whistles that they can easily take 50, 100, or 150 megabytes of hard disk space — you can replace your old drive with one of those new, huge 6-, 10-, or 15-gigabyte disk drives.

You can of course add a second disk drive to your computer, but it's my suggestion that you replace your old disk drive with a new one. In addition to the fact that the new drives are so much bigger, they also read and write data to the hard drive much faster. As a result, your whole system runs faster.

Seagate Technology makes a complete line of hard disk drives. Its newest drive, the Medalist PRO 9140 (ST39140A), has a capacity of 9.1GB, a 9.5 millisecond seek time, and a spindle speed of 7200 RPM. It uses Seagate's Ultra ATA technology and can transfer data from the hard drive to the computer's central processing unit (CPU) at speeds of up to 33.3MB/second.

Look at what's happened in just a few years. Hard-drive capacity has increased ten-fold, and the speed at which data is transferred from the hard drive to the computer has doubled. In 1995, when I wrote the first edition of *Time Management For Dummies,* Seagate's newest drive was the Decathlon 850 (ST5850A). It had a capacity of 850MB and transferred data from the hard drive to the computer's central processing unit at speeds of up to 16MB/second.

Norton Ghost makes copying everything that's on your old hard drive onto your new hard drive easy

Norton Ghost is a software utility program that enables you to copy everything that is on your old hard drive — including the partition tables, operating system, programs, and data files — onto your new hard drive in just a few minutes.

Norton Ghost automatically takes care of some of the most time-consuming aspects of installing and configuring a hard drive. This includes dynamically resizing FAT12, FAT16, FAT32, and NTFS (a file system developed for the Windows NT operating system) partitions as needed.

It also performs disk formatting on the fly — manual procedures involving the FDISK and FORMAT commands are a thing of the past. And when the source and target hard drives are different sizes, Norton Ghost automatically adjusts the position and size of the partition tables.

For more information about Norton Ghost, contact Symantec Corporation, 10201 Torre Ave., Cupertino, CA 95014; phone 800-441-7234. Its Web site is www.symantec.com/ghost.

Installing the Seagate drive in your computer is rather easy. (However, you may want to have your local computer guru do this for you if you're not familiar with the inner workings of your computer.) The instructions that came with the hard drive are very thorough and comprehensive.

Before you do anything with your computer, always call tech support just to see whether there's anything additional you should know. This will help keep you out of trouble.

With a new Seagate hard drive, you'll find that your many programs — your word processor, spreadsheet, graphics and design programs, and everything else you use on your computer — run faster because the access time, the time it takes to read and write information from the hard drive to the computer's memory, is much faster.

The faster your hard drive sends data to your computer's CPU, the more productive you are.

For more information, contact Seagate Technology, 920 Disk Drive, Scotts Valley, CA 95066. To find your nearest Seagate dealer, call 800-468-3472. You can also learn about Seagate's newest products by visiting its Web site at www.seagate.com.

Your Screen Redraws Faster with a New Video Card

If you think that all of your programs are running just a bit too slowly, or if you've just gotten into Web-based multimedia, or you're trying to watch CD-ROM or DVD movies, and everything appears on your screen in slow motion, it may not be your computer that's slowing you down. It may be your video card. Even though you just purchased a super-fast computer, the computer manufacturer may have installed last year's video card, one with only 2MB of memory, in order to keep the price down.

Today's video cards can really make your computer fly. I replaced my old video card with an ATI Technologies ALL-IN-WONDER PRO with 8MB of memory. When I turned my computer on, I couldn't believe how much faster it ran. I didn't notice too much of a difference when I was working in my word processor, because the screen doesn't redraw itself that frequently. But when I started working on my *ACT! in ACTion* newsletter in Adobe PageMaker, a page layout program, I discovered that the images on the screen redrew themselves — in 16 million colors — so fast that I was actually working in real time.

I would have to estimate that my graphics programs are now running several times faster than they were before. It's also done the same thing for my CD-ROMs. And, if you're one of those people who like to play games on your computer, a faster video card will make a world of difference.

These are some of the other things you can do with ATI's ALL-IN-WONDER PRO video card:

- ✔ **Watch TV.** The TV tuner displays cable or broadcast television on the whole screen or in a window.

- ✔ **Capture video images.** You can capture full-color, 24-bit-per-pixel still images from MPEG movies, your camcorder, or television, save them onto your hard drive, and print them.

- ✔ **Capture full-motion video and audio.** You can use the "Digital VCR" to capture a stream of full-motion video plus audio from your video source and save it as an .AVI file.

- ✔ **Play and edit video and audio clips.** Once you've captured a video or audio clip, you can play it back or edit it.

For more information about the ATI Technologies ALL-IN-WONDER PRO graphics card, contact ATI Technologies Inc., 33 Commerce Valley Drive East, Thornhill, ON, Canada L3T 7N6. The phone number for its sales and marketing department is 905-882-2600. ATI's Web site is www.atitech.com.

Improve Your Vision with a New Monitor

If you're using an old monitor or your current monitor is smaller than 17 inches, it may be time to give the old one away and buy a new one. A new monitor can make a world of difference to your daily productivity. If you have to overconcentrate to read the words on your monitor because of either low resolution or small screen size, the muscles in your neck and shoulders become tense — and you get tired. With a new 17-, 19-, or 21-inch monitor, there will be such a substantial increase in your productivity that it will pay for itself in a matter of weeks.

When I recently upgraded my computer, I replaced my old 17-inch monitor with a NEC E900+ 19-inch color monitor (which has an 18-inch viewable image size).

I didn't know what I had been missing until I plugged the monitor into my computer and turned it on. The first things I noticed were the increases in size, clarity, and brightness.

Furthermore, NEC's flat, square screen provides an edge-to-edge viewing area. And its digital on-screen controls allow fine-tuning of nearly every aspect of the monitor's images. This includes size, position, brightness, and contrast.

The MultiSync E900+ is designed for corporate, small-office, and performance-driven home users who want a larger viewable image size but do not have the space or budget for a larger monitor.

NEC makes a complete line of monitors, the newest of which are its True Color LCD Flat-Panel monitors. These monitors are ideal for people who require superior image quality but work in an environment with space and weight constraints. (The MultiSync LCD 2000, for example, is a 20.1-inch monitor that weighs only 22 pounds and has a depth of less than 9 inches.)

For more information about NEC monitors, contact NEC Technologies, Inc., 1250 N. Arlington Heights Dr., Suite 500, Itasca, IL 60143-1248; phone 800-632-4636 or 630-775-7900. NEC's Web site is www.nec.com.

Your Computer Runs Faster When You Add More Memory

Earlier in this chapter, I mention the importance of using a memory manager to make your computer run more efficiently. One of the productivity-improving features of Windows is that it enables you to run three, four, five, or more programs simultaneously if you have enough memory. Needless to say, the more memory you have, the faster these programs run.

If your computer has only 16 or 32MB of memory, it's time to call your computer guru friend and invite him or her over for dinner. After dessert, you can ask your "guest" to put some more memory into your computer. It's not difficult to do, if you know what you're doing.

The price for additional memory continues to drop. Go out and increase your computer's memory to 64MB or 128MB. You'll see the difference in increased performance the moment you turn your computer on.

Improve Your Productivity by Upgrading Your Software

Whenever the developer of your favorite program releases a new version, you should go out and buy a copy. (The developer will let you know about it because you'll get a postcard in the mail every day for at least six months.) These bells and whistles will help you get your work done more quickly.

And that's why we use these machines so much: because we want to produce high-quality work, keep all our clients and customers happy, and then go home for dinner.

Take the time to learn how to use your software. Studies have shown that most computer users use only 15 percent of the features in each of their programs.

Get Yourself a Fast Modem

If you really want to expand your horizons, increase your knowledge, improve your productivity, and give yourself access to an almost unlimited amount of information, get yourself a fast modem and explore the World Wide Web.

Throughout this book, I make references to every company's Web site and list many Web sites that I thought had relevant information. If you're not on the Internet, you are truly missing out on a wonderful resource.

3Com's U.S. Robotics division is the world's leading modem manufacturer. U.S. Robotics makes every kind of internal and external modem. Its product line includes the following modems:

- **56K Faxmodem:** These modems support the new V.90 modem standard.
- **56K Voice Faxmodem:** These modems incorporate voice capabilities, such as voice mail and speaker-phone, into the modem.

- ✔ **V.Everything:** These 56K small-office and home-office modems support business applications — such as remote configuration, dial security, and LAN access with remote control — as well as the local telephone company's Caller ID and Distinctive Ring features.

- ✔ **I-Modem ISDN with V.Everything:** This modem offers ISDN connectivity (at speeds of up to 128 Kbps), plus state-of-the-art analog modem technology and all of the features of the V.Everything modem for the small office and home office.

- ✔ **Megahertz Modem PC Cards:** The Megahertz series offers a large selection of PCMCIA LAN, 56K, and ISDN modem cards for laptop and notebook computers.

To get more information about 3Com's U.S. Robotics modems and the company's other products, contact 3Com Corporation, P.O. Box 58145, 5400 Bayfront Plaza, Santa Clara, CA 95052; phone 800-638-3266 or 408-326-5000; Web site www.3com.com.

Bells and Whistles for Your Next Computer

When you're ready to buy a new computer, read this section for the list of the bells and whistles that I recommend you buy. As far as brand names go, there are many good ones. But remember, the quality of service that the manufacturer or computer store offers is of primary importance.

I feel that the quality of the service offered by a computer store is even more meaningful than low price, because when you've got a question or have a problem, you want to be able to talk with someone who can help you.

I've been buying my computers from EOM Office Systems, Inc. in suburban Chicago for years. Rich Barkoff, EOM's owner, has always given me great service. He's probably forgotten more about computers than I'll ever know. If you need some computer assistance, give Rich a call at 847-647-7304 or visit his Web site, www.eomoffice.com. EOM Office Systems, Inc. is located at 7314 N. Milwaukee Ave., Niles, IL 60714.

That said, here are the bells and whistles I would get in a new computer if money weren't an issue. (But since it probably is, you'll just have to decide which features are more or less important to you.)

Here's some advice about the features to look for in a desktop computer:

- ✔ Get a fast computer. Look into getting the fastest processor chip that is available. This will ensure that your computer will last for two or more years. You'll never be disappointed when you buy a fast computer.

✔ Add lots of memory. Today you need a minimum of 32MB just to get your computer to run. Increase your computer's memory to 64MB, 128MB, or higher. You'll thank yourself each time you turn on the machine.

✔ Include a huge hard drive. You should get at least a 6GB (Gigabyte) hard drive. And for just a little more money, you may want to install a 10- or 15GB hard drive.

✔ Put in a fast video card. Get a video card with at least 8MB of memory. Your graphics programs, CD-ROMS, and games will fly across your screen.

✔ Get a big monitor. When we started using computers, we had these itty-bitty black-and-white (or was it green?) monitors. Today there are 15-, 17-, 19- and 21-inch monitors that display 16 million colors. Treat yourself to a 17-, 19-, or 21-inch monitor and make sure the dot-pitch rating is less than 0.28 millimeters. (The lower the better.) You'll thank yourself for it.

✔ Get a fast CD-ROM. The first CD-ROMs were slow, and it took a lot of time to transfer information from the CD-ROM to the computer. Along came double-speed, triple-speed, and quadruple-speed CD-ROM drives. Today you've got 40-speed CD-ROM drives.

As an alternative to purchasing a CD-ROM, you may want a Digital Video Disk (DVD). A DVD is like a CD-ROM, except it can hold 25 times as much data. DVDs enable you to watch theater-quality, full-length movies on your computer.

✔ Don't forget a sound card with high-quality speakers. If you're going to be using your CD-ROM or downloading multi-media files from the Internet, you need a good sound card and great speakers. Your system should sound as good as the graphics look.

✔ To communicate with the outside world, you need a high-speed modem. Three years ago, we were happy with 14,400bps (bits per second) modems. Last year 28,800bps modems were the rage, and now everybody's using 56K modems.

✔ Most importantly, your computer is the gateway to the Internet and the World Wide Web, so you should give serious consideration to utilizing an ISDN, DSL, or cable connection.

✔ Protect yourself with an automatic backup program. You've got to back up your data on a regular basis. Backup programs are discussed in Chapter 25.

When looking for a laptop computer, you're probably not going to find the perfect computer. In a laptop, you're going to have to make trade-offs and compromises. Here is a list of the things you should consider when purchasing a laptop computer:

- ✔ Price
- ✔ Weight
- ✔ Dimensions (height, length, and depth)
- ✔ Speed of the microprocessor
- ✔ Amount of RAM
- ✔ Battery life
- ✔ Size of the keyboard
- ✔ Size of the hard drive
- ✔ Size of the display screen
- ✔ Speed of the CD-ROM
- ✔ Speed of the modem

As you look at the features that are available in the different laptop computers, all you've got to do is determine which features are more or less important to you and then weigh that against the price. Good luck!

Chapter 22

Handheld Personal Computers: The New Time Management Tool

*T*he hottest products on the market today are handheld personal computers. These lightweight personal computers enable you to keep track of your schedule, read your e-mail, surf the Web, and much much more.

In this chapter, I tell you about three of the most popular handheld personal computers: the 3Com's PalmPilot, Sharp's Mobilon, and Franklin's REX PRO.

The PalmPilot

For many people, the PalmPilot organizer has changed their life. (There are now more than 1,500,000 PalmPilot users.) They carry it everywhere they go. They love it because it enables them to take their name and address book, to-do lists, important phone numbers, passwords, train and flight schedules, and just about everything else that's important to them wherever they go.

The PalmPilot enables you to take all the information you used to carry around in your big, bulky paper organizer — or notebook computer — and put it into a 7-ounce personal computer that's 4.7 inches tall, 3.1 inches wide, and less than an inch thick. It fits in your shirt pocket and runs on two AAA batteries that can power it for up to a month.

The basic PalmPilot includes these features:

✔ **Name and Address Book:** In the name and address book, you can store, organize, and easily locate thousands of names, phone and fax numbers, and e-mail addresses. It holds about 6,000 addresses.

✔ **Appointment Book:** In the appointment book, you've instant access to your agenda for today, tomorrow, and any date in the future. You can schedule recurring meetings, scan for open time slots during the week, attach notes to appointments, and schedule alarms. It holds about 3,000 appointments, which should cover the better part of the next 5 years.

✔ **To Do List:** The interactive To Do list lets you prioritize your daily tasks. Sort items by priority or due date, check off items you've completed, and carry forward those you haven't. You can store about 1,500 to-do items.

✔ **Memo Pad:** With the Memo Pad, you no longer need to make mental notes. You can store about 1,500 memos in the PalmPilot.

✔ **Expense Reporting:** You can capture and track expenses as they occur and then automatically transfer them into an Excel (5.0 or higher) expense-report form or your company's expense template when you synchronize by using the PalmPilot's HotSync technology.

✔ **HotSync Desktop Synchronization:** With the PalmPilot's HotSync Desktop Synchronization feature, you can synchronize your PalmPilot with your PC — in both directions — with the touch of the HotSync button.

You can synchronize your PalmPilot with ACT!, Outlook, Schedule+, Lotus Organizer, Goldmine, and many other contact managers.

The PalmPilot has become a platform for 10,000+ software developers

The best thing about the PalmPilot is that it has become a platform from which about 10,000 software developers have written software.

There are hundreds of Web sites that are devoted exclusively to the PalmPilot. On these sites they offer links to the thousands of third-party add-on products that work with the PalmPilot. Here are three that I found to be extremely helpful:

✔ Pickled PalmPilot: `www.pickled.com`

✔ PalmCentral.Com: `www.palmcentral.com`

✔ PalmtopPlanet: `palmtopplanet.interspeed.net` (There is no `www.` in this address.)

With your PalmPilot and Smartcode Software's HandMAIL software, it's easy to send and receive your e-mail. (You do of course need a PalmPilot modem.) Just download the HandMAIL software from Smartcode's Web site — a free demo version is available — and install it on your PalmPilot. Within minutes, you'll be sending and receiving e-mail from your PalmPilot. For more information, visit Smartcode's Web site at `www.smartcodesoft.com` or contact Smartcode Software, Inc., 5355 Mira Sorrento Place, Suite 100, San Diego, CA 92121; phone 619-597-7544.

For more information about the PalmPilot, visit its Web site at `www.palmpilot.com`. PalmPilot, a 3Com Company, is located at 1565 Charleston Road, Mountainview, CA 94043. Its customer service number is 888-619-7488.

Sharp's HC-4600 Color Mobilon

Sharp Electronics offers a full line of Mobilon products and accessories that give you added flexibility when in the office or on the road. Its Color HC-4600 Mobilon handheld personal computer (H/PC) is the perfect companion for the mobile professional. Here are some of its features:

- ✔ **Built-in Modem:** The built-in 33.6/9.6 Kbps data/fax modem enables you to send and receive e-mail, send faxes, and browse the Web.

- ✔ **Voice Recording:** The voice recording feature lets you record voice memos, even when the Mobilon is off or closed.

- ✔ **One-Touch Application Keys:** The Mobilon's One-Touch application keys make it easy for you to quickly launch your programs.

- ✔ **16MB Memory:** The Mobilon comes with 16 JJM/MB Memory and can be upgraded to 32MB.

- ✔ **IrDA Infrared Port:** Data can be transferred/synchronized through the Mobilon's infrared port.

- ✔ **PC Link Cable and Synchronization Software:** The Mobilon can also be connected to your PC with the bundled PC link cable. Once linked, it's easy to transfer and synchronize information with Microsoft Office.

The Sharp Mobilon comes with Microsoft Windows CE and includes these Microsoft Handheld PC applications: Pocket Word, Pocket Excel, Pocket Outlook (Calendar, Contacts, Tasks, Inbox), Pocket PowerPoint, and Pocket Internet Explorer.

The HC-4600 Color Mobilon also includes Sharp Exclusive software that is designed to make you more productive. These programs includes a PC File Viewer, Photolink image management software, and software that enables you to send and receive faxes.

With Sharp's Color Digital Camera Card (optional) and the Mobilon's built-in fax/modem, you can take digital photos with your Mobilon and send the images — with text and/or voice messages — over Internet e-mail. The images can also be transferred to your PC.

For more information, contact Sharp Electronics Corporation, Sharp Plaza, Mahwah, NJ 07430-2135; phone 800-BE-SHARP or 201-529-8200; Web site www.sharp-usa.com.

Franklin's REX PRO PC Companion

Franklin's REX PRO is a 1.4-ounce credit-card-size electronic organizer (3 ⅜ inches x 2 ⅛ inches). The REX PRO enables mobile professionals to view, enter, or edit appointments, contact information, to-do's, and memos on the go with Starfish's patented SuperKey Light Data Entry System.

It has 512K of RAM memory and can hold up to 6,000 records.

The REX PRO also includes Starfish's TrueSync Plus software for direct synchronization with ACT!, Outlook, Schedule+, Lotus Organizer, and Sidekick 98.

This is what REX PRO enables you to take with you when you leave the office:

- ✔ **Your calendar:** The REX PRO stores daily and recurring events with alarms to keep you on time, all the time.

- ✔ **Your contacts:** You'll have shirt-pocket access to every important phone number and address.

- ✔ **Your to-do/call list:** You'll have a complete list of all the things you need to do and the people you need to call.

- ✔ **Your memos:** You can download talking points, proposals, or outlines for easy reference when you're on the go.

This is how you use the REX PRO:

1. Enter your appointments, address book, and to-do's in your favorite contact manager.

2. Plug the REX PRO into your laptop's PC-Card slot. (Desktop users can synchronize data by using the REX PRO's serial docking station that is connected to a PC serial port.)

3. Run the TrueSync Plus software to synchronize your address and schedule information with your contact manager.

4. Remove the REX PRO from your laptop, or the serial docking station, put it in your pocket, and walk out the door.

For more information about the REX PRO, visit Franklin Electronic Publishers' Web site at www.franklin.com/rex or contact Franklin Electronic Publishers, One Franklin Plaza, Burlington, NJ 08016-4907; phone 800-266-5626.

Chapter 23

Software That Will Save You Time

. . . .

In This Chapter

▶ Discovering software that shaves time off your day

▶ Getting more out of software you may already have

. . . .

Since this is a book about time management, and I'm a time-management expert, I thought it would be appropriate to tell you about some of the computer programs that I use to save me time and help me be more productive. (I know that I'm not supposed to be writing in the first person, but these are the programs that help me, and I'm sure that they can help you.)

Corel WordPerfect

I've been using WordPerfect word processors for years, and I think they're great! I wrote my first three books with WordPerfect 5.1 for DOS, my next five were written with Corel WordPerfect 6.1 for Windows, and this book was written with Corel WordPerfect 8. (I know that almost everybody — or maybe it just seems that way — is using Microsoft Word, but I've found WordPerfect to be much easier to use.)

The productivity-improving features in Corel WordPerfect 8 enable me to spend all my time and energy writing. I don't have to be concerned with the layout or format of the text because WordPerfect does it for me.

Corel WordPerfect is part of the Corel WordPerfect Suite. The Suite includes the following programs:

- ✔ Corel WordPerfect, the word processor.
- ✔ Corel Quattro Pro, a spreadsheet program.
- ✔ Corel Presentations, a presentation program.
- ✔ CorelCentral, a program that offers group scheduling and contact management. You can also use it to send and receive e-mail.

For more information, contact Corel Corporation, 1600 Carling Ave., Ottawa, Ontario, Canada, K1Z 8R7; phone 800-772-6735 or visit the company's Web site at www.corel.com.

ACT!

ACT! runs my life. It's the first computer program I turn on in the morning and the last one I turn off in the evening. By using it, I have been able to automate all of my follow-up tasks — my calls, meetings, and to-do lists — and it has improved my daily productivity three- or fourfold.

In Chapter 5, I explain how you can use ACT! to automate your appointment book, calendar, and Rolodex file. If you haven't read this chapter, I suggest you do so now.

For more information about ACT!, contact Symantec Corporation, 10201 Torre Ave., Cupertino, CA 95014; phone 800-441-7234; Web site www.symantec.com/act.

DAZzle

DAZzle is one of those utility programs that I just can't live without. DAZzle is an envelope- and label-printing program that makes it easy for you to design and print envelopes, labels, and flyers on any size paper.

With just a click of your mouse, you select where you want the return and main addresses to appear. Then you can import graphic images, include messages, and add POSTNET bar codes to the mailing address. (POSTNET bar codes are the ZIP+4 bar codes that identify the destination of the mailing piece: the zip code, delivery point, and carrier route. The presence of the POSTNET bar code is important because your letter will be handled with electronic sorting equipment and will be processed more quickly.)

DAZzle can import information directly from ACT!, other contact management programs, and your word processor, so you don't even have to play the paste-and-cut game. And if you have the person's ZIP+4 zip code, DAZzle prints the POSTNET bar codes on the label or envelope.

Oh, you don't have the ZIP+4? Not to worry! DAZzle has a great feature called Dial-A-ZIP. Once you've imported an address into DAZzle, DAZzle's Dial-A-ZIP dials into a ZIP-Station, a remote CD-ROM directory of addresses in the United States; or logs onto an Internet site.

After it makes a connection, DAZzle gets the ZIP+4 zip code, adds it to the address on your envelope, and updates the person's zip code in your contact management program. The whole process takes about 20 seconds.

For more information about DAZzle, contact Envelope Manager Software, 247 High Street, Palo Alto, CA 94301-1041; phone 800-576-3279; Web site www.envelopemanager.com.

Quicken

Quicken has enabled me to automate all of my financial record keeping. It keeps track of my bank balances, it prints my checks, it categorizes all of my financial transactions (my tax preparation costs have gone down by more than 50 percent), and it helps me stay on top of all my saving and investment programs.

For many people, Quicken has been a reason to go out and buy a computer, and I heartily agree.

For more information about Quicken, contact Intuit, P.O. Box 3014, Menlo Park, CA 94026; phone 800-624-6095; Web site www.intuit.com.

QuickBooks

If you run a small business, you need an easy-to-use accounting program, and Intuit's QuickBooks can help you take care of all your financial record keeping. You can use it to perform the following tasks:

- ✔ Write your checks.
- ✔ Keep your check register.
- ✔ Create and print your invoices.
- ✔ Show the aging of your accounts receivable.
- ✔ Keep track of your accounts payable and balance sheet — your assets, liabilities, and net worth.
- ✔ Create hundreds of different types of reports.

For more information about QuickBooks, contact Intuit, P.O. Box 3014, Menlo Park, CA 94026; phone 800-624-6095; Web site www.intuit.com.

Adobe's PageMaker

Adobe's PageMaker is a high-end desktop publishing program. Anything you want to do with the printed word, or a graphic image, can be done with PageMaker.

✔ You can use PageMaker to create any type of publication, be it an advertisement, a 2-page newsletter, a 500-page book, or a 4-color magazine.

✔ You can create your Web pages with PageMaker, and your own PDF documents. (PDF is an abbreviation for Adobe's Portable Documents Format. PDF documents are fully formatted documents that can be read in Adobe's Acrobat Reader, which is available as a free download from Adobe's Web site.)

I've been using PageMaker for years, and I've found it to be a very powerful desktop publishing program.

For more information about PageMaker and Adobe's other desktop publishing products, including Adobe Illustrator and Adobe Photoshop, contact Adobe Systems Incorporated, 345 Park Ave., San Jose, CA 95110-2704; phone 408-536-6000; Web site www.adobe.com.

AddressGrabber

AddressGrabber helps you to magically copy name and address information from your favorite PIM or contact management program — such as ACT!, Goldmine, Lotus Organizer, and Maximizer — with other programs such as QuickBooks, FedEx Ship, Eudora Pro, Outlook, and Outlook Express.

Just select a record in your PIM or contact manager, click the icon of the program into which you want the name added on AddressGrabber's toolbar, and it magically copies the name and address information into another program.

For more information, contact ProdEx Technologies, 14471 Big Basin Way, Suite E, Saratoga, CA 95070; phone 408-872-3102; Web site www.prodexusa.com/addressgrabber.

ClipMate

ClipMate is a utility that enables you to save and store items that you have copied to the Windows clipboard for future use.

ClipMate makes the Windows clipboard easier to use because it remembers all the items (both text and graphics) that are copied to it. ClipMate then stores them in "collections" for later pasting.

You can, for example, use ClipMate to record all of your personal information, such as your name, address, phone, e-mail address, and so on, so when you register on a new Web site you don't have to retype the same information over and over again.

For more information, contact Thornsoft Development, P.O. Box 26263 Rochester, NY 14626; phone 716 352-4223. You can receive a free 30-day evaluation copy from its Web site at `www.thornsoft.com`.

Chapter 24

Keeping Your Computer Healthy

*F*or most of us, our entire business and personal lives are contained inside our computers. All of our letters, memos, presentations, spreadsheets, and other documents are stored on our hard drives. And we keep all the names, addresses, phone numbers, and e-mail addresses in our personal information managers and contact managers.

But what would you do if something happened to your computer? Hard drives crash every day, and computer viruses can contaminate an entire computer system, making everything unusable, in a matter of minutes.

In this chapter, I tell you about some steps you can take to keep your computer healthy. Keep your computer safe, and you'll save yourself lots of time because you won't ever have any downtime due to the loss of your important data.

Norton Utilities Keeps Your Computer Healthy

Norton Utilities is an integrated suite of programs that can help you find and fix computer problems and improve your computer's performance. It will help you keep your computer in good condition, warn you of potential problems before they become apparent, and minimize your downtime should something go wrong.

These are the programs that will find and fix your computer's problems:

- ✔ Norton WinDoctor checks your system for problems.

- ✔ Norton CrashGuard monitors your system so it can alert you to application crashes as they happen, thus enabling you to save your data before closing your programs.

- ✔ Norton Disk Doctor monitors your hard drive for potential problems.

- ✔ UnErase Wizard recovers deleted files that are protected by Norton Protection, the standard Windows Recycle Bin, or Novell's Salvage (for recovery of files on a network).

- ✔ Norton File Compare compares any two versions of a text file — such as a Windows initialization (INI) file — in order to see what has changed between versions, and selectively undo changes.

These are the programs that are designed to improve performance:

- ✔ Speed Disk defrags and rearrange files for faster access. It also defrags and optimizes the Windows swap file.

- ✔ Norton Optimization Wizard fine-tunes your PC so that applications load faster.

- ✔ Space Wizard identifies files that aren't needed, are used infrequently, or are excessively large. It can also locate duplicate files for you.

Defragment your hard drive once a week

The more you use your computer, the more your hard drive becomes fragmented. (Really, it's not as scary as it sounds.)

When you create a new file — a word processing document, for example — your computer places it somewhere on your hard disk. As you edit and add new material to the document, the file grows in size and becomes larger than the original space in which it was stored. So the computer's thrifty operating system splits the file up into two or more pieces and places them in open spaces elsewhere on the disk drive.

Over time, many of your files become fragmented, that is, split into many pieces,

especially the ones you use and/or make changes to every day. As a result, your computer slows down because it takes longer to gather all the parts of the file when you want to open it.

Norton Utility's Speed Disk analyzes each file on your hard drive. It then takes all the parts of a file that are stored in different places on the disk and places them in one spot on your hard disk. When it's finished, you have a neat, orderly hard disk.

You should make it a point to run Speed Disk at least once a week.

These are the programs that are designed to perform preventive maintenance:

- ✔ Norton System Doctor continuously monitors your computer for problems.

- ✔ Rescue Disk enables you to save and restore your PC's critical setup data.

- ✔ Image saves a "snapshot" of your disk's critical information.

- ✔ Norton Registry Tracker tracks changes to your computer's Registry and other critical files. This utility gives you the ability to restore previous versions of these files should a problem arise.

These are the programs that help you see what's going on inside your computer:

- ✔ System Information tells you everything about your computer. This includes information about your monitor, printer, memory, and lots more.

- ✔ Norton Registry Editor makes it easy for you to manage the Windows registry. You can edit, search, import, and export registry information, as well as track and undo registry changes.

- ✔ Norton Web Services is a subscription-based service that provides a growing library of Web-based utilities like LiveUpdate Pro, which finds and installs the latest updates and bug fixes ("patches") for many of your computer's software programs and device drivers.

I think everyone should have a copy of Norton Utilities. I use it every day, and it helps to keep my computer's disk drive in tip-top shape.

For more information about Norton Utilities, contact Symantec Corporation, 10201 Torre Ave., Cupertino, CA 95014; phone 800-441-7234; Web site `www.symantec.com/nu`.

Protect Your Computer from Viruses

A computer virus is an infectious computer program that makes your computer do weird things. Some viruses are nothing more than mere annoyances that display cute, or not-so-cute, messages.

Other viruses can be very destructive. They lie in wait until a particular date, and then they go on a rampage and destroy files. Sometimes they will erase the entire contents of a person's hard drive.

So let me ask you a few questions. Do you do any of the following?

- ✔ Do you download files from Web sites?
- ✔ Do you exchange files with people over the Internet?
- ✔ Do you ever copy files from other systems by using floppy disks?
- ✔ Are you hooked up to a local-area network (LAN)?

If you answered "Yes" to any of these questions, your computer could easily become infected with a computer virus.

These are the things you should do to keep your system free of viruses:

- ✔ Back up your files regularly. (If your computer is infected with a virus, you must remember to disinfect the restored files.)
- ✔ Never boot your computer with a floppy disk that you haven't scanned and disinfected first. (When you scan your computer with an anti-virus program, you search your computer's memory and program files for viruses. If a virus is found, the anti-virus program will remove the virus from your computer.)
- ✔ Always disinfect every file you download from the Internet, copy from a floppy disk, or copy from a network drive — before running it on your computer.
- ✔ Install an anti-virus program, like Norton AntiVirus, and use the memory-resident virus-spotting feature of the program at all times.

Norton AntiVirus scans your boot records, files, and directories whenever your computer is turned on and monitors your computer for any activity that might indicate the work of a virus in action. It can also scan each floppy disk for viruses before files are copied onto your computer. Should a virus be detected, Norton AntiVirus can quickly repair infected files.

For more information about Norton AntiVirus, contact Symantec Corporation, 10201 Torre Ave., Cupertino, CA 95014; phone 800-441-7234; Web site www.symantec.com/nav.

Clean Up Your Hard Drive

In addition to keeping your computer healthy, you should clean up your computer's hard drive.

I explain how you get organized and clean off all the stuff that's accumulated on the top of your desk in Chapter 2. Now I would like to discuss the importance of getting rid of the stuff that's accumulated inside your computer.

From my perspective, a hard drive is nothing more than an electronic filing cabinet. And no matter how large a hard drive you've got, if you continue to add more files and software programs, without deleting the files you no longer need, or removing the programs you no longer use, your hard drive — like the file drawers in your desk — will eventually become stuffed beyond capacity. Until you actually start getting rid of your old computer files and unused programs, you won't realize how much space is being wasted.

The easiest way to remove unwanted or unneeded files from your computer is with Norton's CleanSweep. This is what CleanSweep does:

✔ **Manages your programs:** You can uninstall a software program, archive a program, back up a program, move a program to a different drive, or transport it so that it can be used on another computer.

✔ **Cleans up your computer:** CleanSweep can search for duplicate files, find orphan files and files that were left behind by programs that have been deleted, and much more.

✔ **Removes Internet files:** CleanSweep can remove programs that were downloaded from the Internet, instantly clean Internet cache files, select and sweep away unwanted Internet cookies, and much more.

✔ **Edits your computer's registry:** CleanSweep makes it easy to edit your computer's registry settings and eliminate unused entries.

For more information about Norton CleanSweep, contact Symantec Corporation, 10201 Torre Ave., Cupertino, CA 95014; phone 800-441-7234; Web site www.symantec.com/sabu/qdeck.

As an alternative to purchasing three separate programs — Norton Utilities, Norton AntiVirus, and Norton CleanSweep — Symantec has created Norton SystemWorks. Norton SystemWorks is a suite of utilities that includes Norton Utilities, Norton AntiVirus, Norton CleanSweep, Norton CrashGuard, and Norton Web Services. For more information about Norton SystemWorks, contact Symantec Corporation, 10201 Torre Ave., Cupertino, CA 95014; phone 800-441-7234; Web site www.symantec.com/sabu/sysworks.

Delete Your Automatic Backup Files

I would also like to mention that you should delete your automatic backup files from time to time.

Many programs, such as your word processor and spreadsheet program, have a feature that automatically backs up a file. You can recognize this type of file because it has the extension *.BK!, *.BAK, or *.WBK.

So if you've been writing a lot of letters, memos, presentations, and reports, and you have been using your word processor and spreadsheet's automatic backup feature, you may have a large number of backup files. And these backup files are certainly taking up valuable space on your hard drive. It's very easy to get rid of your backup files.

This is how you locate files on your computer:

1. Click the Start button and select Find⇨Files And Folders. The Find: All Files dialog box opens.

2. Enter the extension you want to search for, such as *.bk!, *.bak, or *.wbk in the Named field. You need to include the asterisk (*) and period (.) so that your computer knows that you are searching for an extension.

3. Select My Computer from the drop-down list in the Look In field.

4. Click Find Now and Windows searches your computer for any file that has this extension.

Then scroll through the list of files for the ones you want to delete. To delete a single file, just highlight it and press the Delete key. To highlight a group of files that are in sequence, click the first file, press and hold down the Shift key, and then click the last file in the list. To select files that are not next to each other, hold down the Ctrl button while you click each file individually.

Back Up Your Data

The best thing you can do to keep your data safe — and to save yourself lots of time — is to back up your computer every day. You just don't want to waste your precious time trying to re-create documents that were damaged because your computer crashed.

Today you've many backup options, and on the next few pages, I summarize them.

Press Ctrl+S to save your data. Do it often!

Have you ever been working on a document or spreadsheet and then, for no good reason, your computer locked up — crashed — and you lost several hours of work? To protect yourself from losing your data, you should make a habit of pressing Ctrl+S every few minutes. Ctrl+S is the Windows command that saves your current file to your hard drive.

I've gotten so accustomed to saving my documents that I do it whenever I finish writing a paragraph. And when I'm working on my *ACT! in ACTion* newsletter in PageMaker, I press Ctrl+S each time I make a change to the document.

Use your program's automatic backup feature

Many programs, such as WordPerfect and Word, have a setting that automatically backs up a file at regular timed intervals. For myself, I've set my WordPerfect Timed Document feature for 3 minutes. So if I have a computer crash, I'll lose only the last 3 minutes of work.

Store data on floppy disks

Old fashioned floppy disks are still a great way to protect individual files. When you're working on an important document, make it a habit to save a copy of it on a floppy disk.

Years ago I was working on my third book, *Winning The Fight Between You And Your Desk,* and my hard drive blew up on me. Not only did I lose half of my manuscript, my Norton Utilities error report of cross-linked files (I don't know what they are, but they aren't good) ran for 125 pages. This problem cost me weeks of work. Since then, I've made it a habit to save my manuscripts to a floppy disk. I even wrote a macro that saves the file to both my hard drive and a floppy disk at the same time.

As an alternative to using the traditional the 1.44MB floppy disk drive, you can replace it with an Imation SuperDisk 120MB drive. This disk drive can read and write to the old-fashioned 1.44 floppy disk, and can also read and write to 120MB SuperDisk diskettes. For more information about Imation SuperDisk, contact Imation Enterprises Corp., 1 Imation Place, Oakdale, MN 55128-3414; phone 888-466-3456; Web site www.imation.com.

Use high-capacity removable disk drives

A few years ago, Iomega developed the Zip drive — the first high-capacity removable disk drive — and the computing world hasn't been the same since. Today Iomega makes a complete line of high-capacity removable disk drives, some of which transfer data faster than the hard drive of the computer to which they are attached. These make it easy to save large amounts of data on a removable disk instead of a hard drive. These are Iomega's removable disk drives:

✔ **Zip drive:** A Zip drive can store 100MB of data. (A 250MB model is also available.) The parallel port model transfers data at the rate of 25MB per minute. The SCSI model transfers data at the rate of 60MB per minute.

✔ **Jaz drive:** A Jaz drive can store 1 or 2 gigabytes (a gigabyte is 1000 megabytes) of data. It has an average transfer rate of 5.4MB per second, which is faster than many hard drives. (The 2 gigabyte drive has an average transfer rate of 7.4MB per second.)

✔ **Ditto drive:** A Ditto drive can store up to 10 gigabytes of data and has a data transfer rate of between 2MB and 4MB per second.

So if you need more disk space and want to take it with you when you walk out the door, get yourself a Zip, Jaz, or Ditto drive.

For more information, contact Iomega, 1821 West Iomega Way, Roy, UT 84067; phone 801-778-1000; Web site www.iomega.com.

Install a tape backup system

Backing up your hard drive just makes good sense. With an automatic tape backup system, the whole process is very easy. Should something happen to your computer, you'll be able to restore any lost or damaged files in almost no time at all.

Years ago it was easy to back up your hard drive onto floppy disks. But how do you back up a 4 GB, 6 GB or 10GB (gigabyte) hard drive? The only way you can do it is with a cassette tape drive and backup software.

Seagate makes a complete line of Trevan tape drives for the PC. The Hornet 8, for example, is an internal ATAPI or SCSI device. It comes with Seagate's backup software for Windows 95, Windows 98, and Windows NT.

I've found the Seagate tape backup systems to be a great time-saver. I've automated the whole backup process, and it's made my life quite easy. At 12:30 p.m. every day, the backup program automatically turns itself on and backs up all of my ACT! database files. And then at 6:30 p.m., it does the same thing and backs up all the files that have changed since my last full backup. I do a full backup of my entire hard drive once a week.

For more information about Seagate tape backup systems, call Seagate Express at 800-656-2794 or visit www.seagate.com. Seagate Technology, Inc.'s corporate offices are located at 920 Disc Drive, Scotts Valley, CA 95066; phone 408-438-8111.

Back up your computer over the Internet

As an alternative, or in addition to, using a tape or Zip drive to back up the data on your hard drive, you can now back up your data over the Internet.

Connected Online Backup is a data protection subscription service — designed for individuals, small- to medium-size businesses, and people who work out of their homes — that backs up your computer's data over the Internet. The backup process is fully automated, and the software can be set up so that it performs daily unattended backups at scheduled times.

For a free 30-day/100 megabyte trial, visit www.connected.com. For more information, contact Connected Corporation, 63 Fountain St., Framingham, MA 01702; phone 888-922-2587 or 508-270-0000.

If you're not backing up your computer on a regular basis, you're taking an unnecessary risk because sooner or later, something bad is going to happen and you're going to lose some, or all, of your data. So go out and get yourself a backup system. It will give you a lot of security and peace of mind. I've found my backup systems to be both a lifesaver and a huge time-saver.

Part VII

The Part of Tens

In this part . . .

*I*f you happen to be thumbing through the book, take a look at the next few chapters; they're jam-packed with my best tips, tricks, hints, and suggestions. If you've read the whole book to this point, think of this final part as dessert. So sit back and enjoy.

Chapter 25

Ten Tips for a Top-Notch Filing System

In This Chapter

▶ Keeping your documents in order

▶ Knowing where everything goes

*B*ecause my specialty is helping people organize their papers and set up their filing systems, I would be remiss if I didn't include a chapter on how to set up an easy-to-use filing system.

Use File Folders

Instead of leaving letters, memos, reports, and other papers lying on top of your desk, put them in file folders. Remember, though, that with time, a folder will get beat up, dog-eared, and dirty. When it does, you should replace it. Don't waste your valuable time trying to reuse an old, beat-up file folder that only costs a nickel.

Collate Your File Folders

To make it easy to see the labels on your folders, collate them — left, center, and right — so that you can see three labels at once.

If you have a lot of alphabetical files, make the tabs mean something to you. I like using the ⅓ cut files, files that have tabs in three positions: left, center, and right. If you set up your filing system in this manner, it makes pulling files from the drawer and refiling them much easier: Put the letters of the alphabet on the file tabs in this order:

Left	Center	Right
A	B	C
D	E	F
G	H, I	J
K	L	M
N	O	P, Q
R	S	T
U, V	W	X, Y, Z

Label Your Files

Always put a label on your files. If you don't, you won't know what's inside them.

Write Your File Labels by Hand

Keep a supply of file folders in your desk drawer, and when you need one, just pull it out and write on the label with a fine-tipped pen (pencils smudge and soon become illegible). Don't waste your valuable time trying to type a gummed label with a typewriter.

If you do want typed labels, you should go out and purchase a Seiko Smart Label Printer PRO. The SLP Printer Pro attaches to the serial port of your computer and prints labels from a roll, one at a time, instead of from a sheet. It's a great productivity-improvement tool. For more information about Seiko Smart Label Printer PRO, contact Seiko Instruments USA Inc., 1130 Ringwood Court, San Jose, CA 95131; phone 800-888-0817; Web site www.seikosmart.com.

File Labels Should Read Like the Telephone Directory

When you're writing labels for the names of people, they should be written just like you see them in the telephone directory: last name, first name, middle initial.

Get Rid of Your Hanging Folders

Many people use hanging folders to keep their manila folders from falling over. In theory, this system is OK, but in practice, it just doesn't work because the hanging folders themselves can take up to a third of the space in an empty drawer. If you find that your file drawers are filled beyond capacity, get rid of the hanging folders and replace them with expandable file pockets.

Use Expandable File Pockets

As an alternative to hanging folders, use expandable file pockets (also called accordion files). I like the pockets that expand to 3 inches. You put the file folders inside the file pockets and put the pockets into your file drawers. They stand up all by themselves.

Organize Your Files

Files that you use all the time should be placed at the front of the drawer so that they're easy to get to. Files that you use less frequently can be placed behind them. Other files that you need to keep but won't look at very often should be placed in the drawers of your credenza, in other filing cabinets in the office, or in permanent, off-site storage.

Work from Your File Folders

After you set up your filing system, you should get into the habit of working from files so that you can have facts at your fingertips, instead of having to rely on your memory.

Chapter 26

Ten Timesaving Tips for Getting More out of Technical Support

I know that computers never have glitches, and computer programs aren't shipped from the software vendors with bugs in them, so I'm not even sure why I should throw in some tips on how to make dealing with technical support easier. But if a situation were to arise in which you had to call tech support, these tips may make your life easier:

- ✔ Write down the technical support number in the front of the user's manual or highlight the number on the page where it's printed. Either bend a corner of the page or attach a sticky note to it so you can find it quickly. (I put all of my tech support numbers into ACT!.)

- ✔ Next to the number, write down the product's serial number or your user ID number. This way, when you're asked for this information, you won't have to start hunting around for it.

- ✔ Every company has a computerized phone system that has many different menus to chose from. To save yourself time, write down the appropriate sequence of numbers to press so that your call can be quickly routed.

- ✔ If you need to talk with technical support, try to do it first thing in the morning — not where *you're* located but where tech support is located — before everyone else tries to call. Check your user's manual because some software companies' tech support departments are open as early as 7:00 a.m. EST. Remember that the busiest time for technical support is early on Monday morning because everyone was trying to do something with the computer over the weekend and got into trouble.

✔ Don't call tech support during lunch hours — not yours, theirs — which is usually between the hours of 11:30 a.m. and 1:30 p.m. local time. During these hours, departments are generally understaffed, and you'll spend even more time waiting.

✔ If a company has recently started shipping a new product, you can expect the tech support phone lines to be ringing off the hook. There will be thousands of users who have questions or problems. Try calling either very early in the morning or at the end of the day. As a general rule, you should expect to be placed on hold for at least 10 to 15 minutes before you even talk to a technician, so make it a point to be doing something else while you're waiting on the phone.

✔ If you're calling and continue to get a busy signal, use the redial feature on your phone. On many phones, the telephone will automatically redial a busy number if you turn on the speaker and then press the redial button.

✔ Before you install a new piece of software or do something that changes your system's configuration, read the installation manual. Then call tech support and ask whether there's anything more you should know before you install the software, something that may not have been mentioned in the manual. Many times, the tech support person will even walk you through the whole installation process.

✔ And one final thought: Don't make changes to your computer at a time of day when you can't call tech support for help. What are you going to do if your computer quits working and tech support doesn't open until 8:00 a.m.?

Chapter 27

Ten Ways to Make the Most of Your Commuting Time

In This Chapter

▶ Making the most of your commute

▶ Turning a commute into productive time

I know that you probably spend one or two hours each day commuting from your home to your office and back each day, so I'm going to give you some tips you can use to turn your commuting time into productive time.

✔ **Develop a master commuting plan of action:** If you're a commuter, study your Master List of things to do before you go home in the evening to see which items of business you could tackle while you're on the bus, on the train, or in a car pool on your way home in the evening and on your way into the office the following morning.

✔ **Start planning for tomorrow:** Think about the work, tasks, and projects you need to do tomorrow and start getting yourself prepared to tackle the most important tasks as soon as you arrive in the morning.

✔ **Start planning for the future:** Begin to think about the work, tasks, and projects you need to do in the days and weeks ahead. The more time you can spend thinking and planning, the easier it will be for you to complete the work.

✔ **Add new tasks to your Master List:** Think about additional items of business that need to be done. If you're commuting, write them down on your Master List or inside your daily planner. If you're driving, you should write them down when you get to the office.

✔ **Make a few phone calls:** A cell phone is a great way to utilize your time while you're commuting. Use this as an opportunity to make or return some of the phone calls that you didn't have time to get to during the day. And if you're calling people who are in different time zones, use the time differential to your advantage.

✔ **Dictate letters and/or notes to yourself:** Pocket tape recorders are great tools for dictating letters and/or memos that need to be typed and for recording notes to yourself of things you need to do. So always carry your cassette recorder in your briefcase.

✔ **Write e-mail and other correspondence:** If you're taking the train or bus or riding in a car pool, bring your laptop along and use this time to write some letters, work on a spreadsheet, or compose some e-mail. If you're driving, you could work on your correspondence by taping your thoughts into a handheld recorder. (See previous tip.)

✔ **Catch up on your reading:** If you're commuting by bus, train, or car pool, always keep a reading file of articles, magazines, trade journals, and other information that you can put in your briefcase and read while you're coming from and going to work.

✔ **Listen to books on tape:** Use your commuting time to improve your business skills by listening to inspirational and motivational tapes. This is a great way to learn new business strategies. Or, if you just want to be entertained, many best-selling books have been recorded onto cassette tapes.

✔ **Listen to the news, a talk station, or all-sports radio:** If you like to keep up with current events, listen to an all-news station. Or for more stimulating entertainment, tune into your favorite talk radio or all-sports station.

✔ **Listen to music:** After a hard day's work, put in a cassette or CD of your favorite music in the player and relax as you drive or commute home.

✔ **Take a nap:** For those of you who commute by train, bus, or car pool, you may just want to sit back in your seat, close your eyes, relax, and take a brief nap. After a hard day at the office, you've earned a brief rest.

Index

• U •

• V •

• *X* •

• *Y* •

• *Z* •

YOUR ONLINE RESOURCE

WWW.DUMMIES.COM

Discover Dummies™ Online!

The *Dummies* Web Site is your fun and friendly online resource for the latest information about ...*For Dummies*® books on all your favorite topics. From cars to computers, wine to Windows, and investing to the Internet, we've got a shelf full of ...*For Dummies* books waiting for you!

Ten Fun and Useful Things You Can Do at www.dummies.com

1. Register this book and win!
2. Find and buy the ...*For Dummies* books you want online.
3. Get ten great *Dummies Tips*™ every week.
4. Chat with your favorite ...*For Dummies* authors.
5. Subscribe free to *The Dummies Dispatch*™ newsletter.
6. Enter our sweepstakes and win cool stuff.
7. Send a free cartoon postcard to a friend.
8. Download free software.
9. Sample a book before you buy.
10. Talk to us. Make comments, ask questions, and get answers!

Jump online to these ten fun and useful things at
http://www.dummies.com/10useful

For other technology titles from IDG Books Worldwide, go to
www.idgbooks.com

Not online yet? It's easy to get started with *The Internet For Dummies*®, 5th Edition, or *Dummies 101*®: *The Internet For Windows*® 98, available at local retailers everywhere.

IDG BOOKS WORLDWIDE

Find other ...*For Dummies* books on these topics:
Business • Careers • Databases • Food & Beverages • Games • Gardening • Graphics • Hardware
Health & Fitness • Internet and the World Wide Web • Networking • Office Suites
Operating Systems • Personal Finance • Pets • Programming • Recreation • Sports
Spreadsheets • Teacher Resources • Test Prep • Word Processing

IDG BOOKS WORLDWIDE BOOK REGISTRATION